Resilient Europe

This boo

.........-5.

-3. PR.

.........-6.

....

....

....

....

....

....

....

....

....

....

....

....

P44165 F

RESILIENT EUROPE

A study of the years 1870 – 2000

PETER CALVOCORESSI

LONGMAN
LONDON AND NEW YORK

Longman Group UK Limited,
Longman House, Burnt Mill, Harlow,
Essex CM20 2JE, England
and Associated Companies throughout the world.

Published in the United States of America
by Longman Publishing, New York

First published 1991
Second impression 1992

British Library Cataloguing in Publication Data
Calvocoressi, Peter *1912–*
    Resilient Europe: a study of the years 1870–2000.
    1. Europe, 1815–
    I. Title
    940.28

    ISBN 0–582–07853–9
    ISBN 0–582–07854–7 pbk

Library of Congress Cataloging in Publication Data
Calvocoressi, Peter.
    Resilient Europe: a study of the years 1870–2000/by Peter Calvocoressi.
        p.   cm.
    Includes bibliographical references and index.
    ISBN 0–582–07853–9 (cased) — ISBN 0–582–07584–7 (paper)
        1. Europe—Politics and government—1871–1918. 2. Europe—
Politics and government—20th century. 3. Europe—Foreign relations.
I. Title.
D443.C255   1991   90–2188
320.94—dc20   CIP

Produced by Longman Singapore Publishers (Pte) Ltd.
Printed in Singapore

By the Same Author

Nuremberg: The Facts, the Law and the Consequences

Survey of International Affairs 1947–48

Survey of International Affairs 1949–50

Survey of International Affairs 1951

Survey of International Affairs 1952

Survey of International Affairs 1953

Middle East Crisis (with Guy Wint)

South Africa and World Opinion

World Order and New States

Suez: Ten Years After (with Anthony Moncrieff)

World Politics since 1945

Total War (with Guy Wint and John Pritchard)

The British Experience 1945–75

Freedom to Publish (with Ann Bristow)

Top Secret Ultra

Independent Africa and the World

From Byzantium to Eton: A Memoir of a Millennium

A Time for Peace

Who's Who in the Bible

Contents

Part One
The German Menace

CHAPTER ONE
Bismarck's Reich

Throughout modern history Europe, the smallest of the continents and geographically only a minor part of a much larger continent, has been divided into independent sovereign states. This has been a luxury. Europe has been able to afford fragmentation because fragmentation has been coupled with striking technical superiority, material wealth, and skills in political management and organization. Time added legal and popular sanctions: nationalism in small sovereign chunks became sacrosanct. For Europeans the state is almost a fact of nature, although this has never been entirely true of any particular state at any particular moment.

If the state itself has been sacrosanct, its borders have not. These borders have varied with conquest and also with ideas. One state might enlarge itself at the expense of another, but at the same time new states have emerged as the idea of the state has focused on nationalism or self-determination – ideas which make for more fragmentation and have created states with relatively little power. As the number of states increases, so does their disparity.

The existence of numerous states in a comparatively small space required a system for regulating the relations between them. The power of the European states gave them immunity to threats from outside Europe (the Ottoman threat being the conspicuous exception), so that the principal threat to their integrity and prosperity came from each other. To minimize conflict Europe evolved a system which, while consecrating the sovereign state, sought to regulate these states' rivalries by checks and balances, by shifting alliances designed to restrain the overmighty, and by minimal international law. Hence statesmanship, as distinct from the exercise of military might: statesmanship is first and foremost a peculiar form of management.

After the upheavals caused by the French Revolution and Napoleon Europe got back to what it regarded as normalcy by reasserting and in some respects redefining its sovereign states. The more powerful among them established a Concert of Europe, a rudimentary association for the preservation of peace and legitimacy. They were few, and the less powerful were also few. The status of the Ottoman empire, which occupied a large chunk of south eastern Europe, was anomalous but its existence was a useful moderating element in the system's shifting alliances. The biggest shock to the system in the nineteenth century was the conversion of Prussia, already a major factor, into Germany, a much more considerable one. This quantum leap in the power of a single member lay at the root of the two Great Wars which rocked the system in the first half of the twentieth century. The double defeat of the German threat cleared the way for a Russian threat. Delayed by the revolution of 1917 and its aftermath, this new Russian threat emerged only after the ascent of two extra-European (or semi-extra-European) Superpowers had laid bare the end of Europe's world hegemony and self-sufficiency. Thus the Russian threat was not the same as the German threat, or the French threat that preceded the German, because the context had changed before the German threat gave way to the Russian. The German threat was countered by the European states system, the Russian by the United States. Europe's states remained intact and distinct, but they were obliged to ask themselves whether they could any longer afford the luxury of a states system or, indeed, whether it still worked.

In the first Great War Germany defeated Russia but was defeated on its other fronts. This German defeat did nothing to soften the Russian defeat because Russia was disabled for a whole generation by revolution, foreign invasions and civil war. The removal of both Germany and Russia from European affairs created a power vacuum in the spaces between them – *Mitteleuropa* – while the simultaneous dislocation of the Habsburg and Ottoman empires gave birth to a clutch of new sovereign states covering much of that space. After 1919 the European system was therefore profoundly altered: major Powers eliminated, minor ones multiplied. The alliance game, which previously had consisted in the permutations of major Powers, became complicated by the untested possibility of using new minor Powers for old purposes, with the added uncertainty that the absent Powers might one day regain their relevance and, in unspecifiable terms, reclaim their roles. The twenty years between the two Great Wars were therefore plagued by unrealities as well as the uncertainties inseparable from politics.

The Second World War did not lead to an attempt to re-establish the European states system, to pick up the pieces and put them together again. When it ended with Germany's second defeat at the hands (principally) of the Soviet Union and the United States, the system was assumed to be dead. In its place was the contest between these two Superpowers. But Europe's states still existed. Even in the east where Soviet power made a monkey of sovereign independence, legal sovereignty was maintained (except in the case of the Baltic republics whose creation in 1919 was in effect annulled) and superficially the map of Europe looked much the same after the war as it had in 1938. The system was destroyed, not by the sort of threat once posed by Napoleon or Hitler, a threat which Europeans might unite to resist, but by a threat which they felt unable to resist and, in half the continent, could not resist. So the other half co-opted the United States into the ghost of the system, thereby acknowledging its demise. In place of shifting alliances to preserve a balance of power, a new alliance was conjured up to draw and hold a fixed frontier: military might at a premium over statecraft. Fortified by nuclear weapons, and the fear of their use, this confrontation persisted for nearly half a century but it too was riddled with unrealities. It was plausibly credited with keeping the peace in Europe, but its cost in central and eastern Europe was galling and western Europeans became increasingly unconvinced of its durability.

It is no longer clear how many Superpowers there are; nor what the two presumed Superpowers want of one another or in Europe; nor how independent a role Europeans may still play in Europe and beyond, in combination or severally. Even the word 'Europe', in its political sense, has become fudged as some Europeans have formed a quasi-union which they call 'the European Community'. The affinity of Europeans with one another has hardly been diminished by the post–1945 sundering of the Eurosphere, nor has their sense of being rather better off than most of the rest of the world and much better organized. They are teased by their circumstances and puzzled about how best to use the advantages, above all economic and technical advantages, which they still possess and which sometimes tempt them to suppose that their best course is to go on as before, a little depressed in the international scale but not so much so as to be obliged to abandon the luxury of multiple sovereignties. Others suppose otherwise but have failed to step very far away from the pattern which they have inherited.

The essential verity of the old European states system was that, in the last resort, the parts were more important than the whole. The whole was constituted to serve the interests of the parts. It was not, therefore, a system consecrated to the preservation of peace, since a state or states might decide that war – or the risk of war – was expedient. War might be the ultimate evil, but that it was escapable was believed by virtually nobody. The system existed to obviate unwanted wars, not to eliminate war. It existed also to ensure the easier predominance of the great over the not-so-great: the Concert sought to concert the ideas and activities of those upon whom greatness had necessarily conferred authority, responsibility and perhaps wisdom. Since unanimity could not be guaranteed or even expected, it was important to be in the majority; and the system derived its characteristic fluidity from this ceaseless need to construct majorities.

There was a corollary, which was also the system's weakest point. If the parts were more important than the whole, the biggest part – the biggest state – could dominate the whole. How far, and in what way, it might choose to do so rested in its own hands and mood.

The legal doctrine of sovereignty upon which the system rested ascribed to all constituent states equality in law. Some states were manifestly less powerful than others – and were not invited to the more select international conferences – but in the nineteenth century these lesser states were comparatively few and either peripheral (in Scandinavia, for example) or too small to be noticed, such as Andorra or Liechtenstein. In practice the equality of sovereign states meant equal rights to independence and territorial integrity, so that any assault on either was an offence (even when condoned) and a threat not only to the victim but also to the system. The very fact that this putative equality did not correspond with the facts of power laid on the greater Powers an incentive or duty to forestall any such assault and so, in the name of the system and in the interest of all its parts, to negotiate by compromise changes within the system which, if not negotiated, might lead to unwanted war. The greater Powers were guardians of the system which, within limits and incidentally, protected the lesser members of the sovereign family.

The system presupposed that the Great Powers, alongside their rivalries, had a community of interests; and the first of these interests was that no Power should be too great, for that would negate the system. There must not be another Napoleon whose view of the continent turned all other monarchs into sub-monarchs and all states but one into sub-states. If a new Napoleon were to arise, then the system required its members to unite to thwart him. The first generations after Waterloo were nervously alive to the possible appearance of a fresh threat, in France or elsewhere. In the event it came from Germany.

A threat to the system arose when a member had the capacity to override it and the intention to do so. Since intentions are normally veiled the co-existence of these two pre-conditions was normally a matter for surmise. Such was the case with the German threat which loomed after 1870. The new Germany, Prussia writ very large, had – in the phrase of the German historian Ludwig Dehio – a choice between *Gleichgewicht* and *Hegemonie*, balance or dominion. It might work the system or override it. The simple existence of the choice was alarming, whether or not Germany intended, or might intend, to choose *Hegemonie* rather than *Gleichgewicht*. In fact there appears to have been no point at which the Second Reich created by Bismarck deliberately opted before 1914 for *Hegemonie*, and to that extent it is wrong to lay upon Germany, as the Treaty of Versailles did, the guilt for causing the first Great War. Germany was not seeking to replace the Concert system by a European one-state band. But it did contribute powerfully to the break-down of the system.[1]

The German Reich was born powerful, unlike other Powers which gathered power gradually. It was built in a day, on Prussian power, economic and military. This ready-made maturity was one of the things that made it different and alarming. Although it did not embrace all Germans, it nevertheless united Germans far more effectively than Latins or Slavs had ever been united; and the Germans were in the middle of the continent. Geographically substantial, psychologically self-conscious, administratively efficient (by the standards of the day) Germany made rapid economic progress which, based on commercial union, industrial invention and first-class education, enabled it to sustain armed forces of the first order and to entertain wide political ambitions. Like all coun-

---

1. The word 'hegemony' covers a range of predominance. At one end it all but makes a mockery of balance, reducing it to a sham. At the other end, acknowledging that the weights in a balance are unequal, it denotes the heavier weight. *Gleichgewicht* and *Hegemonie* co-exist and Dehio's distinction is one of emphasis rather than antithesis.

tries, particularly new ones, it had weaknesses but a combination of material resources and optimism enabled it to overcome them with remarkable speed. Industrially it lagged behind Great Britain until the end of the century but overtook it in crucial areas such as iron and steel and technical and scientific education. Politically it remained to outward seeming a patchwork with considerable pockets of anti-Prussian resentment, but the reality was rapid unification under the signs of the Hohenzollern monarchy and the imperial army – a military-regal complex, happily supported by old aristocratic Junkers and new plutocratic industrialists. Bismarck himself was made a Prince (Disraeli, who also made his sovereign imperial, became merely an Earl). The tone of the new Germany was aristocratic and military, by contrast with Great Britain which was the standard-bearer of parliamentary liberalism and France where the imperialism personified by the second Napoleon had just been overthrown and discredited. Political parties existed in the new Germany but party politicians were as marginally effective as they were (as such) socially subordinate. Bismarck was no democrat. He treated his adversaries with disdain, opposition as near to treason. His Reich was different therefore from its neighbours in character as well as in its origins, resources, geography and destiny and these differences, which accounted for much mutual distrust, persisted for the better part of a century.

The differences between the leading Powers of Europe were far from absolute but they were sharp enough to define inter-state relations in terms of conflict. The biggest change in Europe since 1870 has been the dissolution of this mood or pattern in the western half of the continent. Whereas in 1870 the German, French and British states seemed made to compete, even to fight, with one another, a hundred years later this was not true. The major changes have come in Germany and the biggest factors in these changes have been the two wars which Germany nearly won but in fact lost and which, by postponing Germany's rise to assured pre-eminence, altered the mood in which Germans assessed their own opportunities. The history of Germany is the main feature in the modern history of Europe. (It is hopeless to study, for example, modern British history in isolation from German history.)

In the nineteenth century the bourgeoisie or upper middle class[2] of western Europe successfully challenged the monopoly of the

2.   A bourgeois was an urban freeman and man of property. Cities were governed by bourgeois or burghers long before nations were.

aristocracy in political power. In Great Britain the aristocracy preserved its position at court and in 'society' and retained its political position in the upper house of parliament which remained an aristocratic preserve for Lords. The middle class occupied the lower house; extended its political base there by promoting successive extensions of the franchise which destroyed aristocratic control over parliamentary constituencies; reversed the dominance of the upper house over the lower; but at the same time increased, with each extension of the franchise, the bourgeoisie's dependence on the votes of yet other classes. The outcome was the creation of a bourgeois parliamentarianism which was not seriously challenged until the twentieth century when, first, the lower classes developed their own political organizations and, secondly, the middle class itself became more sharply differentiated between the established bourgeoisie based on secure and superior wealth and, on the other hand, less prosperous elements in the urban middle class (small retailers, clerks) and the liberal professions: the last were politically ambivalent, while the median middle class of the towns became increasingly resentful of the exclusiveness which the upper middle classes learned from the aristocracy. The bourgeoisie, like the aristocracy, was a minority but, unlike the aristocracy, it relied in politics on numbers, on wooing voters and counting votes. France developed along similar lines in spite of its violent and famous Revolution – which, to the considerable advantage of the bourgeoisie, was aborted by the Napoleonic reaction and by the failure of the revolution of 1848. (The chroniclers of the ups and downs of the French bourgeoisie are Balzac and Zola.) Germany, however, took a different course. The German bourgeoisie gained political power as subservient partners of the *ancien régime* of court, landowning aristocracy and officer caste. To its western neighbours, therefore, the new German state was ideologically suspect as well as uncomfortably powerful.

The main components of the German Reich – landowners and the military – were (as elsewhere) nationalists. The economic aspect of nationalism is autarky. Since Germany was not economically self-sufficient, autarky – or the lack of it – required expansion into, or dominion over, markets and sources of supply. Economic penetration might satisfy these needs only partially or uncertainly: military control would secure them. The principal economic cohorts in Bismarck's Germany were the Junkers in the east, landowning agriculturalists who were protectionist and coveted colonies, and the industrialists of the west who were protectionist too and looked to the state to back them in their competition with foreigners. Unlike contemporary Great Britain, Germany did not feel strong enough to rely on free trade to boost its economic fortunes: even Great Britain had not done so until it was well on the way to superlative wealth. These economic classes were, with the dynasty and the army, the pillars of the Reich and by the time of Bismarck's more liberal successors they were influential enough to block any moves towards more liberal economic and international policies. Their ideal was the widest possible self-sufficiency, to be won through power and to be so firmly established by a combination of private enterprise and state authority as to be indifferent to any need for statecraft. Thus the Reich, for all its military and industrial muscle, was a politically inflexible state. The military and industry, under the dynasty, constituted the state and instead of admitting elements of the middle class to share in its direction (as Great Britain and France were doing) this state regressed under Kaiser William II to a narrower dynastic autocracy which, under the impact of failure in war, turned in 1917 into the brief military dictatorship of Field Marshal Ludendorff and his staff.[3]

As the greatest continental Power, Bismarck's Germany stepped into a position of pivotal responsibility. By defeating Austria in 1866 Bismarck had created a German empire with its capital in Berlin, not Vienna (which had for centuries been to Germans what Paris was to Latins). After 1870 Bismarck adopted for Germany a policy of no territorial claims, but he did not espouse a similar policy for all Europe. Given the decline of the Ottoman empire he could not do so. Territorial changes were clearly impending, with or without the intervention of major Powers to supplement the restlessness of Turkey's subject peoples in south east Europe. The question was whether such changes would be made without war,

---

3. Yet until this catastrophe the German Reich was not more militarist (as distinct from aggressive) than other Great Powers – militarist, that is to say, in the sense of allowing the military an overriding role in the direction of the state. Towards the end of the nineteenth century general staffs tended to become dabblers in high policy, much as the CIA under successive American presidents a hundred years later. This was particularly the case with French and Russian generals who were brought together in amicable professional hobnobbery during and after the conclusion of the Franco-Russian military convention of 1894. On neither side, however, was there any serious intent to usurp the civil power.

with only local wars or to the accompaniment of a Great War. The European system existed to obviate the last possibility and failed to do so, and Bismarck himself contributed to this posthumous failure.

Bismarck's fame rests on the startlingly sharp Prussian victories of 1866 and 1870 over Austria and France, victories which appear in retrospect to be fore-ordained but were at the time great surprises. They placed upon Bismarck the chief responsibility for handling the outcome. His task was to consolidate and at least maintain the power of the new Reich. To the west he had nothing to fear, but to the east the outlook was menacingly uncertain. To the west the verdict of 1870 was a decisive stroke, but to the east the verdict of 1866 was peripheral to the contest between the Austro-Hungarian and Russian empires over the disposal of the Ottoman empire in Europe. The Ottoman retreat was by far the most likely source of a major war in Europe, a war from which Bismarck and the Reich had nothing to gain. When, in the previous century, the central territorial question had been the disposal of Poland, the three monarchs with designs on it had taken the relatively easy course of partitioning it among themselves, but unlike Frederick the Great in the Polish case Bismarck in the Ottoman case had no wish to take a piece of the Ottoman inheritance nor any prospect of doing so. He was therefore in the position of a mediator, not a co-conspirator or predator, and Germany's role in the same trio of monarchs was to manage the other two and prevent their rivalry in Europe's far east from obstructing Germany's interests in Europe as a whole. Given the magnitude of the issue Bismarck did not contemplate opting out of it, but given too his comparative remoteness from the scene of action his intervention could succeed only upon the assumption that Habsburg and Russian spheres of ambition might be delimited and reconciled. But this assumption was not valid and as early as 1878 – at the Congress of Berlin convoked to cut Russia down to size after its victory over the Turks – Bismarck assumed the dominant role in settling the affairs of Europe at the expense of taking the lead in thwarting Russia. This bias was emphasized a year later by the German-Austrian treaty which tied Germany to Austria's Balkan policies, undermined Germany's role as mediator between Vienna and St Petersburg and became the trigger for war in 1914. Bismarck left Germany more shackled than, owing to its military efficiency and its power to surprise, it appeared to be, and this unperceived weakness was compounded by a second cardinal miscalculation. While the treaty of 1879 tied Germany's hands in the east, the annexation of Alsace and Lorraine from France after 1870 hobbled the states system which Bismarck wished to operate. With France and Germany fixed in hostility the system was deprived of one of its principal permutations, of part of its essential fluidity; the room for manoeuvre of Bismarck's successors was constricted. The annexation of the two provinces gave Franco-German enmity the appearance of a fact of nature which dominated the diplomacy of Europe for the better part of a hundred years.

If the annexation was one of those acts of choice which might have been eschewed, Bismarck's more fateful move in the 1870s – his drift into an alliance with Austria – was not so much a choice as a response to circumstances beyond his influence. The German Reich was not the German nation state required by nineteenth-century principles and by many Germans. The anomaly was caused above all by the existence of the Austrian empire. The temper of the times pointed to a German state embracing all, or nearly all, Germans. The first part of the century had seen the creation of a north German customs union and nascent economic union which, however politically insignificant to begin with, had provided Bismarck with a base from which to annex southern Germany and so create a German empire. He did so, however, by defeating Austria in battle and by excluding Austrian Germans from the new German Reich. This turned out to be a more lasting, even a more disturbing, event than his more famous victory over France a few years later. For almost all the years since that time – all except 1938–45 – Austrians have been excluded from Germany and still are.

An extension of the German union to embrace Austria was in Bismarck's time a political impossibility. The very existence of the Habsburg monarchy forbade it. Hohenzollerns could swallow much, but not Habsburgs. Further, the extent of Habsburg rule over various non-German lands made it foolhardy to contemplate a German-Austrian union. Not until Austria had become detached from empire by defeat in the First World War could anybody (in the event Hitler) set about incorporating it in a German Reich. The consequences were tremendous. In German eyes Austria could never be the same as other states. Paradoxically its defeat in 1866 both highlighted its Germanity and made it less German, making the problem both more blatant and more intractable. Conspicuously excluded from the German Reich it was nevertheless the core of another and older Reich which was at least more German than anything else; but it was driven to convert itself from Habsburg into Dual Monarchy – dual with the Hungarians. This conversion was effected by the *Ausgleich* or Compromise. The *Ausgleich* was a deal struck under compulsion between the Habsburg dynasty in Vienna and the Hungarian nobility in Budapest. It registered, even if it did not avow, two things: that 1866 forced Austria to renounce any role in Germany and therefore to look east and, secondly, that the Habsburgs must share power with the Hungarians who were relentlessly opposed to sharing it with anybody else – that is to say, with those Slavs who were inside the Dual Monarchy and far from untouched by the currents of nationalism. The Habsburgs were thenceforward not merely subdued by Bismarck's Reich but also rendered dependent on the Hungarians who, unlike the Reich Germans, were not their kin. Habsburg legitimacy had been dynastic – anachronistic maybe as the nineteenth century wore on – but intelligible and long established. After the *Ausgleich* it was in effect contractual in Hungary, increasingly national as well as dynastic in the hereditary Austrian lands, and evanescent everywhere else. Within the Dual Monarchy neither Austrians nor Hungarians were a majority in their own spheres; and together they accounted for less than half of the empire's population. At the census of 1910 the Germans in the Austrian half numbered ten million out of twenty-eight million, the Hungarians in the other half ten out of seventeen million. The empire contained substantial groups of Czechs, Poles, Italians, Croats, Romanians, Slovaks and Slovenes. (The Germans were not all contiguous either with Bismarck's Reich or with one another. They were scattered throughout the Habsburg empire and indeed beyond it, for Germans had travelled far afield over the centuries. There were three million Germans in what later became Czechoslovakia alongside six and a half million Czechs; and between the wars there were three quarters of a million Germans in Poland, as many in Romania, more than half a million in Hungary and as many in Yugoslavia – altogether 15–16 million Germans living between the German Reich and Russia, not counting people of German descent living in Russia.)

Bismarck's solution to this peculiarly German dilemma was sensible but flawed. Given the demographic mishmash of the Habsburg empire he decreed the existence of two distinct empires. He preferred to renounce the incorporation of Austrian and other Germans in the new German Reich if that meant incorporating also thirty million non-Germans. But this solution had two grave weaknesses: it could not escape a special relationship between the two empires and it offended nationalist pan-Germans.

The special relationship embroiled the German Reich in the

affairs of central and eastern Europe, hamstrung Germany's capacity to manage Austro-Russian conflict in the spoliation of the Ottoman empire and eventually, when mismanaged by Bismarck's successors, precipitated the First World War through Berlin's irresponsibility in egging Vienna on in the disaster-laden crisis of August 1914.

In 1871, the year when the German princes made the Prussian king emperor in Germany, the German and Austrian emperors held a much advertised meeting which celebrated the special amity of their dynasties and realms. It confirmed Bismarck's policy of hands-off Austria, but it also foreshadowed a policy of hand-in-glove with Austria. In the same year the direction of affairs in Vienna was entrusted to Count Julius Andrassy, a congenital anti-Russian Hungarian, and although Bismarck tried two years later to keep his options open by constructing the *Dreikaiserbund* (League of Three Emperors), this showpiece of his diplomacy proved little more than a sham. The reality was his treaty with Austria in 1879, concluded after Russia's alarmingly successful war against Turkey in 1877 and after the Congress of Berlin where the Great Powers sanctioned Austria's *Drang nach Osten* to stem Russian expansion. Europe's Great Powers could keep in concert only by becoming more anti-Russian than anti-Turkish, and in various crises thereafter Austria felt confident enough of German support against Russia to risk war which, when it came in 1914, turned from a Balkan war into a world war. While nothing that happened in the 1870s made anything in the 1900s a foregone conclusion, it may be said that from the first years of the Second Reich Bismarck compromised or maimed the European states system, rendering Great Power rivalries much more difficult to handle without war. There was therefore a German threat to the system, a threat which arose partly from the sheer power of Germany but more from the course of German diplomacy than from any malevolent intention of Germany's rulers. Neither Bismarck nor his successors as Chancellor nor Kaiser William II aimed to subvert the system *à la* Napoleon, but they failed the system in the period when, German power reaching to its apogee, German mismanagement mattered more than that of any other state.

There was, too, another unresolved problem: the aggrandizement of Germany. If in Bismarck's vision Germany was to limit its role in central Europe to diplomacy without territorial expansion, there were other visions both before and after Bismarck. The nationalist spirit of the age was flavoured by exciting new technology which beckoned the venturesome. A Berlin-to-Baghdad railway was first mooted in 1846, coupled with the idea of German settlements in Asia Minor: something like the plantation of Ulster by King James I or of the highlands of Kenya by British ex-servicemen after the First World War. With the aid of the new technology Germans might create in western Asia an alternative to those empires which the British and others had captured by sea in the Americas, Africa and the Far East, while the road to the east might – as a certain Baron Bruck from the Rhineland urged on Metternich – be made safe for Germans by building an entirely new port at Trieste with railways radiating from it in all directions to create a commercial and political dominion in central and eastern Europe. Germans of this era were ebullient and idealist and at the same time acquisitive. The cosiness admired by an earlier generation was out of fashion. Germans were on the move, on the make and sometimes on the march. It was not always easy to distinguish the moving, the making and the marching. The aims could be elevating or deplorable. In either mode they usually began with a broadening of the German base. In the wake of the revolutions of 1848 the German Assembly convoked at Frankfurt – an assembly dominated by liberals – envisaged a greater Germany which would certainly be a fine thing for Germans but splendid for everybody else too. It was inchoate and premature, but its sinking was not without trace. The king of Prussia indignantly refused an all-German crown offered to him by revolutionary democrats; the Assembly turned to an amiable, if aged, Austrian archduke (he had commanded an army against the French in 1800) but he too refused; the Assembly disintegrated, princes of all degrees resumed their several sways, and soon afterwards Bismarck set about uniting Germany within narrower horizons.

But emotions cannot always be contained by statesmen and before the great Chancellor's fall in 1890 Germany was full of voices enthusing over schemes for continental expansion. These schemes were various and vague. The Pan-German Verband, founded in 1886, began as a lobby for overseas colonies, developed a romantic hankering after the defunct Holy Roman Empire and then more concrete plans for German domination over central Europe. Some champions of a German forward policy were racist (Paul Lagarde), others were not (Friedrich Naumann). The chorus included men of letters, professors, captains of industry, publicists and pamphleteers, and a sprinkling of lunatics. In their widest and wildest dreams these enthusiasts foresaw Germany lording it not

only over central Europe but also, to west and east, over France
and Turkey. In the milder versions of this German apotheosis
dominance might be less rather than more heavy-handed, but in
all of them the German role was that of master. The notion of
seeking national advantage through international cooperation or
confederation was foreign to them. Like Japanese between the two
world wars, Germans before them designed a Greater European
Co-prosperity Sphere in which they themselves came clearly first
and top. They were insensitive to the point that their plans were
less attractive to others.

So long as Bismarck and Bismarckian ideas ruled, *Mitteleuropa*
as a political programme was peripheral, but neither Bismarck
nor anybody else could alter the fact that Germany was a central
European Power and by the turn of the century the use of that
power to secure German dominion in central Europe was back on
the political agenda. In 1911 General Bernhardi, who had taken
to literature after being sacked from the general staff, published
an influential treatise entitled 'Germany and the Next War', in
which he advocated the military defeat of France, expansion of the
German colonial empire, and German control over central Europe.
Behind this ample programme was fear as well as greed – fear that
a tide was turning; that time was no longer on Germany's side
(Hitler, too, was later obsessed with the need to strike before it
was too late); that Russia, now allied with France, was a fearful
menace to Germany and incidentally to civilization; that those
other cultural outlaws, the Turks, were no longer Europe's enemy
number one and that as they retreated down the Danube their
place along and about the great river must not be taken by Russians
but by Austrian Germans or German protégés.

To popular sentiment and military calculation were added other
urges. Germany was a great and growing industrial Power with a
manufacturing economy's needs for markets, investment opportunities and raw materials. These needs might be satisfied in central
Europe or elsewhere. If nationalism was one of the dynamics of
the nineteenth century state, overseas imperialism was another. In
theory Bismarck might have refused to join the imperial competition which characterized the last quarter of the century, although it
is difficult to see how he could have done so for his successors. He
was not congenitally attracted by the notion of acquiring colonies
in distant continents, but the evolution of the new German state
after the Franco-Prussian War made him think again. The new
state was the most populous in Europe except Russia and was

becoming the most productive. Rich in people and techniques it needed markets. German pride found it unbecoming to be left out of the imperial league in which not only Great Britain and France (the latter increasingly after its defeat in 1870) but also the new Italy and King Leopold II of Belgium were performing. German industrialists were casting round for *Ergänzungsräume*, supplementary zones of economic activity such as Great Britain and France had acquired by colonization beyond Europe. Bismarck began to toy with the idea of colonies and after him William II, in his cruder way, coveted a stake in Africa or the Pacific. The line between imperialism and economic self-fulfilment is hard to discern. *Ergänzungsräume* became *Lebensraum*: the latter term, with its additional demographic implications, appeared in serious academic parlance about 1900. But Germany did not have to go to Africa to satisfy its economic needs. If economic penetration were the object Germany, unlike Great Britain or France, had lands of economic opportunity close to its own borders. Some of these were even peopled by Germans, although others were not. A modest expansion eastward to incorporate Austria in the German state would create a greater German state; a more ambitious *Drang nach Osten* would create one of the world's greatest empires. *Mitteleuropa* might mean economic penetration or military domination: its meaning depended on who was using the term. Politically this ambiguity was part of its unsettling impact on non-Germans. Geographically it meant at its narrowest the Danubian lands, but for those with the sharpest vision it extended as far as the mind could reach to Asia Minor, the Middle East, the Persian Gulf. If the British could build a railway from the Cape to Cairo, the Germans could build another from Berlin to Baghdad. (Neither did.)

The First World War began – that is to say, the shooting began – in Bosnia with the assassination by Serbian nationalists of the Archduke Francis Ferdinand, the heir to the imperial throne of the Habsburgs. The Archduke was a protagonist of a reform of the empire which would put an end to the *Ausgleich* or at least modify it by raising some Slavs to the status reserved for Austro-Germans and Hungarians. This was not a new idea. It was almost certainly held by Francis Ferdinand's cousin and previous heir to the throne, the Archduke Rudolf, who committed suicide at Mayerling in 1898 after killing his teenage mistress. But the idea was anathema to the Hungarian magnates who were fiercely anti-Slav. For the German Reich it was a perilous idea because any upheaval in

the Habsburg Reich, coinciding with the further weakening of
the Ottoman empire by the recent Balkan wars, must enhance
the Austro-Russian competition in south east Europe and embroil
Germany on the Austrian side. Western Europeans who think
of eastern Europe as a secondary zone forget that its economic
inferiority has not prevented it – in the past and in the present –
from being politically the prime motor in the continent's affairs.

In July 1914 the Hungarian government was more prescient than
Vienna or Berlin. The Hungarians feared war. They feared that
war would ensure the collapse of the Habsburg empire and leave
Hungary a helpless minor state between Germans and Russians:
which is what happened. Hungary, although fond of hectoring
its Austrian partner, could no more do without the partnership
than Austria could; and Hungarians, however much they despised
the Slavs, did not want to chastise them in such a way as to
bring retribution upon themselves. Berlin, on the other hand,
raised the stakes and pushed Vienna into war, virtually dictating
the ultimatum presented by Vienna to Serbia in the knowledge
that its unacceptable terms and language must start a war. So
Germany went the way that Bismarck had planned to avoid. By
over-commitment to the Habsburgs and to the politics of central
Europe Germany wrecked its prospects as a world Power.

After initial German successes on all fronts the war settled
into an inertial pattern of trench warfare and blockade. The
blockade concentrated German minds perforce on continental
Europe, particularly central Europe. The two most important men
in Germany, after the Kaiser, were the Chancellor Theobald von
Bethmann Hollweg and the Chief of Staff Erich von Falkenhayn.
Both were in some degree continental expansionists. Before the
war the Chancellor had ruminated over schemes for a German-
Austrian-Hungarian customs union, flanked both west and east
by secondary partners such as France and Turkey. The war seemed
an opportunity to put flesh on such schemes and to inflate them
so that only the British and Russian empires would be left outside.
The rest of Europe would be a German empire and the world would
progress from a network of competitive nation states to a network
of competitive imperial conglomerations. Bethmann envisaged a
German-dominated continent outfacing not only the British and
Russians but also the waxing world power of the United States
of America. During the war Falkenhayn, somewhat less grandiose
but closer to the Kaiser's ear, dreamed up a Central European
Federation comprising not only Germany and Austro-Hungary

but also the wartime allies Bulgaria and Turkey and, if possible, neutrals like Romania and Greece.

To these musings in high places there was added, towards the end of 1915, something quite different: a book. Its title was *Mitteleuropa* and its author was Friedrich Naumann. It was written in clear straightforward German, it hit a mood and became a best-seller. Naumann was a liberal clergyman. He was also something of a pessimist who discounted the euphoria which had characterized so much German thinking earlier in the century. He saw Germany caught in east–west pincers. He counselled the abandonment of a German world role and propounded instead a continental confederation. He ducked the tricky question of its constitution but advocated in a general way full respect for the national susceptibilities of all peoples and races. Naumann was in the Bismarckian tradition in as much as his Europe was to be constructed round the German Reich and not round a combined German-Austrian core, but nothing could conceal the fact that the liberal Naumann, like the conservative Bethmann and the military Falkenhayn, had in mind a German hegemony which was unacceptable to non-Germans. In his own country Naumann was criticized by those in industry and finance who wanted world, not merely European, markets and he was equally opposed by pan-Germans who disguised neither their conviction that the Germans were a superior race nor their annexationist war aims.

In retrospect *Mitteleuropa* looks like a mirage. Nevertheless, there was a moment when it seemed to have arrived. Serbia was beaten and Russia reeling. When Bulgaria joined the war on the German side Germany became linked once more, by the Danube and by sea and rail, all the way to Turkey and the far confines of the Ottoman empire. An intensified British blockade confirmed the Eurocentrist view of Germany's destiny. But at about this time Germany's war leadership was changed. Falkenhayn, who had hoped to win the war on the western front and had failed, was dismissed in 1916 and so too next year was Bethmann Hollweg. Falkenhayn's effective successor, Ludendorff, became an even more supreme warlord than the Kaiser himself. The Hohenzollern monarchy was replaced by a Ludendorff dictatorship. Russia, paralyzed by revolution, collapsed. The Bolsheviks who seized power in 1917 were divided between those who wanted to make peace and those who wanted to fight on. The peace-makers, foremost among them Lenin who was convinced of the hopelessness of fighting on, prevailed and signed in March 1918 the Treaty of Brest-Litovsk which ended Germany's war on two fronts. Germany imposed treaties – in effect surrender – on Russia and also on Romania and an allegedly independent Ukraine. Compared with these feats Ludendorff could contemplate with equanimity the tottering of the Habsburg empire, accelerated by the death in 1917 of its aged symbol, the emperor, and by the pull of the Russian revolution on the Slavs under Austrian and Hungarian rule. In the spring of 1918 Ludendorff seemed to have victory in the west in his grasp too. But it was not to be. The great German offensive of that year petered out and a few months later Germany sued for peace.

Mitteleuropa was dead. Or was it merely pickled? Ludendorff had no use for it. He regarded south east Europe as a sideshow and its inhabitants as inferior and undependable. His strategy was eastern, not south eastern; his aims were to defeat Russia and win *Lebensraum* by dismembering the Russian empire and prising the Ukraine and other western provinces away from it. If *Mitteleuropa* meant anything to Ludendorff it meant not the Danube basin but the lands further north between Germany and Russia. That too was the vision of Ludendorff's colleague in the failed postwar putsch of 1923, Adolf Hitler. *Mitteleuropa* as a political programme might fade away but central Europe was still there.

There is, finally, one of history's might-have-beens. Between the Franco-Prussian War and the first Great War there was in Europe's states system one permutation which could have altered the face of European affairs, had it been pursued – a German-British entente.

To the British the German threat which arose after 1870 was not what it looked like on the mainland. Great Britain was still the greatest economic Power and (with the possible but deceptive exception of France) the only European Power which was also a World Power. It was committed to preventing the domination of the continent by a single Power and wedded, therefore, to the variable states system, but this deep-rooted doctrine did not preclude an Anglo-German partnership. Throughout most of the nineteenth century the British supposed that France continued to cherish hegemonial designs, so that the French defeat in the Franco-Prussian War was more surprising than unwelcome. In the same generation moreover British distrust of Russia as a rival in Asia was augmented while Great Britain's confidence that it could do without allies was eroded. Logically an Anglo-German alliance was on the cards. What aborted it were non-continental issues: naval hegemony and an indefinable emotional incompatibility.

Great Britain was as firmly committed to retaining naval hegemony as it was opposed to any other state's continental hegemony.
If sharing power with Germany in Europe meant allowing Germany to build commensurate naval power, then the deal was
off. Great Britain might be attracted by a European duumvirate
but was loftily uninterested in a world duumvirate. At sea Great
Britain was not so much supreme as unique, and it intended to
remain so. Neither the British nor the Germans were dead set on
a quarrel, let alone on war. With brief exceptions Anglo-German
relations at official level have been good from the creation of
the German state to the present day. Neither the Kaiser (Queen
Victoria's grandson – her eldest child's eldest child) nor Hitler saw
any need for a war with Great Britain or wanted one. Both the
one and the other found himself in a war with the British more
through ignorance than design. On the British side, as on the
German, a *pax Anglo-Teutonica*, giving other breeds a good example
and good governance, exerted sporadic fascination. But there was
also, in the last quarter of the last century, a fair degree of mistrust
in the ruling and commercial classes (repeated in and fanned
by the press) and too much mutual ignorance. The collecting of
information and its assessment were by modern standards ama-
teurish, and their shortcomings fostered mistakes which tripped
up groping approaches to friendship. The Kaiser, a well-meaning
but gauche and ill-educated man, struck a series of wrong notes,
most spectacularly in his flashy telegram to President Kruger of
the Transvaal Republic which convinced the British that the Kaiser
was impossible personally and his regime a threat to the British
empire. More persistently throughout a fateful decade the German
challenge to British naval superiority, personified by Admiral von
Tirpitz, was incompatible with an Anglo-German entente and put
the lid on it. At the turn of the century Great Britain's naval
superiority was massive and growing, but British self-confidence
was dented by humiliations in the Boer War and a still vague sense
of the ebbing of economic pre-eminence. Hence the abandonment
of glorious isolation from continental affairs and at the same time
a stubborn insistence on continuing naval power. Great Britain
resolved a variety of Anglo-French disputes outside Europe and
allowed this Franco-British *entente cordiale* to be merged with the
Franco-Russian military convention[4] to form the Triple Alliance.

4.   This accord was vital for both parties and yet only skin deep. The
      bond was fear of Germany. It was weakened by Russia's unexpected

The German naval challenge was parried by 1906 at the latest but when, eight years later, war broke out the British had no doubt which side they were on – or, at the very least, that they were not on the German side. Firm and lasting Anglo-German goodwill had to wait until neither country could hope to boast the greatest navy in the world. The naval issue touched raw nerves in Great Britain and ranged the British alongside the French and Russians, whom they did not much like or trust. Alliance with Russia in a war against Germany in 1914 was hardly less surprising than the same alliance in 1941. It came about in 1914 on the concrete issue of naval power and the less easily weighed, but no less potent, element of mood – an anti-German mood fostered by the forays and tempers of the Reich and the antics of its emperor.

Bismarck put Germany on the political map of Europe – literally, since before Bismarck it was not there. Geographically central and economically successful Germany became the strongest state on the continent. In the twentieth century it was defeated in two terrible wars but it was not erased and one hundred years after Bismarck's fall Germany, although shorn of some of its eastern parts and denied nuclear weapons, was the strongest state in western Europe. By some reckonings it might be accounted stronger than the Soviet Union.

defeat by Japan in 1905 and by the revolution of the same year which exposed the Tsarist regime's vulnerability. It had no common positive aims. Neither party was interested in what the other might get out of a general war. France stood to recover Alsace and Lorraine (but had no intention of going to war for them); Russia was entirely uninterested in these provinces. Russia wanted to turn the Black Sea into a Russian lake and get more than Austria out of any Ottoman stumble or fall; France had no special animosity against either the Austrian or Ottoman empire.

CHAPTER TWO
Interreich

The 1920s and 1930s turned out to be an interlude in two parts between two German Reichs and two Great Wars. In the first half of this period Germany was a stricken giant, in the second it was rampant. The new Reich appeared in 1933 and the second war began in 1939.

In retrospect this period is dominated, first, by the peace settlement of 1919 and, secondly, by the Great Depression which began a mere ten years later. In this context it fell, first, to Great Britain and France and, later, to these two states and Germany to manage the affairs of Europe.

Great Britain and France were not up to this task, not so much because of the mediocre talents of their leaders or because for much of the time they were in disagreement, but because they did not have the material resources for a role which the first war had magnified. They were swamped and had to fight again. Germany, once restored to power halfway through the interwar years, had by then designs which were not collaborative but destructive. Hitler's obsession with Germany's need for *Lebensraum* led him not merely to dismantle the Versailles settlement but also to take for Germany lands which could not be taken without fighting.

The first Great War was an enormous shock. It overturned confidence. One effect of industrial and commercial success in the last decades of the nineteenth century had been a population explosion which, France excepted, emboldened the peoples of western Europe to regard rising birth and survival rates as evidence of unstoppable well-being. The problems of having more and more people to feed and employ were veiled by steady economic growth and by emigration. Confidence became unquestioning and axiomatic. The war, by contrast, induced a mood of guilt in which the tragedy of war was seen as nemesis for over-indulgence in national pride and material wealth. Also, the war lasted much longer than most people expected and was far more horrible. Its cost was commensurately huge and dismaying.

The war caused the Austro-Hungarian empire to collapse; the Russian empire was destroyed by revolution and replaced by the Soviet Union which was disabled by civil war, foreign invasions and gross mismanagement throughout the interwar years; the Ottoman empire also disintegrated, although a successor Turkish state retained a foothold in Europe. In the European system the balance between greater and lesser Powers shifted, the former reduced in number and the latter greatly increased. Before the war there were five (or, by some calculations, six) Great Powers but after the war only two and a half (Italy, dubiously a Power at this level, and after the advent of fascism more than dubiously a cooperative member of the system). Lesser states rose therefore in significance as well as in numbers, and since they were all in the eastern half of Europe long-standing differences between east and west were accentuated. The problem of how to make the lesser states supply the place of departed greater Powers engaged the French in particular and was never solved. Self-determination, which was meant to give eastern Europe a western democratic savour, did more to reveal the gulf between western and eastern economies.

Although Germany reappeared as a major force halfway between the two wars, Russia did not and the United States opted out of European affairs. The Bolshevik revolution, although it achieved nothing tangible outside Russia's frontiers, spread clouds of mistrust and immoderate fears of submerged dangers which were held to threaten the very fabric of society and the entire moral order. How to cope with such threats was unknown. The United States, now the most powerful state in the world, was anxious to keep clear of Europe and for a while to pursue economic prosperity without political or military commitments. Permanently or temporarily the Superpowers of the future, as well as a majority of the Great Powers of the past, were off-stage, dead or on the sidelines.

The principal survivors, Great Britain and France, were weakened not only by the war itself and their solitariness on the European scene but by over-commitment in the wider world, from which they had been thought to derive extra strength. The extra-European context turned burdensome. Great Britain in particular was distracted, in both senses of the word, by the twentieth century's most startling political phenomenon – Japan – and by fears of what Japan could and might do to British territories, British wealth, British prestige and British promises (to Australia and New Zealand) in Asia and the Pacific.

This was the nemesis of empire. Europeans have never ignored the wider world which, given the size of Europe, is not very far away. From Herodotus to Livingstone it has intrigued and excited travellers, scholars, merchants and missionaries, but it was of minor political account until the venturings of these special groups were transformed in the nineteenth century into imperial extensions of state power and state responsibility. The exercise of this power and the discharge of these responsibilities required additional resources, material and intellectual, which in the twentieth century were hard to come by or begrudged.

The Treaty of Versailles provided the foreground and framework for the events which, in a broader sense, were conditioned by these trends. The making of the treaty was dominated by the experience of war, its havoc and emotions. The principal aims of the peace-makers were to prevent another war, by which they tacitly understood another war started by Germany. This was to be done by a combination of physical measures directed against Germany and the creation of machinery for the better exercise of statecraft. The outbreak of war twenty years later signalized the failure of both these endeavours.

The treaty was not negotiated, except among the victors themselves. When Napoleon was defeated in 1814 and again in 1815 the ensuing Congress at Vienna was attended by France as a principal party to the proceedings. When Germany was defeated in 1918 the Kaiser, like Napoleon, was obliged to abdicate, but the new rulers of Germany were summoned to Paris not to negotiate but to be told what had been decided. They were forced to admit German guilt for the war, pay for it and submit to special restrictions on their sovereignty. (The war guilt clause in the treaty was not merely an accusation. It provided the justificatory basis for the heavy reparations which the victors intended to exact.) This way of concluding a war was not unusual so much as unwise, particularly if the aim was to turn the conclusion of the war into a basis for peace. Every peace treaty is to some extent a *Diktat*. Circumstances make it so – and for some lawyers, employing the analogy of the law of contract, invalidate it. But the makers of the Versailles treaty so feared and hated Germany that they shut their eyes to a future which would certainly contain a Germany fit and able to operate as a major European state. They tried to rule out this eventuality or at least to postpone it beyond the reach of practical thinking, and since there were in the next few years no pressing reasons for reintroducing an impoverished and discredited Germany to the comity of nations, its full rehabilitation was postponed until it was in a position to rejoin on its own terms and as an outsider intent upon shaking things up rather than helping to manage them. Even the British, who had fought the Germans only once in living memory and were readier than the French with their memories of 1870 to treat the Great War as a singular aberration, did not abandon strident anti-Germanism until the first postwar general election was out of the way.

The Americans, represented at the peace conference by President Woodrow Wilson in person, were less concerned with the punishment of Germany than the re-patterning of Europe on the basis of national self-determination (something of a mirage and a disruptive one at that), together with the establishment of standing international machinery for the settlement of disputes without recourse to war: i.e. the League of Nations, to which French and British groups also made contributions but without the force or conviction which derive from heads of government.

In a neat and tidy continent such as did not exist the principle of self-determination would have produced discrete national states. In practice its application produced, in Czechoslovakia and Yugoslavia, national amalgams and, in relation to Germany, anomalies by banning a German-Austrian union, excluding three million Germans allotted to Czechoslovakia and giving the new Poland an unfair slice of Silesia. Other Germans, in Tyrol, were barred from inclusion in Austria, and Austria's erstwhile yokefellow Hungary lost to Romania the Hungarians who lived in Transylvania. Ethnic patterning was particularly thwarted by the events of 1917–21 in the east which left large numbers of White Russians and Ukrainians inside Poland. (The new face of Europe's eastern half is the subject of the next chapter.)

France wanted but had to forego the partition of Germany, a policy which was again mooted and again abandoned during the Second World War. If rationalized, this policy meant that self-determination did not apply to peoples who made wars, or perhaps to peoples whose union would be uncomfortably powerful, or perhaps uniquely to Germans whose central location and assumed propensities made them a special case. Denied the dismemberment of their principal enemy, the French (and Belgians) had to be content with the demilitarization of the Rhineland, the occupation of parts of it and the Saar, the disarmament of Germany, crippling reparation payments, and a promise of an Anglo-American alliance against renewed German aggression. This was an impressive package but it began to fall to pieces at once with the refusal of the United States Senate to ratify the treaty and the consequent evaporation of the Anglo-American pledge. (The United States then made a separate peace with Germany.) France entered upon the postwar era with a deep distrust of the United States and Great Britain.

For Germany the core of the treaty was twofold: heavy reparation payments, and the denial of all but a puny army and navy or any air force. Besides these impositions, both of which were eventually evaded, loss of territory and a limited occupation were comparatively bearable. The retrocession of Alsace and Lorraine and a small readjustment of the frontier with Belgium were neither to be avoided nor wondered at; the resurrection of Poland partly at German expense was more irksome but a recognized price of losing in war. In the long roster of treaties between victors and vanquished the Treaty of Versailles was unremarkable in that it did what such treaties were expected to do by way of penalizing and shackling the losers. Such treaties normally endure until the losers are strong enough to renegotiate parts of them. Germany succeeded in renegotiating the essence of the treaty within a generation, for a complex of reasons: Germany was inherently a strong state, only temporarily incapacitated; the alliance which won the war broke up, as such alliances frequently do; the unilateral disarmament of Germany came to seem anomalous, when the general disarmament envisaged at the peace conference did not follow; the war guilt clause, its original purpose forgotten, got a bad name which strengthened the case for revision of the treaty; the economic burden of reparations was represented as both excessive and damaging to the European economy as a whole as well as to Germany. The treaty's main aim – to keep Germany down – was overtaken by the question how to engage with a Germany which was on the way up and this question divided the principal erstwhile allies as well as opinion within each of them. Enforcement of the treaty failed spectacularly when France and Belgium, in exercise of their rights, reoccupied the Ruhr at the beginning of 1923 upon the failure of Germany to maintain reparation payments. The British disapproved and the Americans, although not a party to the Versailles Treaty, intervened to effect a compromise. Although from this early date the enforcement of the treaty was seen to be impractical, its revision was never comprehensively tackled. Only the size of the reparations bill was continuously debated.

The payment of reparations was a well-established practice. The costs of the war, which had been largely met by borrowing, were unprecedented and the victors intended to recover these costs over and above recouping the material damage which they had suffered. Undeterred by the lone warnings of J. M. Keynes, who argued that the treaty was unworkable (not that it was unjust),[1] the victors were guided by the example of the Franco-Prussian War, after which France had paid heavy reparations with surprising ease. At the 1919 peace conference there was no agreement on how much Germany should pay and the arithmetic was referred to a Reparations Commission which fixed the amount in 1921. The assessment was bedevilled by a number of disputes, such as whether reparations should cover pensions payable to relicts and the disabled as well as damage to property (which was mainly French and Belgian); whether the measure should be the damage suffered or Germany's capacity to pay. It was further bedevilled from opposite sides by those, mostly German, who said that the total was grossly unfair and unpayable; and others, mostly British, who argued that the exaction of large sums would do grave harm to the European and world economies by devastating the German market which was vital to their manufacturers and merchants. And thirdly, the reparations question was bedevilled by inter-allied war debts. Keynes, besides urging a modest reparations bill, proposed that all inter-allied debts be cancelled, but the Americans, much the biggest creditors, could not see the sense of this and insisted on keeping the two issues separate. France, a net debtor by a factor of two to one, complained that only through reparations from Germany could it pay its debts to the United States. It was also anxious

1.   Keynes regarded some aspects of the treaty as dishonourable but his main argument was that reparations claims were absurdly and self-defeatingly high. He assessed Germany's capacity to pay at £2 billion spread over fifteen years against £8 billion canvassed at Versailles and £6 billion fixed in 1921. After resigning from the British team at Versailles he was offered no official position until the next war.

to extract money from Germany as an alternative to heavy domestic taxes. Great Britain, heavily indebted to the United States but a net creditor, was ambivalent. The Franco-Belgian occupation of the Ruhr brought the issue to a head but only to a limited extent and to the advantage of Germany, since the Americans maintained their (ultimately futile) insistence on getting their loans back through bilateral deals with their allied debtors while intervening to present Germany with a revised schedule of reparation payments in return for a Franco-Belgian retreat. The Dawes Plan (1924) settled what Germany should pay over the next five years and gave Germany an American loan to sweeten the payments. Five years later the Young Plan revised and extended the Dawes Plan (to 1988), but less than another five years further on reparations and inter-allied debts were in practice abandoned by the Lausanne conference of 1932. The Depression killed them off.

The Dawes Plan was the first and most precise in a series of attempts to modify the postwar settlement instead of enforcing it. The Locarno Treaty (1925) was the next. It provided France and Belgium with the military guarantee which they had been vainly promised at the peace conference, but at the price of instituting a system which put them on an equal footing with Germany by giving Germany an equivalent guarantee against aggression. The language of Locarno was that of equals among themselves, as distinct from Versailles' overt and even offensive division of the principal European states into good victors and sinful losers. Germany's simultaneous admission to the League of Nations emphasized this new attitude. But Locarno, unlike the 1919 settlement, was restricted to western Europe by Great Britain's refusal to involve itself in eastern Europe either by giving the new states of the east similar guarantees or by supporting the sub-system nurtured by France in the east to create there an inhibiting threat to Germany's remoter frontiers.

There ensued the most important diplomatic bout of the decade, between Aristide Briand and Gustav Stresemann. Briand was French Foreign Minister for nearly seven years (1925–32) with a break of only a few weeks. Stresemann was German Foreign Minister for six years from August 1923. Stresemann, having partially secured his eastern front by a treaty of neutrality with the Soviet Union, opened talks with Briand after Locarno. His main aims were to accelerate the end of the Franco-British occupation of the Rhineland and the Saar, to secure a modification of Germany's frontier with Poland in Silesia, and to erase some of the more unpalatable aspects of the Treaty of Versailles such as the war guilt clause. To some observers, then and since, Stresemann was working Germany's passage back into the European Concert; to others his policies were the thin end of a wedge, prelude to a fresh attempt to dominate Europe or too much of it. This is a question about Stresemann's intentions. He could not achieve the first without at least facilitating the second, but historically it is of secondary importance to determine whether or not he wished the second.

The statesmen of the Weimar Republic had enormous tasks and, as it turned out, very little time in which to perform them. Defeat in war brought not only the burdens and humiliations imposed by Versailles but also domestic political upheavals of two kinds. On the one hand radical revolution, akin to the successful Bolshevik revolution, threatened the new German state from its inauguration in 1919 until around 1923. The threat was real, even if not as great as it was widely thought to be. On the other hand, it was the business of the new state to effect a different but hardly less radical reformation by substituting, for the military-industrial-landowning complex which had ruled the Second Reich, a parliamentary democracy on the British or French model. The politicians of Weimar leaned to the left rather than the right but were pushed to the right by the threat of communist revolution which, together with the first (failed) Nazi putsch by Hitler and Ludendorff in 1923, made them dependent on what was left of the army. They never tamed the army. In Germany, and elsewhere in Europe, the Bolshevik revolution, which so alarmed the right, in fact weakened the left by splitting it into communist and socialist sections which failed to reunite even to oppose fascism and Nazism (the French Popular Front, formed in 1934 and briefly in government from 1936, being the exception which pathetically proved the rule). This portentous split was partly methodological and partly doctrinal. It divided those prepared to use violence from those who renounced it; and it reflected the fundamental mistake of those communists who, believing fascism to be the last stage in the collapse of capitalism, opposed socialists whose willingness to take part in left–right politics seemed, in communist eyes, only to preserve the capitalist system and its injustices for a little longer. The Bolshevik revolution did great harm to the European left throughout the 1920s and 1930s.

In Germany the Kaiser had gone and the agricultural Junker interest was in decline, the army had been dissolved and industry shattered. But the new small army retained prestige and became exceptionally efficient and a focus for the cruder kind of patriotism. Industry rebounded in the boom of the late 1920s and, like the army, was ready to abandon Weimar for anybody (Hitler, for example) who might eradicate Versailles faster than the Weimar politicians, whom in any case these old pillars of the German state despised as socially inferior, politically suspect and unreliable champions of the sort of Germany which they wished to restore. Weimar weathered some exceedingly rough storms – communist and Nazi insurgence, the hyper-inflation of 1923, the occupation of the Ruhr – but the Depression proved too much for it.

A decade is a fearfully short period and the 1920s were unnaturally abbreviated by postwar miseries at one end and the Depression which was just round the next corner. The 1920s was a decade of postwar bewilderment in which an entirely new political pattern was imposed on a continent struggling to recover its prewar poise and prosperity in the wake of the Versailles and kindred peace treaties and (to a lesser extent) the Bolshevik revolution. The complexities were compounded by a similar fragmentation and impoverishment of the international economic order which, until this period, had been dominated and stabilized by Great Britain. Under the signs of free trade and the gold standard the economic relations between sovereign states, expressed in the exchange rates of their national currencies, had been held steady, with manageable balances measured and adjusted in gold. As in the political sphere the national units were comparatively few after the consolidation of the German world in the third quarter of the nineteenth century, but the war set in train the destruction of this adequate, if fragile, system by greatly reducing the value of all currencies, even more greatly altering the relations between them, and by creating in the new post-Versailles states new and weak national economies: economic weaklings destined to be puppets or shuttlecocks. Reparations therefore and inter-allied debts were only part of systemic economic disorder.

The United States declined the role of regulator which the British had filled. The British half thought they could go on filling it. The decline of the British economy in relative terms since before the end of the previous century was a commonplace, but its extent and significance were imperfectly assessed, the principal European competitor (Germany) had been eliminated, and victory in war fostered illusions, particularly about the British empire which had significantly strengthened the British war effort and was regarded as a continuing source of strength in peacetime. Yet British imperialism had become doubly negative: negative in the sense that Great Britain was no longer seeking lands to conquer, and negative too in the sense that the imperial role was imposing impossible burdens on the British budget. The role had been sustained by industrial wealth and commercial muscle, but much of the wealth came from declining industries so that Great Britain was slowly ceasing to be the dominant element in the world's economy and, as it did so, was equally slowly turning away from free trade to an imperial sub-system in which British dominions and colonies could be relied upon to go on buying British manufactured goods and supplying Great Britain with mineral and agricultural products. Great Britain was becoming the centre of a large economic system which, however, was smaller than the total world system and it was withdrawing into this secondary role because, consciously or (probably) not, it was ceasing to be equipped for the greater.

Nevertheless, Great Britain, having lost its predominance (to nobody in particular), strained to get back to the prewar order by restoring the convertibility on demand of sterling into gold, at the prewar rate of exchange with the dollar: the albatross of an overvalued currency. Since this rate was unrealistically high it could be maintained only by a policy of deflation which (as later in the 1980s) constricted industrial output, maximized unemployment and excluded Great Britain from the modest boom of the late 1920s. (At the same time the French franc was also stabilized at the wrong rate, but one which was too low rather than too high.)

In October 1929 stock prices on the New York stock exchange crashed. A rising boom turned into catastrophe because buyers went on buying on 'spec' until the boom got out of hand. This was one of those local affairs which, given a certain context, may turn into an epidemic. By 1931 the American stock market disaster had become a world economic disaster. Among its multiple causes one, perhaps the chief, was an expansion of credit which had been gathering pace from the early 1920s and which had stimulated an unrestrained speculative rise in stock prices far outstripping the simultaneous economic boom: the rise in prices lost sight of the rise in values. The modest economic boom and the immodest stock market boom in the United States had a major effect in Europe because they diverted into American activities large sums of money which had been flowing into Europe. As after the Second World War, so after the First, the destruction or loss of assets at home and abroad forced European countries into dependence on American funds, which were at first plentifully available and then not. American investment in Europe helped European enterprises to recover and when investment petered out it was for a time succeeded by American loans, but from about 1928 American funds of all kinds began to dry up and then virtually disappeared. The economic distortions caused by the war and by the peace settlement – by material destruction, financial dislocation, reparations, inter-allied debts, inflated credit – were exacerbated by a consequent trend to protectionism and by maniacal speculation in the United States. One kind of crash begat another: first stock prices, then banks which, in the United States, had lent too much to farmers and, in Europe, had lent too much to renascent industries.

An attempt was made in 1927 under League auspices to reverse the protectionist trend which threatened to clog world trade by turning every national economy inwards on to itself. The World Economic Conference held in London proposed a truce to tariff increases and quota restrictions, but its qualified success was quickly overturned when President Hoover felt obliged to take action to protect American farmers (who were overproducing and were deeply in debt to their banks) and in 1930 the Congress approved the severe Smoot-Hawley tariffs. The agricultural crisis in the United States was a main trigger of the world depression. During the war American agricultural production had expanded to fill the gap made when good European farmlands were given over to trenches and shells, but after the war European agriculture recovered, causing overproduction in the United States and falling prices and incomes: American administrations tried to protect farmers' incomes without doing anything about the overproduction, giving farmers more loans, subsidies and the haven of stockpiles (the last a temporary expedient which cut neither production nor farm debts). When the stock market crashed and the credit balloon was pricked, purchasing power collapsed too, industrial production did likewise and the menace of inflation turned into the menace of deflation.

In Europe bankruptcies began with small and relatively unnoticed enterprises but spread to the largest, including (in 1931) Austria's biggest bank and two months later one of the four big German banks. Unprecedented unemployment ensued, causing great misery, fear and deprivation and a slump in confidence in government, accompanied in a number of countries by violence and renewed fears of the revolution which many thought had been only narrowly averted in the first years after the end of the war. The shocks of 1929–31 scared statesmen into convening an International

Conference on Monetary and Economic Questions. It took place in London in 1933. Its scope was wide and its consequences negligible. It was to embrace topics such as currency stability, loans and liquidity, reparations, tariffs and quotas. It revealed the subordination of international cooperation to national self-interest, not least from the Americans who failed to give any leadership and then killed the conference off. As international trade withered, the terms of trade improved for European manufacturing countries but the improvement was valueless since there was little trade. Attempts to revive industry by promoting external consumer demand were doomed to failure, leaving only the remedy of boosting internal demand by investment and extended credit. By adopting such Keynesian methods Great Britain began to recover in 1932, sooner than its neighbours. The policies of the 1920s were jettisoned, bank rate was reduced to 2 per cent (where it remained until 1951 except for one brief interval during the second war), substantial sums were invested in building, and manufacturing output rose by 50 per cent. In France, on the other hand, which suffered later but more severely than other leading European countries, governments embraced deflation, gold and balanced budgets; lent huge sums of money to banks and other enterprises and lost them; refused until 1936 to devalue the franc; cut real wages, forced women out of the labour market, and so added social unrest and political instability to economic disorder. The tactics of sticking a finger into a crumbling dyke converted France into a Power no longer to be reckoned with. The Popular Front government led by Leon Blum tried to reverse this tide by raising wages by law, cutting working hours and introducing holidays with pay – only to find that such measures were ineffective or worse without a coordinated international strategy. Blum was forced out of office in 1937 (he returned briefly in 1938) and was treated by half of France as a menace greater than Hitler.

There was no revolution in France but there was in Germany. In 1931 the centrist government of Heinrich Brüning, hagridden by recollections of Germany's prodigious inflation only eight years earlier (which ended with the introduction of a new mark worth one million old marks), clung to deflation with its inevitable concomitant of falling wages and rising unemployment until, too late, he abandoned it in 1932. Unemployment quadrupled in three years. Amid increasing turmoil and brutality the flagging Nazi party revived spectacularly, winning 107 seats in the Reichstag in 1930 in place of only 12 two years earlier, and in 1932 a majority. At the beginning of 1933 President von Hindenburg, the Second Reich's most emblematic Field Marshal, made Hitler Chancellor of the Third. The Nazis set about refashioning German society and politics and preparing the country for war in a chaotically ill-organized but purposeful exercise of power which solved some economic problems – particularly unemployment and output in heavy industry. Production of tanks and aircraft, although only about half what British intelligence calculated it to be, cancelled some of the more painful aspects of the Depression, aided by Hitler's short-term concentration on conflict which led him to accelerate Weimar's comparatively modest rearmament programmes, spurn the cautiously conservative economic policies of Hjalmar Schacht (who was replaced by Hermann Goering as economic supremo in 1936) and go for quick results regardless of long-term economic logic. In the long term Germany's economic problems would be transformed because Germany itself would be transfigured.

Both before and after Hitler came to power in 1933 Germany's overriding national aim was to redress not only the failures in the field of 1918 but also the real, if exaggerated, injustices inflicted by the peace treaty of 1919. Before 1933 Stresemann, after that date Hitler, pursued the same ends by very different means. Stresemann, like Adenauer in a comparable situation after the Second World War, wanted to work Germany's passage back to the comity of European nations. Hitler, by contrast, defied those nations. Stresemann, unlike Adenauer, was shackled by economic crises, notably the postwar inflation which destroyed the German economy and middle classes; and, unlike Hitler, spoke for no more than a small minority of his countrymen and women. The second great economic crisis of the interwar years – that of 1929, to which Germany was more vulnerable than its principal European neighbours - transformed German politics from a conflict around the political centre to one between the extremes of communism and Nazism which Hitler easily won with his programme of reasserting German pride, rearming the German forces and reviving plans for a German empire over much of continental Europe. (Hitler would have liked to establish this empire with the connivance of Great Britain. He turned to an alliance with Italy only because British attitudes were ambiguous and Italy was thrust into his path by the Ethiopian crisis.)

The short history of the interwar years was one of experiments and expedients whose main purpose was security – in diplomatic parlance making Europe safe from war, in reality making it safe from Germany. The Versailles Treaty was the basic blueprint; the Locarno Treaty of 1925 a second attempt, but confined to western Europe. The authors of the Versailles Treaty hoped to sidestep another war by rearranging the map of Europe and by general, not merely German, disarmament – by reducing the causes of war and its instruments. But there could be no disarmament before security, which neither Versailles nor Locarno provided. There were marginal achievements such as international protocols on gas warfare and submarine warfare, but the long-heralded Disarmament Conference was postponed beyond the 1920s and then straddled (1930-34) the Nazi conquest of power in Germany; it was dispersed without issue by that event. Thereafter the question was not disarmament but rearmament. The recovery of Germany and the advent of Hitler, marked by Germany's departure from the Disarmament Conference and then from the League of Nations, signalled the end of Anglo-French control over the agenda of European affairs. They signalled too the collapse of the attempt to provide Europe's states with security. Great Britain and France had failed to do this during the eclipse of Germany, and Germany revived set greater store by other things.

When Weimar Germany, with which Briand had tried to reach accommodation in the 1920s, was annihilated it fell to Great Britain to try in the 1930s to reach accommodation with Nazi Germany. The British aim was to prevent another war. It failed. Hitler's aim was to create in Europe a New Order. He failed too – but only just and at a terrible price all round.

CHAPTER THREE
The Changed Face of Central and Eastern Europe

The First World War changed the face of eastern Europe. It did nothing comparable in western Europe. The agents of this change were the collapse of the three empires which had dominated central and eastern Europe for centuries together with the principle of national self-determination. The new eastern Europe looked on a map like western Europe, a neatly defined patchwork of sovereign, nearly national states, each with its precise boundaries, a place in the broader international network of states, and the appropriate symbols of national flag, national anthem and national bank. They were, however, profoundly different from the states of western Europe, for whereas in the west nationalism had proved more constructive than destabilizing – the prime examples were France and England whose strong centralizing monarchies and mutual hostilities had been at work creating these states from the Middle Ages – in central and eastern Europe nationalism created acute conflicts both between states and within them. In addition their economies were in western terms backward or very backward. Their statehood therefore was vulnerable, their independence severely circumscribed, and although ostensibly actors in international affairs they were constantly on the verge of becoming somebody's puppets.

The Low Countries have been called the cockpit of Europe but that name belongs more accurately to central Europe whose wide-open spaces have been repeatedly ravaged by invaders and perennially disputed between Germans, Slavs and Magyars. Central Europe has been Europe's most turbulent zone. From the time of the Goths in the second century, followed by Huns, Vandals, Avars, Magyars, Mongols and Turks, this zone was constantly and more ferociously exposed to invasion than the west. The Magyars (or Hungarians as other people called them) were vigorous enough to reach the Loire and Bremen before settling down in the Danubian plain where they still are. The Tatar Mongols raided as far as Warsaw and dominated Russia from the eleventh to the sixteenth century. The Byzantine empire, which persisted for a thousand years after the dissolution of the Roman empire in the west, was more Asian than European for most of that time and was succeeded by the even more alien empire of (Muslim) Ottoman Turks which lasted into the present century. Bouts of instability alternated with bouts of stagnation. The Turks killed the Black Sea trade, cared little for any except local industries in their European provinces, neglected roads and allowed even cities to fall into decay: Athens lost even its name. The Slavs, the largest ethnic group, stretching from the Baltic to the Adriatic and the Black Sea, were split by successive waves of Avars, Magyars and Turks and never formed a consolidated state or even a single language. Given their demographic preponderance this incoherence has been an important factor in the instability of the area and an invitation to predators.

A sense of national identity did not produce the strong states characteristic of western Europe, even where that identity was most pronounced (Hungary, Poland). In the west kings created compact and efficient states, prevailing over unruly barons, promoting urban economies (which they could tax) and substituting central authority for local caprice. But further east royal dynasties were most often foreign, short and bullied by a nobility which obstructed the growth of central authority.[1] Although towns appeared in the later Middle Ages they flourished less vigorously than their western counterparts, partly because there was no farming hinterland

---

1.   Hungary had six royal lines between 1301 and 1526. Only one king (Matthias, 1458–90) was native and his roots were as much Vlach as Magyar. The other lines came from Anjou, Luxembourg, Austria, Poland and Bohemia. Bohemia itself in the same period had a line of Luxemburgers, one of whom was killed fighting miles away at Crécy, and native and Polish interludes before being gathered into the Habsburg fold. In Poland the nobles imposed an elective monarchy which produced kings from here, there and everywhere, puppets either of the nobles or of some foreign state. Contrast France where every king from the tenth century to the last was a direct descendant in a male line from Hugh Capet.

prosperous enough to feed them. Between towns and countryside there was a chasm, often ethnic, sharper than any known in the west, and no comparable agricultural revolution. Agriculture, the most important economic activity by far, was stunted for centuries by an exploitative landowning aristocracy too ill-educated to realize that an abused and half-starved peasantry, regularly debilitated by malaria and plague, was no instrument for raising agricultural yields. Central Europe was remoter than the west from the great seas, thinner in population and poorer in natural resources. Its commerce, education and invention were commensurately retarded.

On the western flank of this relatively poor and inchoate zone were the Germans, represented in the north by the Teutonic knights, by their Hohenzollern cousins of Brandenburg-Prussia and eventually by Bismarck's Reich and Hitler's: the principal antagonists of these Germans were first Poles and then Russians. To the south were their Austrian kinsmen, whose antagonists from the sixteenth century were the Ottoman Turks.

When the kingdom of Hungary was destroyed by the Turks and its king killed at the traumatic battle of Mohacs in 1526 the Habsburg duke of Austria, who was the king's brother-in-law, was forced into the front line of the defence of Christendom against Islam. After Mohacs most of Hungary became Ottoman territory, the rest Habsburg. Besides inheriting a tattered Hungarian crown the Austrian duke was also, or soon became, king of Bohemia, Holy Roman Emperor, ruler over assorted Slavs and Italians, and so overlord of poly-ethnic central Europe. For good measure he was also the champion of the Roman Catholic counter-reformation as well as Christianity's standard bearer against the Turks. The Habsburgs were thenceforward committed to the policies, including the religious policies, of central Europe, a German outcrop in a non-German world. Although Turkish power reached its apogee in the sixteenth century nobody at the time knew that this was so. Vienna was besieged towards the end of the next century but was saved by the Pole John Sobieski. The Ottoman reflux was slow and its sluggishness was the most important thing about it, since the duel between Austrians and Turks was still undecided when a third Power appeared on the scene. This third Power was Russia. Alone of all these three imperial Powers, Russia survived the First World War and then went on to win the second. Between the wars central and eastern Europe were penetrated by Germany gradually until 1938–41 when Hitler, preparing to attack the Soviet

Union, deemed it necessary to subjugate the whole area (except Albania) and had no difficulty in doing so.

The map of 1919 represented broadly what the new states (other than those which had been on the losing side) wanted and were able to win as a consequence of the defeat of the imperial Powers and the substitution, with eager American backing, of the principle of national self-determination.[2] But the Americans

2. The principle of self-determination is not as simple as it looks. It offers justice and satisfaction to groups but, not infrequently, discomfort to individuals belonging to the group. It asserts that a body of people which constitutes a nation is entitled to govern itself as an independent state. It is therefore a disruptive principle. Many of its results have been unhappy. At the political level it has created states which have been unable to support themselves or improve the lot of their citizens. Some have been less than good at governing themselves. Self-determination after the First World War removed (mainly) Turkish, Austro-German or Hungarian over-lords but replaced them in a number of instances by class-conscious military castes with ruinously expensive chauvinist policies. The principle of self-determination has also contributed to the view that groups, notably ethnic minorities, have rights. Yet rights pertain to individuals and not to groups. Groups mean well by the individuals whom they represent but sometimes subordinate the well-being of these individuals to the preservation of their group identity or to values or traditions not shared by the whole group. Groups which demand rights for themselves *qua* groups do so on the assumption that rights cannot be secured to individuals without a constitutional separation of the group, even its political independence. This may be true in some circumstances of some religious or other cultural attributes but it is not true of all civil or political rights. The insistence on being distinct is more often than not disruptive and invades the greater happiness of a great number. The individual has the right to make the choice between distinctiveness and happiness, but the group does not have the right to make that choice for him and there is no justification for the general claim that the preservation of group attributes ranks above the happiness of the individual. The champions of minority group rights condemn assimilation, even when assimilation may be the better path to happiness. This conflict is an aspect of the antithesis between the collective and the personal ideals – an unstoppable pendulum which has animated western civilization for good and ill since, at least, the time when it marked the transition from classical to hellenistic Greece, from the ethos of the *polis* to the ethos of individualism.

quickly lost interest in their foundlings; the British were no less determined to keep out of eastern European affairs; the French were concerned for the new states only as a second-best substitute for their lost Russian alliance and as a buttress for the anti-German pattern of the 1919 treaties. Of the two Powers traditionally and geographically involved in the area Germany was absent for half the interwar period and Russia for the whole of it. In the absence of these two Powers the settlement was essentially provisional and the reappearance in the 1930s of the one without the other placed the whole area at the mercy of Germany. For a brief period a German *Mitteleuropa* came about by default.

The peace treaties of 1919[3] elaborated a patchwork of new states, or states with new boundaries, which were part of, or contained fragments of, the Habsburg and Ottoman empires. The frontiers of these states were drawn with scant regard to economics. Austria was marooned, Hungary amputated. Industries everywhere found themselves cut off from their sources of supply and their markets. So was agriculture. Cities were deprived of food. Waterways, railways and telephone services were chopped up into smaller segments, which were less efficient and more expensive. People lost their jobs because they had the wrong nationality. The flow of goods, capital and labour was impeded by new administrative and legal barriers. President Tomas Masaryk of Czechoslovakia mooted a federation of all central and eastern Europe excluding Russia but including Poland and Greece, but the response to this and other proposals for economic cooperation was faint. After some economic advances in the late 1920s all these states were felled by the Depression. Their agricultural economies, hampered initially by the fragmentation of landholdings, were battered by the slump in world prices for their produce. Czechoslovakia, with an industrial base in its western half, was a partial exception and the three Baltic republics converted with some success to animal husbandry, but attempts by the Danubian states to industrialize led to competition between them without fruitful diversification by the time of the general economic collapse of the early 1930s. They were accorded only a decade to match political independence

3. Besides the Treaty of Versailles with Germany there were the Treaties of St. Germain with Austria, Trianon with Hungary, Neuilly with Bulgaria and Sèvres with the Ottoman empire. The last was a dead letter and was replaced in 1923 by the Treaty of Lausanne.

with economic independence and, like the Third World in later years, found that the more prosperous countries which were their principal customers had selfish reasons for conceding as little as possible: Great Britain, for example, because of its special commitments to the Dominions; France for fear of offending its rural voters. The Depression, which arrived a mere decade after the end of the war, accentuated and exposed the vulnerability of the whole area and the inability of the new states to defend their independence. They were minor, relatively helpless but not therefore insignificant counters in a states system which had been constructed as a Great Power system but had been shorn of its Great Powers in this zone.

Eastward from Germany there were eight of these states with, to the north of them, the resurrected Poland, three new Baltic republics and Finland. France, trying to make up for the disappearance of its Russian ally, made an alliance with Poland (1921) and constructed the Little Entente with Czechoslovakia, Romania and Yugoslavia, beneficiaries of Versailles and therefore hopefully clients of France. These were anti-German insurances of questionable value and so less than satisfactory for all parties: a *pis aller*. Italy, puzzling over the expediency of fishing in Danubian and Adriatic waters, toyed with the idea of sponsoring a Danubian association with Austria, Hungary and Romania and was specially concerned about the new Yugoslavia and the older Albania, neighbours and adversaries across the Adriatic. But Italy got no help from its wartime allies in its claim to annex Fiume (as well as Trieste) from the Austro-Hungarian collapse, and when Fiume was seized by the madly nationalist poet Gabriele D'annunzio the Italian government was itself obliged to remove him. Italy was also forced to desist from meddling in Albania and was condemned and again forced down after bombarding Corfu in the course of a dispute with Greece. After more than a decade of unproductive ventures in European affairs Mussolini, while never oblivious of Italian interests on the further shores of the Adriatic, decided that he could do better in Africa.[4] Only Great Britain was consistently disinterested

4. Italy's Adriatic and Balkan policies were fashioned by the Nationalist Party of Luigi Federzoni rather than by Mussolini and the Fascists. The Nationalists were included in Mussolini's first government and then swallowed by the Fascists. Mussolini's obsession with Africa echoed that of Francesco Crispi half a century earlier and proved equally disastrous.

in central and eastern Europe until the last year of peace. When
a British prime minister declared that Great Britain's frontier was
on the Rhine, he meant what he said: the Rhine, not the Danube.
The British endorsed the principle of national self-determination,
supported the independence of the several states (Great Britain had
no prospect of making them dependent on itself), deplored French
designs for using them to construct anti-German combinations,
was worried by their economic instability and favoured in the
abstract any measures likely to reduce it. But the British were
more concerned to keep away from troubles than to put them
right in a part of the world which, until a second Great War
became obviously imminent, occupied a low place in the British
international agenda.

Germany had only one serious rival in the area: France. French
strength lay in its financial resources – it had money to lend – and,
in the special case of Austria, in the letter of the law. Germany
offered trade which, particularly after the Depression, proved a
more potent instrument and, particularly after the Nazi seizure
of power, enjoyed the advantage of being able to ride roughshod
over its agricultural lobbies whose protests were no longer backed
by effective votes in a German parliament.

The first round of the Franco-German contest was fought over
a German proposal for a customs union with Austria. France,
fearful of the making of a new Reich, objected that it would be
a breach of the Treaty of St Germain and of undertakings given
by Austria when it was rescued from financial disaster by the
Geneva Protocol of 1922.[5] At this juncture one of the principal
Austrian banks, the *Creditanstalt für Handel und Gewerbe*, went
broke (May 1931); there were doubts about Austria's ability to
service its foreign debts; and France seized the opportunity to
get Austria, in return for financial aid, to abjure unilaterally the
idea of a customs union with Germany, thus consigning itself
to economic limbo. France proceeded to overplay its hand. The
economic crisis which had destroyed the *Creditanstalt* spread from
Austria to Germany and beyond and was no more than checked
by the moratorium on payments for reparations and inter-allied
debts sponsored by President Hoover. France too was a victim

5. The French case was subsequently rejected by the Permanent Court
    of International Justice in respect of the treaty but upheld in respect
    of the Protocol, in each case by eight votes to seven.

and when it resolved to follow up its success over Austria by negotiating preferential trade treaties with Danubian countries it discovered that Germany could play the same game better.

French treaties with Hungary, Yugoslavia and Romania were robbed of most of their economic and all their political consequences by the French farming lobby which in effect vetoed French foreign policy. German farmers were as hostile as French to commercial agreements which helped foreign growers to compete with them but in Germany, both before and more pressingly after the Nazis won power, governments went further than the French in overriding farmers' lobbies in order to exploit strategic opportunities – an unusual example of the prevailing of foreign policy over domestic concerns but one readily available to Hitler because he had eliminated genuine elections in Germany. Pre-Nazi treaties with Hungary and Romania (1931) had been scuppered in practice by German farmers' lobbies but after 1931 Nazi Germany established a stranglehold over the Danubian and Balkan countries by paying scant attention to the short-term grumbles of German farmers. In effect Hitler enslaved foreign countries at some expense to the German economy but damned the expense.

The concept of Europe split into two parts by the Second World War and the Cold War has become a commonplace of postwar discourse. Yet eastern and western Europe were sharply divided long before the present century; central and eastern Europe, while sharing disadvantages *vis à vis* the west, were themselves different from one another; and within each sector further differences alienated the several states from each other.

Central Europe had experienced in the nineteenth century some urbanization and the slow growth of commercial and professional middle classes which were mildly tinged with liberalism. These classes espoused a romantic nationalism, secular rather than ecclesiastical (and so different from Balkan nationalism). Politically they were overshadowed by landowning aristocracies or a foreign upper crust and although they discussed and advocated constitutional and social reforms they looked for upper class leaders to champion change and were easily scared when (as in the year of revolutions, 1848) initial moderate success incited a radical fringe to press for more. In the next century these classes became more numerous and politically more robust, and after the First World War they inherited unforeseen responsibilities when the ruling classes were swept away by their display of ineptitude. The war had opened in the east with spectacular incompetence by Austria against Serbia.

Germany intervened to ensure the capitulation of the Serbs – grudgingly, as it did in 1941 in North Africa to redress a similar failure by an ally – but the Austro-Hungarian empire collapsed none the less and what was left of its core was divided into two small and secondary states. Central Europe ceased to be controlled by an Austro-Hungarian partnership and was refashioned as the three mutually suspicious states of Hungary, Czechoslovakia and Poland took most of its place. Poland had twice the population of Czechoslovakia which had twice the population of Hungary. There were Czechs in Poland, Poles and Hungarians in Czechoslovakia, Slovaks in Hungary. There were substantial German and Jewish minorities in all three countries: the Germans in Czechoslovakia amounted to nearly a quarter of the population, the Jews in Poland to nearly a tenth. Hungary contained Slovaks, Croats, Slovenes, Serbs and (as listeners to Liszt or Bartok know) gypsies[6] but was less conscious of its domestic ethnic anomalies than of the Hungarians in Transylvania which it had been obliged to cede to Romania.

Poland had a strong identity, fortified by the loss of independence for 123 years which had concentrated the aspirations of Poles on the recovery of statehood. But this national consciousness was without secure location. No country in Europe has moved or been moved about as has Poland. It reappeared on the map at a time when, by a strange coincidence, both its major enemies, Russia and Germany, had been temporarily knocked out and the third author of its partition in the eighteenth century – imperial Austria – had disintegrated for good. Poland had a history of expansion which had been foiled in the eighteenth century by the rising Powers of Russia and Prussia. Re-born it re-embarked on the foreign adventures which many Poles regarded as delayed retribution and the best way to prevent another subjugation. The victory of the Bolsheviks in Russia presented them with allies in the shape of anti-communist Ukrainians and enabled them to storm across Europe to Kiev. Baulked in their extremer aims they retained nevertheless territories peopled by five million Ukrainians and Byelorussians (White Russians) and they also seized and kept the Lithuanian capital of Vilna (Vilnius) in despite of the newly created Lithuanian republic. To the west and south Poland recovered lands

6. Perhaps as many as half a million and at the bottom of the socio-economic pile.

from Germany and Austria in an untidy settlement which was never accepted by Germany or deemed adequate by Poles. Poland gained territory to the north west round Poznan, but not the city of Danzig with its mostly German inhabitants; and parts of Upper Silesia after much wrangling, but not the whole territory of Teschen (Tezin) which was divided with Czechoslovakia – unfairly to the Poles – and seized by them in 1938. This quarrel drew Poland to Hungary which harboured even greater resentment against Czechoslovakia.

Czechoslovakia comprised the so-called historic lands of Bohemia and Moravia, part of Silesia abstracted from Germany, and Slovakia and Sub-Carpathian Ruthenia both formerly under Hungarian rule. Not all the victorious allies were wholehearted in this act of creation. The British in particular had hoped to keep an Austro-Hungarian state in being. Besides its quarrel with Poland over the apportionment of Teschen (and its coal) Czechoslovakia was threatened at birth with the loss of Slovakia which Hungary briefly occupied. Ruthenia, whose people were neither Czechs nor Slovaks, was promised a degree of self-rule which was never implemented. In the historic lands Germans were numerous enough to claim autonomous status as a distinct province in northern Bohemia, and it was even suggested at the peace conference that this province might be attached in some way to Austria, with which it had no frontier.

The pattern of politics in Czechoslovakia between the wars was the familiar western spectrum from right to left, with the left splitting into socialist and communist parties and the right divided between a conservative agrarian party and a nationalist or chauvinist strand which tended to fascism. The politics of the historic lands were secular in tone, but in Slovakia the highly politicized and conservative Roman Catholic church dominated affairs. Externally the Czechs looked to Romania and Yugoslavia which had similar sources of friction with Hungary, while Slovaks – always halfhearted about their association with the historic lands and increasingly right wing as the years went by – were more favourable to an accord with Hungary and Austria: a new model of the old empire rather than a league to prevent its revival. To Czechs and others a rehabilitation of Hungary raised some of the same apprehensions as had the Russian attempt to establish a big Bulgaria in 1878 – a big brother protected by a bigger one – while any alliance or federal scheme which focused on one of the old imperial capitals smelled too much of the *ancien régime* to be palatable to the new states born out of its ashes. These fears perpetuated the fragmentation of the area. Beyond the area Czechoslovakia's principal support was France, an alliance epitomized by the Franco-Czechoslovak treaty of 1924 and its uselessness in 1938. The small communist party hoped for Russian support against a German revival, particularly after the Nazi seizure of power in 1933, but communists were perennially uneasy about Muscovite regimentation. The German minority became more and more disaffected as it espied a willing backer over the border in a Germany reinvigorated under the Nazis. These tensions eventually wrecked the state, browbeaten by international agreement at Munich in 1938 and taken over by Hitler and dismembered six months later. Virtually all its surviving Germans fled or were evicted in 1945.

For Hungary the First World War was a disaster. A re-birth of Magyar consciousness in the nineteenth century had made it culturally confident and even aggressive, and the *Ausgleich* with Austria had raised it to a dual partnership which relegated other possible partners to an inferior place. Defeat in 1919 represented the revenge of these subordinates.

Hungary's territory was reduced by two thirds. Transylvania alone, shuttled back to Romania, was larger than what was left of Hungary, which lost other lands too to Czechoslovakia and Yugoslavia.[7] Its plight fomented the revolution of 1919 led by Bela Kun whose communist regime was overthrown with the help of invading Romanian and Czech forces – a reminder of the defeat of the 1848 revolution in Hungary by Russian invaders going to the aid of the Habsburg monarchy. The counter-revolution which followed the defeat of Kun was exceptionally savage. It proclaimed Hungary a kingdom, but when the last king, the Habsburg emperor

7.   Transylvania has been attached to Hungary for most of the last thousand years but has never had a majority of Hungarians in its population. It was Hungarian property from about 100AD to the destruction of Hungary by the Ottoman Turks in 1526, when it became a province of the Ottoman empire. The Turkish withdrawal at the end of the seventeenth century transferred it to the Habsburg empire as an autonomous province in which Hungarians were lords over a Romanian peasantry. The Austro-Hungarian *Ausgleich* of 1867 turned it over to Hungary. In 1920 most of it was given to Romania. In 1940 Hungary recovered most of what it lost in 1920, only to lose it again in 1947. By 1990 Hungarians constituted about one sixth of a population of 7.5 million.

Charles, arrived in Budapest to claim the throne he was told that Habsburgs were no longer welcome. A subsequent attempt to secure the crown by force failed and Admiral Nicholas Horthy was appointed regent of a kingdom which remained without a king until he and it foundered in 1944. Economically Hungary was comparatively well favoured. It produced a surplus of food and was able itself to finance modest industrialization out of the proceeds of agricultural exports and therewith to develop its infrastructure and education and win access to supplemental foreign investment. Before the war its large landowners, politically dominant, enlarged their mental horizons as they participated in diverse economic activities. After 1919, however, these landowners and the attendant gentry and middle classes went down in the world and the depression midway between the wars further depressed them and encouraged the growth of Italian-style fascism. Hungary hitched its small waggon to Hitler's juggernaut, won back by his good graces much of the lands lost in 1919, paid for them with grievous losses of life in fighting with the Germans in southern Russia, was occupied by the Germans in 1944 when trying to escape from German tutelage, and was occupied a few months later by the Soviet army.

When central Europeans were being ruled or fought over by other Europeans, eastern Europeans were under the even more alien rule of the Ottoman Turks. Their nationalism was rooted in the researches and propaganda of ardent *savants* who, in the eighteenth and nineteenth centuries, revived and dignified vernacular languages in order to foster national pride and self-consciousness in alliance with no less ardent ecclesiastical leaders who combined religious zeal with political ambition. Their nationalism was inescapably militant. Its aim was political independence and it needed help from outside. The jealousies and disputes among major Powers provided it. The Russians wanted to supplant Turkish power and to block the extension of Austro-Hungarian power; the Germans became embroiled in the Russo-Hungarian conflict over the Ottoman heritage and then succeeded the Austro-Hungarians as Russia's main adversary. The principal concern therefore of native nationalists was to pick the right power of which to be the client. Territorial changes were the outcome of these choices; and territorial changes were the stuff of politics since nationalism was not satisfied by the removal of alien imperial governors but entailed also contests over liberated areas with mixed populations. To a far greater degree than in western or even central Europe the expression 'nation state' concealed grave discrepancies between nation and state and committed political leaders to the business of removing anomalies which they regarded as national disgrace.

Eastern European societies were overwhelmingly agrarian. There were no indigenous aristocracies and only a small bourgeoisie, cautiously open to liberal ideas imported from France or Great Britain but otherwise suspicious of foreigners (and Jews) who were regarded as predators, not always unjustly. Industrial development was embryonic and dependent on foreign capital and knowledge; it tended therefore to be haphazard and prone to over-indebtedness, a pitfall which reappeared after the second war. Urbanization and industrial development were sluggish in the 1920s and reversed in the 1930s. Both before and after the First World War these states were mainly in the hands of cliques which were extravagant, snobbish and fond of large armies. Turkish forms of government which had prevailed over centuries gave way only slowly and politicians who described themselves as party leaders often exhibited for generation after generation the style and attributes of pashas. Their parties, although they might be called Peasant Parties or Liberal Parties, were the personal followings of individuals whose programmes were pursued by intrigue and demagoguery. The few radicals were allied neither with the hapless peasantry nor with the exiguous proletariat. The peasantry, the great majority of the people, was poor and chronically in debt; had shabby housing or none, inadequate food and no education; and was despised. Surplus agricultural products, where they occurred, were generally unexportable because of their poor quality. Emigration was a dream realized by few. To the economic misfortunes of the Great Depression these countries responded not by closing ranks but by enhanced distrust of one another and increasingly authoritarian or incompetent government: the autocratic Yugoslav monarchy became more autocratic, Romania a kingdom of pals, Bulgaria a political shambles.

All the states of eastern Europe had ancient pedigrees which they revered and which were magnified by the often romantic historicism of the nineteenth century when history was an adjunct of politics, less an academic discipline than a boost to parochialism (of which all traces have not disappeared). Romanians traced their ancestry to Roman times and settlement, and the two provinces of Moldavia and Wallachia whose union created the modern Romania antedated the Turkish conquest of the Middle Ages. The birth of the modern state was a by-product of the Russian defeat in the Crimean War, coupled with but delayed by Austrian and British inclination to prop up the Ottoman empire which was the proprietor of the two provinces. When the Crimean War ended, Austrian and British diplomacy prevented the union of the provinces which, however, circumvented the ban by choosing in 1859 the same foreign prince to preside over both. This union was acknowledged three years later and independence followed after the next war, when Russia defeated Turkey in 1878 (by which time the first German prince had been replaced by the Hohenzollern line which lasted until 1948). There was, however, a third province, Transylvania, which to Romanians was no less a constituent part of Romania but whose inhabitants included Hungarians, German immigrants over many centuries from the late Middle Ages, and sprinklings of Ruthenians and Jews. The defeat of the Austro-Hungarian empire in 1918 gave Transylvania to Romania and also the Austrian territory of northern Bukovina. The defeat of Russia gave it Bessarabia – long contested between Slavic Ukrainians and non-Slavs, ceded to Russia by Turkey in 1811 and retroceded to Turkey after the Crimean War. Romanians became a minority in their own country. In 1940 Hitler gave Transylvania back to Hungary but his defeat reversed this award, as likewise his award to Bulgaria of southern Dobruja which had been won by Romania in the Balkan Wars of 1912-13 (the Black Sea coast being a recurrent bone of contention between the two countries). In the same year Stalin annexed Bessarabia and turned it into the Soviet Union's Moldavian Socialist Republic.

Bulgarians could not look back to the Roman empire since they did not arrive until the seventh century AD, but they were able to recall two Bulgarian empires which had flourished on the decaying outskirts of the Byzantine empire. Ethnically Slav and in religion Orthodox they were a natural instrument and grateful client of Tsarist Russia against, not only ruling Turks and Latin Romanians, but also the Orthodox but non-Slav Greeks and even the Orthodox and Slav Serbs: both the Greeks and the Serbs constituted autocephalous or autonomous churches within the community of Orthodox churches, a distinction not granted by the Ecumenical Patriarchate to the Bulgarians until 1870 – a source of much spleen. The Russian connection brought the Bulgarians great advantages and commensurate disappointments. A rising in 1876 was put down by the Turks with savage slaughter; it was the occasion for Gladstone's philippics against the Turks. The Turks went on to belabour the Serbs and staved off the diplomatic protests of the Great Powers with diplomatic deviousness until the Russians, matching impatience with opportunity, declared war and won it. At San Stefano near Istanbul[8] they imposed on the Ottoman empire a peace which included the creation of a large Bulgarian state which was to embrace most of what later became southern Serbia and Greek Macedonia and was manifestly to be an outpost of the Russian empire in south east Europe. The other major Powers immediately intervened and under the presidency of Bismarck in Berlin in 1878 insisted that Bulgaria be greatly curtailed, divided into two and remain under Ottoman suzerainty.

The Berlin settlement satisfied nobody since even those who gained thought they should have got more. A first attempt in 1885 to unite the two segments of Bulgaria was unsuccessful and shortly afterwards the Battenberg prince installed by the Powers in 1878 was replaced by a Saxe-Coburg prince chosen by the Bulgarians themselves. In 1908 he declared a united Bulgaria to be an independent kingdom (in this formative period the interests of imported monarchs and native nationalists coincided). But this coup had its price. The advancement of Bulgaria only thirty years after the rebuff of 1878 was achieved with the connivance of Austria which simultaneously annexed the Ottoman provinces of Bosnia and Herzegovina – a coup which, besides angering the Turks, aggravated the ill will between Bulgarians and Serbs and confirmed them as rivals rather than partners among the southern Slavs. Although their rivalry was briefly suspended for the first Balkan War against the Turks, it was resumed in the second Balkan War in which the other anti-Turkish allies – Romania and Greece – combined with Serbia against Bulgaria and deprived the latter of its gains. The outcome of the Balkan Wars was as great a setback for Bulgaria as the Treaty of Berlin of 1878, and it was compounded when Bulgaria joined the losing side in the First World War. These conflicts were further embittered by the Macedonian question which pitted Bulgaria against Serbia and Greece.

Macedonia was an ancient name – a kingdom which produced one of the world's most spectacular conquerors in Alexander the Great and had retained a nominal identity as a province in successive empires from the Roman to the Ottoman. The Macedonians, as an identifiable people, arrived a century or so before the Bulgarians

---

8.   In a house belonging to the author's great grandparents. San Stefano is now Yesilköy.

reached the Balkans. They occupied an area rather larger than
Iceland, well endowed agriculturally and lying across the main
routes from central Europe to the Aegean and the Mediterranean. They spoke an undeniably Slav language, but how distinct
they were, or thought themselves to be, was a fiercely debated
question. They might be Bulgarians or Serbs or neither. Seeds of
conflict first began to germinate with the help of holy water. The
establishment of the autocephalous Bulgarian Orthodox church in
1870, displeasing to Serbs and Greeks, inaugurated a contest for the
souls and allegiance of the Macedonians which became politicized
as the Turkish withdrawal came evidently closer. At the very end
of the century an Internal Macedonian Revolutionary Organization
(IMRO) was founded in the Bulgarian capital, mainly in support
of Bulgarian ambitions but partly in favour of an independent
Macedonian entity in a Balkan federation. IMRO used violence
from the start (it had little else to use) and eventually degenerated
into a racketeering mafia. The Balkan Wars and the First World
War, an almost uninterrupted sequence of warfare, pushed the
competing states into partition agreements which, after 1918, left
Bulgaria with no more than a tenth of Macedonia, Yugoslavia
with four tenths and Greece with half. Greece was then removed
from the tangle because a great part of the Macedonians in Greek
Macedonia departed for Bulgaria, leaving it overwhelmingly Greek
in character. An exchange of populations under the Treaty of
Neuilly, implemented over the ensuing twelve years, transported
25,000 Slavs from Greece's eastern Macedonia into Bulgaria. The
Slavs of Greek western Macedonia, whose affinities were with
Yugoslavia, were unaffected and many stayed where they were.
More significant for Greek Macedonia was the Treaty of Lausanne
of 1923 which engineered the exchange of 350,000 Turks from
northern Greece for 640,000 Greeks from Turkey, many of whom
settled in Macedonia.

The most obtrusive change brought about in eastern Europe
by the First World War was the creation in 1921 of Yugoslavia
(meaning south Slavs, but excluding some of them). To Serbs,
Yugoslavia was Serbia writ large: Serbs accounted for more than
a third of the population and nearly half the area and provided the
king. The Serbs, like the Bulgarians, cherished memories of a medieval empire which, in the fourteenth century, dominated much
of the European territories of the Byzantine empire before being
abruptly extinguished by the Ottoman Turks. The Turks advanced
to the Adriatic coast – most Albanians and many Bosnians being

converted to Islam – and to the walls of Vienna, receded gradually from about 1600 onwards, but remained a substantial presence into the twentieth century. They did not conquer the Croatian or Slovene Slavs who fell into the sphere of Austrian and Hungarian imperialism and aspired to share power in the Austro-Hungarian empire rather than to join the Serbs in a new Slav state. Serbia, being on the western fringe of the Ottoman empire, outpaced its neighbours on the road to independence and, unlike Greece, Romania, Bulgaria or Albania, acquired native instead of imported dynasties. A national rising in 1804 began the expulsion of the Turks and secured autonomy under the rule of an hereditary Serbian prince which was later converted into an independent kingdom. Serbia's geography put it in the front line of the clash between the Austro-Hungarian and Ottoman empires, while its nationalist ambitions concentrated its mind on expanding its borders at the expense of whoever happened to occupy, or might wish to occupy, lands regarded as Serbian: in particular, Bosnia which was under Turkish rule until appropriated by Austria in 1908, and Macedonia which was under Turkish rule until 1912.

The creation of Yugoslavia satisfied many Serbian aspirations but substituted a Yugoslav for a Serbian state. Yugoslavia, as its name divulged, was an amalgam (like Czechoslovakia) and the largest and most heterogenous state in south east Europe. It embraced an enlarged Serbia, Bosnia and Herzegovina, Slovenia, Croatia with Dalmatia, Montenegro and much of Macedonia. Half a million Croats and Slovenes were outside the new state in Italy, and the inclusion of the Dalmatia coastline displeased Italy which had hoped to win it out of the collapse of Austria. The annexation of Vojvodina to Serbia created a running dispute with Hungary. An unsuccessful attempt to include Albania soured relations with the Albanian inhabitants of Kosovo and Metohia (the Kosmet) in Serbia. The incorporation of nearly half Macedonia perpetuated Serb-Bulgarian animosity. The incorporation of Montenegro – the first of all the Balkan states to declare war on the Ottoman empire in 1912 – followed a decision in Montenegro in favour of union with Serbia but entailed the extinction of the state and its native dynasty. Croats, outnumbered two to one by Serbs and mistrustful of them, wanted an independent Croatia; the Croat Ante Pevelic established in 1929 the *ustachi* which were the spearhead of secession, contrived in 1934 the murder of King Alexander I (a Serb but also a genuine partisan of the federal state) and in the Second World War divorced Croatia from Serbia by turning it into a puppet kingdom under an absentee Italian prince. Religion added its discords, particularly between Orthodox Serbs and Roman Catholic Croats. Yugoslavia included at its birth half a million Germans and almost as many Hungarians. It concluded in 1934 the Balkan Pact with Romania and Greece, leaving Bulgaria still the odd man out, but by this date regional politics were becoming overlaid by Great Power politics as Hitler revived the German Reich and prepared to engulf central and eastern Europe in the prelude to his attack on the Soviet Union. All else was suspended.

CHAPTER FOUR
Hitler's Reich

Hitler's ambitions ran contrary to the one hopeful way of giving post-1919 Europe an international framework for the interplay of its national conflicts without war. By 1933 three states – France, Great Britain and Germany – each had markedly more power than any but themselves. Anything upon which they were agreed they could most probably bring about. The historical importance of Hitler (or part of it) is that he postponed any prospect of such agreement for a generation and in doing so transposed this possible three-way association into an entirely different European context.

After 1919 France was once more Europe's leading continental Power but had lost its principal European ally, Russia; Great Britain, still Europe's most powerful world Power, lost the lynchpin of its world policies, its alliance with Japan. A German revival would find both these Powers less well placed for a war with Germany than they had been in 1914, but after 1933 avoiding war with Germany meant allowing Hitler a free hand in central and eastern Europe. Eventually they fought Hitler's Reich to prevent this expansion of German territory and power.

Hitler knew broadly what he wanted. He had been thinking for years about the one subject that enthralled him and he had written a book about it. *Mein Kampf* was a blueprint for Germany's *Kampf* for *Lebensraum*. The two words are equally indicative. Hitler believed that a nation or *Volk*, like a plant, must grow or die, that in order to grow it must have room or living space, and that war was a permissible and indeed admirable way to get it. He thought fighting was a healthy occupation, good for the body politic. He despised peoples who were not 'Aryan' and in the case of Jews (and gypsies) he believed them to be not merely inferior but positively evil. He wanted to rid Germany of Jews but had no way of doing so until the war presented him with a way of doing far more. Baulked by a somewhat hazy scheme for transplanting German Jews overseas (for which he needed but lacked a dumping ground and control of the seas) he found himself in 1942 in a position to round up nearly all Europe's Jews as well as Germany's and transport them to Poland where some six million of them were killed. This appalling crime, unparalleled in European history except perhaps by the slave trade, displayed two of Hitler's principal characteristics: obsessive determination and opportune planning. He was not a man of many ideas, good or bad, but those ideas which he had he held obdurately and pursued fiercely when occasion arose. His territorial aggrandizement of Germany was non-negotiable but it was sketchily planned.

Hitler triumphed in 1933 through a combination of circumstances: the economic confusion which scared many Germans of all classes and destroyed faith in the existing political system; long-standing nationalist indignation against the discriminatory clauses of the Treaty of Versailles, together with the conviction that Germany was now strong enough to right these postwar wrongs; and the frightening disorder and violence which the Nazis had themselves done most to create and were therefore best qualified to curb. All these circumstances gave the Nazis an appeal which was classless. In 1932 they won 37 per cent of the vote in a general election, the highest score achieved by any party in any election during the Weimar period. Initially Hitler's power seemed limited by other groups with whose help he had won power, and foreign statesmen who wanted to persuade themselves that Hitler was a national leader like any other (if a bit uncouth) sought comfort in the belief that he was less a dictator than a partner in a coalition. But this was a complete misinterpretation of the circumstances and of the character of a Führer who might accept useful associates but had no use for partners with any claims to independence. German army officers and industrialists shared his aims sufficiently to give him enough rope to hang them. In external affairs foreign leaders were treated in much the same way, used until discarded.

Hitler's Reich was like Bismarck's in being a country on the march and powerful enough to be a menace. It was unlike Bismarck's in both its European and world contexts. While Bismarck's Germany had been one Great Power among five or six, Hitler's peers in Europe were only two. A balance of power system with only three main levers is more difficult to maintain than one with six. Nor was Hitler interested in working a participatory states system for its own sake. He had neither the disposition nor the talents for such statesmanship. His assessment of German power, which proved in 1941–42 to be only marginally (if disastrously) wrong, was based on his readings of recent history and on his racial prejudices. He was misled by the first Great War which went reasonably well for Germany except at its very end and included the comprehensive defeat of Russia: Hitler himself never served on the Russian front and knew at first hand only about the final outcome, not the rigours, of the eastern campaigns. He also misjudged Great Britain. Unlike von Tirpitz he was not keen to challenge Great Britain at sea and had only the haziest notions about extending German power beyond Europe. But he was again misled – partly perhaps by British eagerness for a bilateral Anglo-German naval agreement in 1935 – into thinking that Great Britain would give him a free hand on the continent and would welcome a German attack on communist Russia: a misjudgement which might possibly have been valid if Great Britain had not already been at war with Germany when he launched his invasion of the Soviet Union. What he got most damagingly wrong was not the aversion of British statesmen to communism or to continental entanglements of any kind but the strength of British popular persistence in a war once it was in train. The growth of German power alarmed British statesmen and kindled their atavistic hostility to the continental dominance of any one Power; they went to war in 1939 – or, more precisely, took steps which made that war inevitable – because they judged that German power had become too great and must be curtailed before it became a monopoly. They were concerned primarily about the extent of that power rather than its beastliness. But concurrently Nazi excesses, which were not themselves a cause of war, ensured the continuance of the war through their cumulative impact on the susceptibilities and emotions of decent people. As in 1914, so in 1939, the British had become slowly but powerfully convinced that Germany was bad. Churchill, who conceded a case for negotiating peace in the winter of 1939–40 (between the invasions of Poland and the west), was in tune with British public opinion when he refused to consider such a step after the spring of 1940. Finally, Hitler was no less mistaken about the Americans, whom he despised sufficiently to declare war on them. He was in many crucial matters an ignorant man, although shrewd enough and intelligent in the limited areas which appealed to his temperament.

Hitler's foreign policy might be summed up in two words: Go east. The causes of the war that began in 1939 lay in eastern Europe. There were no causes in western Europe. The war began because Hitler was determined to gain territory in the east by war if necessary, and accepted the necessity. In 1933 there was still much to be done before he could get going, rearmament being the first item on the agenda. There was also the question what, if anything, western Powers would do about Germany's eastern adventures into south east Europe in the first place and then against the Soviet Union. He was impeded in 1938 by the existence of western commitments to Czechoslovaks but circumvented them; he was interrupted in 1939 when the western Powers declared war on him for his invasion of Poland, but the interruption was brief. These were subordinate matters. From 1933 to 1939 Hitler was engaged to the eastward in clearing the way for his attack on the Soviet Union in 1941 and short of the Soviet borders he met no serious opposition to his *Drang nach Osten* because eastern Europe was a power vacuum.

Hitler had his eye on central Europe from the first. Austria, besides being his birthplace, was for him a natural piece of Germany and so too was Czechoslovakia with its substantial German minority and long history of association with the Holy Roman Empire: Prague had once been its capital. Hitler had also a personal hatred of the Czechs from the times before 1914 when he had seen too many of them for his liking in Vienna. He planned to kill half of them and turn the other half into a denationalized helotry. Strategically both Austria and Czechoslovakia, which he originally proposed to subjugate in a single coup, were a staging post in his envelopment and conquest of *Lebensraum*. So too was Poland. They had to be subjugated. Other countries might have to be subjugated and easily could be. Hitler's well-advertised aims, together with his hectoring style and rearmament, forced all central and eastern Europe to give prior and pressing attention to relations with Germany rather than France which, worsted in middle Europe and at arm's length from Great Britain, reverted to its older policy of alliance with Russia but did so very much less than wholeheartedly. The treaty negotiated by Louis Barthou in 1934, although ratified by Pierre Laval after Barthou's assassination, was then pigeonholed. As Hitler shaped up to war with the Soviet Union eastern Europe was increasingly divorced from western Europe. Only the Franco-Czechoslovak treaty of 1924, which exposed him to a French attack in the west whenever he decided to invade Czechoslovakia on his way to the Soviet Union, might stay Hitler's hand.

Although Great Britain had no such commitment to Czechoslovakia, Hitler risked a British declaration of war in support of France. This gave him pause and scared some of his senior generals. It was to pose the most serious obstacle to his foreign policy, so much so that in 1938 he compromised and agreed at Munich to a limited dismemberment of Czechoslovakia which, although only a temporary check, was an unpalatable rebuff forced upon him by a rare display of Anglo-French solidarity.

The prewar subjugation of central Europe by Germany showed that the European states system, which had worked reasonably well until 1914, was inappropriate after 1919, when a plethora of minor states occupied an area of strategic significance. These states could not sustain either their formal sovereignty or their effective independence. Their subjugation was an exercise of economic power by a state which was not content with economic penetration but was bent on using economic power to pave the way for military dominion. If Germany had been willing to regard central and eastern Europe as distinct and separate parts of Europe economic control would have sufficed, but in the pursuit of *Lebensraum* these areas were a strategic as well as an economic zone – particularly on account of British power in the eastern Mediterranean and the presence of British forces in Egypt and the Middle East. Economic subordination was therefore supplemented by political assimilation, leading at the crucial moment to military invasion and occupation. (The instrument of political assimilation was the Tripartite or Anti-Comintern Pact, first concluded in 1936 by Germany and Japan, almost immediately joined by Italy and later by Spain, and eventually rammed down sundry eastern throats.) This was the end of independence for half a century for nearly all the states created or enlarged by the 1919 settlement, for there proved to be no escape from Hitler's rule except by subjection to Stalin's.

Besides the vulnerability of central and eastern Europe as constituted after the First World War, Hitler had a second big advantage. He had no extra-European distractions. France on the other hand had, and Great Britain had more. Although British commitments beyond Europe were no new thing, their impact on British power and policies was changed. Great Britain was a Power distracted, and its distractions were the major source of the absence between the wars of any effective Anglo-French entente or any consistent British European policy.

From 1936 a substantial segment of the British army was in Palestine. The Royal Navy was, according to its own chiefs, dangerously stretched. At the Dominions Conference of 1937 Great Britain renewed pledges which, notably to Australia and New Zealand in the event of Japanese aggression, the navy could not honour if there were also war in Europe or the need to deploy naval forces in the expectation of war. (The influence of the Dominions on British policy was considerable. Kept extensively informed by London the governments of the Dominions were well equipped to bring timely pressure to bear on the British cabinet. They had their ears to the ground floors of British policy-making.)

Both the Middle East and the Far East were regarded as vital areas for British interests, no less vital than Europe. The combination was unsustainable. The majesty of British power, demonstrated by its great capital ships and the fortifications of Singapore, was no counter to the loss of the prewar Japanese alliance. By defeating China in 1895 and Russia in 1905 Japan had become the greatest Power in Asia and (in Manchuria from 1905) a mainland Power. From 1902 it was an ally of Great Britain. This alliance was lost at the postwar naval conference (1921–22) when Great Britain toed the American line and forced Japan to accept naval ratios offensive to its newborn pride. Thereafter Great Britain oscillated between mending relations with Japan and displays of assertiveness. The touchstone was Japanese aggression in China which, by requiring Great Britain to stand up and be counted, exposed its desperate ambivalence. The affairs of east Asia impinged on the politics of Europe by forcing the British to keep looking over their shoulders.

In 1927 Japan occupied the Shantung peninsula which it had successfully claimed in 1919. In 1929 the Soviet Union sent forces to protect the Chinese Eastern Railway, which was Russian property. The Japanese army engineered the Mukden Incident to enable it to conquer Manchuria and extend its empire from island to mainland (as when the Venetian island republic took what became the Veneto). The sources were militant nationalism, plus fear of a reintegration and reinvigoration of China by the Kuomintang, plus the need to protect Japanese export industries hit by the Depression.

Great Britain could not recognize Japan's conquest of Manchuria without offending China and flouting the Covenant of the League, nor help China with loans without offending Japan, nor – any longer – treat Far Eastern affairs as an independent group of problems. Japan's aggression in China and fears of what Japan might do in south east Asia and the Pacific had repercussions in Europe which were altogether new. In the past Europe had done things in Asia, not the other way round. The change was confusing. While some, including Churchill, underrated and even despised the Japanese 'Asiatics', others – especially admirals – were alarmed by them. British politicians, including Chamberlain, distrusted the Americans, hankered after the old alliance with Japan, but could not convince themselves that its revival was worth the risk of American alienation. The handling of European affairs was greatly complicated by the intrusion of these other continents. Only Hitler did not need to bother about them since Germany no longer possessed anything in Asia. In the event the Japanese inflicted humiliating defeats on the British and other European imperialists, were comprehensively defeated in their turn by the Americans and became a Great Power again in next to no time.

Great Britain had no wish to get into a conflict with Germany in Europe or anywhere else, and least of all in south east Europe which it regarded as remote and inconsequential. Germany might dominate the area provided it refrained from the blatant use of physical force. Great Britain's overriding aim was peace, not the preservation of the territorial status quo. Boundaries might be shifted within reason, if thereby peace might be made more secure.

This was an honourable aim. Throughout the years between the wars most British Ministers were men who had fought in one war and were resolved to save the next generation from having to fight in another. To achieve its aim Great Britain sought to reincorporate Germany into a states system, on terms appropriate to its strength and position, as quickly as possible; France, by contrast, aimed principally at keeping Germany in durance for as long as possible. There were arguments for either policy, but nothing to be said for the more or less simultaneous pursuit of both by Powers supposed to be allies.

The British regarded the French as revanchist and obstructive; the French regarded the British as foolish and unreliable. The British foresaw a German menace which they were trying to prevent, the French saw a German menace which they were trying to contain. The characteristic British contribution to international politics was the belief in rational dialogue, a belief taken to irrational lengths when extended to talking Hitler out of conquering *Lebensraum*.

To many in France Great Britain's approaches to Germany, which developed into the policy aptly called appeasement, were a cloak or pretext for a new alignment in Europe, and when Hitler's advent to power sharpened well-grounded French fears of Germany the French Foreign Minister, Louis Barthou, set to work to construct a counter alliance with the Little Entente, Italy and the Soviet Union. He was, however, assassinated in October 1934 and his plans bore no fruit because France had lost its capacity to make or lead such an alliance; French political will was sapped by the Depression; French governments were ill-assorted coalitions, indecisive and short-lived; French society was plagued by apocalyptic visions of a new French Revolution engineered by Soviet communists or the socialists led by Leon Blum or both. Increasingly pessimistic French politicians belittled France's capacity for war and deliberately exaggerated Germany's military might in spite of the fact that French war production remained superior overall to Germany's until the last days of peace in 1939 (but defective in some areas, notably aircraft).

Concurrently with the demise of Barthou and his policy Italy took its first decisive step towards joining Hitler's bandwagon. Ever ambivalent, as both Great Wars demonstrated, Mussolini's Italy caught the pseudo-imperialist bug which is sometimes latent, sometimes patent in the Mediterranean – historic home of great civilizations.

Mussolini's swagger was regarded north of the Alps as footling but no worse, until in 1935 he falsified a minor episode in Ethiopia, invaded it by way of the Red Sea and Eritrea, slaughtered the ill-armed Ethiopians with modern firearms and gas, appropriated three quarters of the country and, emulating Disraeli, called his king its emperor. The British and French were offended by this *parvenu* attempt to emulate their imperial status in Africa, were alarmed by the obstacles it created to good relations with Italy and calm in the Mediterranean, and were caught in a dilemma between upholding at Italian expense the clearly violated Covenant of the League of Nations and, on the other hand, enticing Italy to their side against Hitler. Great Britain in particular was loath to take any meaningful action against Italy, not because the Italian navy was a serious threat to the British, but because, as the admiralty advised the cabinet, the Royal Navy could not cope simultaneously with war in European and eastern waters; any need to reinforce the fleet in the Mediterranean could encourage Japan to make hay in Asia and the Pacific.

This dilemma produced two disastrous compromises. Great

Britain and France took the lead in proposing international sanctions against Italy as required by the Covenant of the League, but since the measures taken excluded those (an oil embargo in particular or closing the Suez Canal to the passage of warships and arms) of real effectiveness, the outcome was severely to hamper Italy without stopping its operations, to alienate Italians and to discredit the League. Secondly, a Franco-British plan to give Italy as much as it wanted of Ethiopia to keep on good terms with France and Great Britain was prematurely disclosed, publicly excoriated and abandoned – with similar consequences. The Ethiopian crisis made French and British leaders look sillier and shiftier than Mussolini, a remarkable achievement. It also increased distrust between them.

Civil war in Spain (1936–39), beginning as a military revolt against the government of the Spanish republic and ending with the victory of the insurgents, was conducted in ideological terms, right against left. The French and British ruling classes were on the whole on the government's side but more out of respect for legitimacy than on the ideological grounds in which the conflict was portrayed. Socialists and Radicals (moderate conservatives) in France, the bulk of the Conservative Party in Great Britain, were uneasy and fumbled. When General Francisco Franco won with German and Italian help they were lucky that he opted for a quiet life inside his peninsula and refused to contribute more than a token anti-Soviet division to the ensuing Great War. Franco, recalling perhaps the way Napoleon and the British had turned Spain into a major battlefield, preferred to keep it on the European sidelines where it had been for most of the time since the early seventeenth century. The Spanish civil war accentuated European fears of the long arm of Soviet communism and, chiefly owing to the open and active participation of the German air force, was the single greatest element in the growing popular conviction that a bigger war was inevitable.

In 1938 Hitler annexed Austria. Mussolini gave this *Anschluss*, which he had feared and opposed, his blessing. Others acquiesced, telling themselves that after all the Austrians were Germans of a kind and there was nothing they could do to reverse the union anyway. In the same year Hitler pushed on his plans against Czechoslovakia, which he had intended to appropriate at the same time as Austria, but the circumstances were different because only a minority in Czechoslovakia were Germans and there were people who could do something: there was the Franco-Czechoslovak treaty of 1924 and there was a distinct possibility that if France were to fight for Czechoslovakia the British would not leave France to fight alone. The British peace-above-all policy required therefore that France did not fight for Czechoslovakia.

Hitler's method was to exploit the grievances of the German minority in Czechoslovakia who, like the Slovaks at the other end of the country, felt ill used by the Czechs. There were three million of these Germans, mostly clustered in the Sudetenland and increasingly politicized by their leader Konrad Henlein who was himself increasingly drawn to the German Nazi party and obedient to Hitler. President Benes of Czechoslovakia made a number of concessions to Henlein's demands for autonomy but every concession was met on Hitler's advice by demands for more. Hitler was less interested in the situation and rights of the Sudeten Germans than in the subjugation of the whole country. He grossly exaggerated the plight of the Sudeten Germans and insisted that there was no solution to it short of redrawing the frontiers to bring them into the German Reich. The violence of his language supported the general belief that he wanted conflict with Czechoslovakia rather than accommodation, and the stronger the impression that he was bent on war the greater the pressures on Great Britain to find concessions that would prevent it. Most senior German generals were opposed to war with Czechoslovakia because in 1938 it was in every way except one (manpower reserves) better equipped for war than Germany, quite apart from the fact that its treaty with France would expose Germany to war on two fronts. Some Germans contemplated a coup against Hitler in order to prevent this war and put out feelers for a determined and open Anglo-French opposition to Hitler in support of Czechoslovakia, as a preliminary to a coup. They were, however, unwilling to take a first step on their own and their tentative rebellion against their own government was not treated as a serious factor in the situation. Chamberlain moreover was convinced that Czechoslovakia could not be saved. His aim, in the course of three visits to Hitler (at Berchtesgaden, Bad Godesberg and the Munich conference) was not to save Czechoslovakia but to save the peace.

Daladier, his French opposite number, was prepared to fight although some of his cabinet colleagues were not, and Chamberlain promised that if France went to war Great Britain would do so too. This promise made it imperative to prevent the emergence of a *casus foederis* under the Franco-Czechoslovak treaty. On the other hand, the existence of the treaty was useful to Chamberlain since

Hitler could not be sure that he was not rushing into the war on two fronts for which he was not equipped and his generals had no stomach. The combination of Hitler's doubts and Chamberlain's ruthless pursuit of peace produced the Munich settlement. Chamberlain and Daladier told the Czechs that they would get no French help. They caved in. Hitler accepted a piecemeal adjustment of his frontier with Czechoslovakia instead of the immediate and more drastic surgical operation which he had been demanding; besides shifting the bulk of the Sudeten Germans into the Reich it undermined Czechoslovakia's daunting defences. In effect Czechoslovakia was eliminated at Munich, although Hitler was forced to take two bites at the cherry and spread the dismemberment of the country over six months.

In the following spring Hitler engineered a separatist coup in Slovakia to make it a German puppet and occupied the Czech provinces of Bohemia and Moravia. Great Britain and France, which had guaranteed post-Munich Czechoslovakia, observed with staggering speciousness that after the defection of Slovakia there was no Czechoslovakia left, so that their guarantee had lapsed. In Poland, where Hitler's handling of Czechoslovakia caused fear but little sorrow, Colonel Josef Beck was trying belatedly to build defences against an all too obvious threat. He said that he was ready to reinvigorate the Polish-German treaty of 1934 and to talk about frontiers, and he tried to organize a league of secondary states: Poland, Hungary and perhaps Italy too. But these were futile moves. Hitler strung Beck along so long as Czechoslovakia remained unfinished business and then made it plain that his price for leaving Poland alone was Danzig – a city peopled by Germans, assigned none the less to Poland in 1919, made a Free City under the aegis of the League, and in whatever guise a threat to Poland if ever it were incorporated in the German Reich. Hitler's price, therefore, like the severance of the Sudetenland from Czechoslovakia, was a permanent German threat to Poland's political freedom and to its very existence.

Poland's treaty with France (1921) was presumably of no more value than Czechoslovakia's had been, that is to say, next to nothing. But such calculations were baffingly jumbled by a British decision to give Poland (and Romania) undertakings of military help in the event of their being attacked. This surprising move reversed at the eleventh hour the British aversion to commitments in eastern Europe and the recent British refusal to bolster Czechoslovakia. It showed that Chamberlain's victory at Munich in staving off war was acknowledged to be a pyrrhic victory. It did Poland no good. Hitler used it as a pretext for breaking off talks with Poland and when he attacked later in the year the promised British military help never came. In the intervening months Great Britain and France continued, for want of being able to do anything else, to treat the Polish question as a dispute about frontiers. Hitler, however, had other things uppermost in his mind. He was drawing nearer to the Soviet frontiers which he must breach in order to secure the *Lebensraum* which he judged necessary for the future of the German race. But just as the Franco-Czechoslovakia treaty had made him pause at Munich, so the British undertakings to Poland forced him seriously to envisage a war in the west when he attacked Poland. Contingency plans for war with Great Britain already existed but they had been prepared in a spirit of prudent precaution and with the hope on Hitler's part that they would remain in the relevant files of the general staff. The British guarantee to Poland obliged him to reflect that his attack on Poland might entail more than a *promenade militaire*. A serious campaign would be a distraction, although – given the disparity in their warmaking capacities – a less daunting one than the prospect of joint Czech and western campaigns against him: it would interfere with his timetable but hardly wreck his grand strategy. How long a time he had allotted in his mind between the subjugation of Poland and an invasion of the Soviet Union is unknown, but war in the west could impose a longer rather than a shorter interval, and in that interval he must have untroubled relations with the Soviet Union. While he did not fear the Soviet Union, it must in his scheme of things await its turn and not take any initiative of its own. So a holding agreement with Stalin was much to be desired, even if it meant partitioning Poland with the Soviet Union temporarily and postponing the wholesale slaughter of Poles (eventually the Germans killed 15–20 per cent of them) and other preparatory moves on the Soviet southern flank in the Balkans.

Making an agreement which you do not intend to keep is not difficult. The details hardly matter. Stalin was as keen as Hitler to make a pact. He had been as obsessed as the British with a Japanese rather than a German threat. He coveted the fruits of a predatory partnership with Hitler and he desperately needed time since Hitler was almost certainly a partner in bad faith and an enemy. A substantial part of his army was engaged in Asia and all of it had very recently been demoralized by an insensate purge of its officers from top to bottom. His rule was at least as unpopular as the Tsar's had been a generation earlier; he had no allies and no faith in the belated and unenthusiastic approaches made to him by Great Britain and France; his war industries were untested and incomplete and in the wrong places. Making a deal with Hitler took little time because it was a necessity. The Soviet-German pact of 1939 was an agreement between two Powers but an agreement only in name, the manifestation of a passing common interest. It lasted two years. In 1941 Hitler broke it. But as in 1914 the German general staff had planned to defeat France in the months between high summer and Christmas and failed, so in 1941 Hitler tried to do the same to the Soviet Union and he failed too.

In both cases the outcome was the collapse of Europe's central Power. Less than four years after Hitler's invasion Soviet forces took Berlin and Hitler's armies surrendered unconditionally, most of them to Soviet conquerors. Soviet armies dominated half Europe. Never before had Russian power been so widespread in Europe.

This monopoly of Soviet power over half Europe was one of the consequences of the ill-fated policy of appeasing Hitler too long and too soft-headedly, the policy which dictated the abandonment of Czechoslovakia in 1938 by Great Britain and France and so ensured that Czechoslovakia and Poland too would be eliminated before the serious fighting began in the east – and ensured, further that a German defeat in the east must, therefore, be an exclusively Soviet victory entailing exclusively Soviet control over Europe east of the German lands (Greece alone excepted).

The appeasement of Hitler by Great Britain was a rational policy carried to irrational extremes. It was a characteristically British policy, an attempt by discussion and argument to keep the peace in a Europe in which Germany was indubitably a major piece and German grievances were at once appreciable and dangerous. It was doomed to fail because there was never a way of arguing Hitler out of his conquest of *Lebensraum* – or, if there had been a way, it had disappeared years before 1938. It was not Chamberlain's aim to promote a war between Germany and the Soviet Union. Although such a war might in his eyes have been far from deplorable, it would have given Hitler a continental dominance unacceptable to Great Britain and vastly more menacing than any Soviet dominance foreseeable at that time; alternatively, since the outcome of war is never safely predictable, there was the danger that a Russo-German war might bring Russia back into central

Europe. Chamberlain's aim really was peace. His cardinal fault
was to conclude at Munich an agreement which bought peace for
a few months at the price of making war, when it came, much
more difficult to win.

Chamberlain was blinded by his good intentions and by his
characteristically English insularity. His loathing of war, coupled
with a dismissive distrust of foreigners whom he did not trouble
to get to know, forced him into a false calculation of the value
of Czechoslovakia to Great Britain. So long as an independent
Czechoslovakia existed Hitler had an enemy to the east which
he could not defeat without pitting his entire ground and air
forces against formidable static defences and against armoured
divisions equal to his own. He would have nothing to spare for a
western front where the French forces, however inadequate they
subsequently turned out to be, would have had a walkover, a
promenade militaire, and above all he would have had no squadrons
to spare for air attacks on Great Britain nor the bases in France and
in Belgium essential for such attacks. In 1938 the Luftwaffe could
not reach Great Britain for more than the odd reconnaissance. By
postponing the war in a futile attempt to prevent it the appeasers
of 1938 gave Hitler the means to bomb Great Britain two years later
and gave Stalin the opportunity to dominate eastern Europe. Their
intentions were as good as their policies were disastrous. When the
war of 1939–45 ended the prospect of German hegemony in Europe
was gone and replaced by nightmares of Soviet hegemony.

Part Two
The Russian Menace

CHAPTER FIVE
Moscow to Berlin

Russia became a major Power by evicting the Tatar Mongols who had been in Russia since the eleventh century, by consolidating diverse principalities into a single monarchy with its capital at Moscow, and by defeating enemies to the west whose place as the principal Slav opponent of the Germans it took. Before the eighteenth century Russia was frightening but remote, or merely remote. From the eighteenth century it was a major factor in European affairs. After Napoleon's defeat the Tsar Alexander I rode into Paris and played one of the decisive roles at the Congress of Vienna. In Hitler's defeat Stalin's armies took Berlin and subjugated all the lands between Germans and Russians.

The ponderous steadiness of this *Drang nach Westen*, which came to be likened to a steamroller, crushed above all the Poles. So long as the Russians remained preoccupied with the Mongols the most extensive Power in central Europe had been the Polish-Lithuanian empire which grew from the union by marriage in 1385 of the crowns of the Grand Duchy of Lithuania and the Kingdom of Poland. This empire covered what were later called Russia's western lands (White Russia and the Ukraine), reached to within a hundred miles of Moscow and embraced also parts of the later East Prussia, Czechoslovakia and Romania. At first the partnership was more Lithuanian than Polish but the balance shifted and the empire's upper crust became Polonised, particularly after the extinction in 1572 of the ruling Lithuanian line of Jagellon whose capital was Vilna. The Polish ruling classes developed a vigorous contempt for the Russians whom they regarded as Asiatic barbarians and an equally sharp Roman Catholic antagonism to the Russian Orthodox church. But the base of the empire was ramshackle. The exceedingly numerous Polish nobles obstructed the growth of an efficient central authority; strangled the economy by oppressing the peasantry, which they treated as subhuman; and lacked the sense to see where these primitive emotions would land them. In the late sixteenth century, coinciding with Russia's Time of Troubles (contests for the throne not unlike England's Wars of the Roses), Polish pretenders joined the scramble for the Russian throne and one king of Poland – who was a Swede – was crowned Tsar in Moscow in 1610. Moscow and Muscovy were occupied by Poland for a number of years. But Polish power disintegrated when the princes of Moscow founded modern Russia. A new Russian dynasty, the Romanovs, prevailed over its own barons and its foreign enemies and in the eighteenth century Polish kings were reduced to being clients of the Tsars: the last of them was an ex-lover of the Empress Catherine the Great. Before the century's end Russia joined the German Powers, Prussia and Austria, to partition Poland and after the Napoleonic wars the greater part of it was made an hereditary duchy, property of the Romanovs.

Russia grew as Poland declined and disappeared as an independent state. Powered by demography, improvements in food production (particularly grain) and a couple of remarkable monarchs Russia defeated a cheeky bid for empire from Sweden; reached the Urals, the Baltic and the Black Sea, with an entry to the Mediterranean by way of Istanbul (if it could be forced against the Turks); added White Russia and Ukraine to its Muscovite core,[1] and came into permanent contact with Prussians and Austrians

---

1. These accretions were Slavic but not Great Russian, components therefore in a Russian empire or federation but not indisputably parts of a unitary Russian state. The word 'Ukraine' means march or mark, as in Ostmark, Mark Brandenburg, Markgraf. 'Ukrainian', or borderer, was a name adopted by a branch of the Russian family, otherwise known as Ruthenian or Little Russian. The words 'Ruthenian' and 'Russian' have the same root. The Great Russians, who founded the Duchy of Moscow which became the Russian state, chose to designate other Russians as Ruthenians. These Ruthenians called themselves Ukrainians. The Ukraine was devastated from the east in the thirteenth century; rose again in the fourteenth; became a part of the Lithuanian-Polish empire; staged sporadic revolts against Polish Roman Catholic overlords; was partitioned in the seventeenth century between Muscovy and Poland with a small southern segment under fading Tatar control; raised its independent head briefly

to the west and south. In 1812 Russians learned that the west was now more dangerous than the east. This *volte face* coincided with the acknowledgement of Russia as one of Europe's Great Powers.

Yet the Tsarist state was peculiarly fragile. It was a compound of different assertive groups, all of them acquisitive in their own ways – nationalist, commercial or strategic. It had no certain frontiers to west or south or east. To counter these internal and peripheral stresses the empire's rulers needed to strengthen the core of the state (which meant also the dynasty) by firm political organization and quickening industrial development, and to protect its sovereign legitimacy and affirm its prestige by taking part in the European states system.

To other Europeans Russia had special features: it was huge and so in that crude sense menacing; it was also backward, above all culturally backward and so in another sense menacing, unaffected by the great movements of the Renaissance and Enlightenment by which the rest of Europe was wont to chart its progress. But the menace was partially offset by the appearance of being politically disordered and economically and technically primitive. In all these respects it was strange, although less strange than one other empire in Europe. If Russia loomed on the continent's eastern edge with uncertain import, the Ottoman empire, which occupied a large chunk of south eastern Europe and controlled half the Danube, had no business to be there at all. Alien in religion and race and manners, it had to be taken into account but was regarded even by its most persistent sympathizers (the British, most of the time) as an awkward and unnatural presence, probably on its way

---

when the Tsarist empire foundered; and became anomalously a part of the Soviet Union and a member in its own right of the UN. Whether Ukrainian/Ruthenian ranks as a distinct language has been much disputed, not without political and religious overtones. It covers the Ukraine, Bessarabia, Bukovina, eastern Galicia and Carpatho-Ruthenia. This last segment of the Ruthenian family, its south eastern corner, was transferred in 1919 from Hungary to the new Czechoslovak state but was seized back by Hungary with Hitler's encouragement, in two bites in 1938/39. Six years later it was once more lost to Hungary, this time to the Soviet Union. White Russians, distinct from Little Russians and further north, are also a border people but their language is not Ruthenian. (NB: ruthenium is a metal not found anywhere near Ruthenia.)

out. For the Russians it was item number one on the agenda of external affairs, not a threat but an obstacle. The Ottoman capital was the only capital city in Europe which another Power actively and optimistically coveted, and that Power was Russia. Other European Powers were sufficiently alive to Russia's designs to toy with schemes to thwart them: these included, as early as the 1830s, a federation of Danubian states to contain Russian expansion southward. The longest and costliest war fought in Europe between 1815 and 1914 was the Crimean War, whose purpose was the same.

In the First World War the Ottoman empire took the wrong side and disintegrated, but its capital did not pass to the Russian empire, which also disappeared. The Turkish empires in Europe and Asia were dismantled and although the new Turkish state retained a foothold in Europe, the 'Eastern Question' which had preoccupied European statesmen for a century and more was expunged and so answered.[2] With the simultaneous disappearance of the Habsburg empire, which had been Russia's principal adversary over the disposal of the Ottoman remains, the politics of central and eastern Europe were forever changed, but a Russian triumph was postponed and this whole area was remodelled on western democratic and nationalist lines and in the absence of every powerful eastern influence. The Bolshevik Revolution of 1917, followed by multiple foreign invasions, civil war and cruel domestic disruption and incompetence on a vast scale, disabled Russia militarily, economically[3] and politically, so that between 1917 and the Russo-German treaty of 1939 the Soviet state was not a factor in European affairs.

Nor, outside the imagination, was the Revolution. Fears of communist subversion spreading from Russia were ill-founded, and no state outside Russia became communist for more than a few weeks until the end of the Second World War a generation later. So far from becoming the vanguard of a new revolutionary order

2. Turkey's foothold in Europe was important to the new Turkish state as its isolation in western Asia, its border disputes with the Soviet Union and a thirst for modernization sharpened its need for friends in the west.
3. The modernization of Russia which was gathering pace before the First World War was arrested not only by these upheavals and disasters but also by the drying up of French investment, occasioned in part by the cancellation of Tsarist debts by the new regime.

in Europe, the Soviet Union was isolated, Lenin having hugely misjudged the revolutionary fervour in Europe which had been moribund for seventy years. Although the Soviet Union resumed diplomatic and commercial relations, made treaties, joined the League of Nations in 1934 and conformed with most of the shibboleths of an interstate system, its positive impact in Europe was smaller than at any time since the beginning of the reign of Peter the Great.

This occlusion of Russian power was effected in the first place by Germany. Whether or not there would have been a revolution of some kind in Russia at about this date, the immediate cause of the revolution that in fact occurred was the defeat of Russia by Germany – the defeat which is the most striking difference between the two Great European Wars. In the first Russia was defeated by Germany before Germany succumbed to defeat on its western fronts, whereas in the second the Russians defeated the Germans: the fact that the Germans came near to winning in 1941 did not detract from the overwhelming scope of their collapse in 1945. A second crucial difference lay within Russia itself. The revolution of 1917, at first precarious but eventually confirmed, put an end to the monarchy of the Tsars in a fashion that permeated Europe with a fear greater than any fear inspired by the Russian *ancien régime*. Thus the Soviet victory in 1945 was not merely a reversal of the verdict of the earlier war; nor was it simply the substitution of a Russian for a German threat to the European states system. It propelled into the heart of European affairs, in which pragmatism had been the ruling principle, the elusive but pungent smoke of ideology. The Russians who settled upon central and eastern Europe in 1945 were not only reminders of the lapsed Tsarist might. They also incarnated the emotions of the revolution and were commanded by a generalissimo who had been one of the four or five top players in 1917 and owed his supreme title to ideological leadership rather than to regimental valour.

The man who, more than any other, brought the Soviet Union back to the centre of European affairs was Hitler when, having invaded the Soviet Union, he got defeated there. Hitler's designs on the Soviet Union had been openly expressed in *Mein Kampf* but Stalin, like the British cabinet, was mesmerized by Japan. He was heir on the Russian side to generations of mutual suspicions deriving from Russian expansion into Asia in Tsarist times and he was more alarmed by Japan's occupation of Manchuria than by

Hitler's seizure of power a year later. By 1939, however, he urgently needed to stave off a German attack. Two years earlier he had purged his officer corps and so enfeebled his armed forces: about half of the officers had been sacked and shot or exiled, including nine out of every ten generals. Political purges, which began after the murder of the Leningrad party chief Kirov in December 1934, had fortified Stalin's personal position by removing his more eminent colleagues but had produced turmoil, and Stalin must have had some idea through his secret police of the perilous state of his regime and his own unpopularity. His agricultural policies had been consistently disastrous and his industrial development, although in some respects remarkable, nevertheless inadequate. He had no allies and was as suspicious of France and Great Britain as they were of him. In a war against Germany the odds were very much in Germany's favour. Even if he could not secure a dependable peace with Hitler he must buy time. Hardly less urgently, he must prevent a rapprochement between Hitler and the French and British democracies, which could lead to a joint western attack on the Soviet Union. So if war were coming, as seemed very likely, the best thing for Stalin was a long war between Hitler on the one hand and the French and British on the other, with the Soviet Union left out of it.

To many in western Europe the Soviet-German pact of 1939 looked more genuine than it was. In Great Britain Churchill was one of the few who saw it as a sham and predicted an early war between the two partners. In retrospect it is surprising to see how many apparently well-informed people (who, however, had not bothered to read *Mein Kampf*) took the pact at its face value and foresaw a Soviet-German condominium in Europe. When the Soviet Union tried to browbeat the Finns and then invaded Finland in November 1939 in order to extend the Soviet defences against a possible German attack, there was much popular support for the Finns and also covert wariness in high places where any Soviet forward moves in the Baltic area were regarded as bastions against Hitler's overwhelming ambitions. The same ambivalence attended Stalin's occupation of the three Baltic republics in June 1940. There was considerable divergence in London between those who saw Stalin as Hitler's partner – and thought of making air attacks on Caspian oil targets – and those who hoped the Soviet-German pact would turn into a Soviet-German deadlock. The confusion was not resolved until Hitler put an end to it by invading the Soviet Union.

Stalin's pact with Hitler failed to win him much time. On the other hand his fears of a three-Power alliance against him did not materialize and when, less than two years after the signing of the pact, Hitler attacked the Soviet Union Stalin acquired a ready-made ally since Great Britain was still at war with Germany – a circumstance which led to the Anglo-Soviet alliance which neither Power had expected or much wanted. This fortuitous alliance was the foundation of the wider alliance with the United States which won the war in Europe.

The making of the alliance was not simple. Stalin's first requirements when he was attacked in June 1941 were military supplies and, so precarious was his position, armed support in the form of fighting units to be despatched to the Soviet Union itself. But before the end of the year Stalin, having weathered the first and worst storm, was formulating political aims too, notably a no-separate-peace agreement and the endorsement by his new allies of the territorial gains conceded in his pact with Hitler: his 1941 frontiers, including the Baltic, Polish and Balkan dividends of his deal with Hitler. Eden, in Moscow in December 1941, refused to endorse these gains on the spot but returned to London in favour of doing so on the grounds that if Stalin won his war he would again be in sole and undislodgeable occupation of what he wanted. Churchill, however, was not so minded, and the British Conservative Party even less so. When a few months later Molotov came to London, he could get no more than a vague treaty of mutual assistance, during the war and after, with a repetition of the mutual pledge, previously made by Molotov and Sir Stafford Cripps (British ambassador in Moscow), not to enter into separate negotiations with Germany. Molotov was also unsuccessful in his pleas to Churchill to open a new front against the Germans in Europe that year. In his own mind Churchill envisaged raids on the French coast in 1942 and a full-scale invasion in 1943, but he was making no promises.

By this time the United States was at war too, following Hitler's declaration of war on the morrow of the Japanese attack on Pearl Harbor. Molotov went from London to Washington where Roosevelt promised him a second front in 1942. The timing of this second front – which always meant a front in Europe – became the greatest source of allied distrust and friction, with the possible exception of the Polish question. When Churchill followed Molotov to Washington he won Roosevelt over to his plans for an invasion in 1942, not of Europe but of North Africa – a plan which ruled out any invasion of France that year or, as it turned out, the next. Churchill then went to Moscow for his first meeting with Stalin, which proved to be tempestuous but not disastrous: each leader needed the other too much to allow recriminations and frustrations to get altogether out of hand. Bonhomie prevailed. Whether the two men liked one another, or understood one another, it is difficult to judge, but Stalin had to accept that there would be no second front in Europe before 1943 and he may have been persuaded that the temporary cessation of Arctic convoys to the Soviet Union – a matter of even more urgent alarm and distrust – was an operational necessity and not a sign of malice or betrayal (the convoys were resumed when cover of darkness returned with the autumn). But there is in the records little evidence of a meeting of minds in spite of the bursts of camaraderie with which this unlikely but crucial alliance was held together. From mid-1941 to mid-1944 almost the entire front line strength of the German army, and much of the German air force, were deployed on Hitler's eastern fronts (the one substantial exception being the forces fighting in North Africa until May 1943), prolonging the issue between Germany and the Soviet Union and feeding Stalin's suspicions of his allies – particularly Great Britain which, in the earlier part of this period, exercised considerable influence in Anglo-American strategies, opposed incautious American undertakings to launch an early invasion of northern France, and deflected the first American thrusts in the European theatre to the roundabout approach via Algeria and Italy. Whatever the merits of this British strategy it was inevitably seen by Stalin as a painful delay and a sinister augury of British indifference to the fate of the Soviet Union.

Unlike Napoleon, Hitler failed in 1941 to take Moscow – or Leningrad – but the Russian plight was extremely grave and a year later Stalingrad on the Volga was invested. It survived, and its survival entailed the surrender on 2 February 1943 of an entire German army group. Stalin was no longer on the defensive; he could take a deep breath and think about what choices he had. Or, if he did not do so at this point, he must have done so a few months later after the Soviet army's smashing victories in the battles round Kursk. Negotiating with Hitler was, in spite of the Molotov–Cripps agreement, a possibility – a possible way of ending the war, albeit at the price of foregoing the opportunity to eliminate German power in Europe for a lengthy period. In considering whether to let his allies down, Stalin must have weighed the likelihood of their letting him down in the same way. But in mid-1943 he publicly, if without much conviction, adhered to the demand for unconditional German surrender made by Roosevelt and (also without conviction) Churchill at Casablanca at the beginning of the year. Stalin's horizons were lifting. He was feeling his way into central Europe, thinking about his relations with governments in countries adjacent to his own. He dissolved the Comintern, not – as was widely assumed at the time – to please Roosevelt and Churchill, but because he intended to deal separately with each member country on a government-to-government basis: Stalin, apostle of socialism in one country, had never had much use for the internationalism favoured by his more intellectual or visionary colleagues and embodied in the Comintern. He wanted a free hand in half Europe but since he still needed allied aid against Germany he had to discover how free a hand his allies would give him at each stage of his progress and how freely it might be expedient to disclose his own hand. He was, in other words, ready to test the political waters in face-to-face discussions with Roosevelt and Churchill. So began the conference season which, from Teheran in November 1943 to Yalta in February 1945, added political to military strategy. On the political side these conferences were about eastern, not western, Europe; on the military side the reverse.

The political agenda kept pace with military events. Soviet troops entered the Baltic states and Poland in January 1944, Czechoslovakia in April, Hungary in December. The western allies landed in France in June 1944. Soviet troops entered the German Reich in January 1945 and the western allies crossed the Rhine in March. This was decisive background martial music.

The Teheran conference lasted a week, Yalta four days. In Teheran, the nineteenth-century capital of Iran (chosen for the conference because it was as far from the Soviet Union as Stalin would go), the Russian and British embassies occupied large and nearly adjacent sites in the middle of the city, each with an imperial ambassadorial residence and a cluster of other buildings. Roosevelt accepted an invitation to occupy quarters in the Russian compound. Yalta, a nineteenth-century imperial resort on the Black Sea, was even better suited to a mixed programme of set meetings, unscheduled encounters and entertainments devoted to the cultivation of friendship and trust. There was no formal agenda at either conference and the proceedings were designedly not very businesslike. Setting an agenda in advance would have proved difficult and it was considered more appropriate that each of the leaders should be free to bring up the topics he most wished to air. Hence an atmosphere of *conversazione*, controlled by courtesies rather than rules. There were set pieces about the latest military developments and immediate prospects, followed by the relegation of more detailed discussion to the military chiefs accompanying the statesmen. On political topics the talk was more gingerly. Although each leader had two or three problems uppermost in his mind, none had much idea what was in the others' minds. Militarily they were united in their overriding determination to defeat Germany as soon as possible and reasonably accurately informed about one another's capacities and intentions: and where they were not precisely informed, they could make good guesses. But in the political field this was not so. Beyond a certain point all three were vague in their own minds and ignorant of their allies'. The vagueness and ignorance compounded the suspiciousness which, particularly between Stalin and the western leaders but also between Roosevelt and Churchill (on colonies, for example), underlay their prewar attitudes and postwar designs.

The central political question was what to do with a defeated Germany. Yet what happened to Germany in the five years after the end of the war did not happen because of anything said or agreed at the wartime conferences. During the war Roosevelt and Churchill got little further than their demand for unconditional surrender, made at a time when, with the African campaigns in sight of a finish, they could not agree on what to do next (except go on bashing Germany from the air). For Americans, the phrase, recalling General Ulysses Grant, had a reassuring ring: for Churchill it was agreeably bellicose and politically non-committal. In relation to Italy, to which it initially applied as much as to Germany, it was abandoned in favour of opportune negotiation.

Later in the same year Roosevelt and Churchill, meeting at Quebec, fell for the so-called Morgenthau plan for turning Germany into a nation of pastoralists, a scheme which was received with incredulous horror by their principal political advisers. Churchill remained vaguely intent on curbing and isolating Prussia, a purpose which seemed to imply a partition of Germany and the creation of a kind of German anti-body round the ancient Bavarian and Austrian duchies (both, as it happened, more closely linked than Prussia with Hitler and the Nazis). Stalin, having abandoned (if he ever entertained) the notion of negotiating with Hitler after Stalingrad and having endorsed unconditional surrender before going to Teheran, also fostered a phantom German government-in-exile in Moscow. But he did little to help it beyond permitting it to exist. Neither at Teheran nor at Yalta was there any meeting of minds over Germany if for no better reason than that minds had not been made up and so could not meet. By the time the leaders – or, in two cases, their successors – met at Potsdam after the end of the European war they had all come round to opposing a partition of Germany. Yet Germany was partitioned. What Poland had been in the eighteenth century, Germany became for a while in the twentieth.

Whereas the future of Germany occupied singularly little of the leaders' time together, Poland occupied a great deal. It was the biggest single cause of inter-allied disagreement in the political (as was the second front in the military) field. As it progressed the Polish Question appeared to resolve itself into a conflict between two sets of Poles, of which Stalin liked the one but not the other. It is, however, probably truer to conclude that Stalin liked no Poles – nor they him. He was determined to dominate Poland, which was far more important to him than any other state in a Europe from which Germany was at least temporarily removed, but until the middle of the war the embodiment of the Polish state consisted of an anti-communist government-in-exile in London where, in Stalin's eyes, it was a British puppet and not a Soviet one. The rooted hostility between the Russian and Polish peoples, stretching back for centuries, had been exacerbated in Stalin's lifetime by the successful Polish invasion of Russia after the first Great War,[4] by unsettled frontier claims by both sides between the recreation of the Polish state in 1919 and its extinction by Hitler and Stalin in 1939, and by the murder shortly thereafter of several thousand Polish officers in the Katyn forest. This last fact became known in April 1943. For some time people in the west tried to believe (and did believe) the untenable proposition that the perpetrators

4. The Poles took the Ukrainian capital Kiev. They were then forced back and almost lost their own capital Warsaw. This venture was the first in a series of perverse attempts in the twentieth century to bring back the past. At the same time the Greeks, mistaking themselves for neo-Byzantines, dreamed of taking Constantinople, invaded Asia Minor and were chastized by the Turks. A few years later Mussolini proclaimed a new Roman empire which recalled only the seamier side of its illustrious parent. Later still neo-Israelites tried to recreate the kingdom of David and Solomon. A little history is a dangerous thing when it goes to the head of politicians.

of this crime were German and not Soviet. When the London Poles pressed for an investigation by the Red Cross, the Soviet Union broke off relations with them.

The Polish Prime Minister in London, General Sikorski, was a man of ability and vision. He was killed in an accident in July 1943. Whether he might have come to terms with Stalin is unknowable; what is clear is that no other London Pole could. The main issues were two: the frontiers of postwar Poland and the composition of its government. The Poles wanted to restore the 1939 frontiers in existence before the German and Soviet incursions of that year. The Soviet Union wanted the frontier which it had reached through the Soviet-German partition but was willing to settle for the slightly less favourable Curzon line, delineated by Lord Curzon in 1920 and opportunely resurrected by Eden. As a potential government Stalin disliked the London Poles not only because they were anti-communist and in London, but also because they controlled an underground army in Poland itself (the Home Army, in Polish AK) which was likely to impede his own military advance directly or indirectly. The alternative Polish group, dubbed the Lublin Poles from the city where they established themselves as a Committee of National Liberation, began during 1943 also to create an army and to try to transform themselves into a recognized government-in-waiting. Stalin was at first dubious about the Lublin Poles and put out feelers both to the London Poles and to individual Poles in the substantial Polish minority in the United States. The Lublin Poles also put out feelers to American Poles. In July 1944, however, Stalin gave the Lublin Committee his formal approval but without allowing it the title of government and without any engagement about frontiers, east or west. So long as the war lasted Stalin was wary of taking any steps which would too gravely offend his allies, but he was never less than determined to secure in postwar Poland a government subservient to the Soviet Union.

Churchill felt strongly committed to Poland since its invasion had been the cause of the British declaration of war against Germany in 1939 and the British guarantee to Poland had been an unedifyingly empty promise which the British of the day had made no attempt to fulfil. But he also became much irritated with the London Poles whom he described as their own worst enemies, and he was far from unsympathetic to the Soviet aim of having friendly govern-ments in neighbouring countries, especially those through which or with which Hitler had attacked the Soviet Union. At Teheran, therefore, he tried to find a compromise but his power to influence the course of events ebbed as the Soviet armies advanced into Poland during 1944.

To the London Poles this advance became the signal for desperate measures. Together with their underground army in Poland they organized a rising against the Germans in Warsaw with the object not merely of revenge on the Germans but more crucially of re-establishing their own authority in the Polish capital before the Soviet forces got there. Their rising, therefore, was as much anti-Soviet as anti-German, and understandably they told the Soviet authorities nothing about it. But German resistance proved tougher than anticipated and the insurgents were forced to appeal for Soviet help. This Stalin refused to send until it was too late. He also obstructed British and American attempts to give help by refusing to put airfields east of Warsaw at their disposal. Stalin had some justification for calling the rising reckless and for protesting against the insurgents' failure to reveal their plans in advance. He may also have had good tactical reasons for not responding to their appeals since his own advance had just been held up, but the failure of the rising and the discomfiture of the London Poles and their Home Army were undoubted political gains for him, to which he cannot have been insensible and to which his inaction made a decisive contribution. If the London Poles were reckless, Stalin exploited their recklessness. After the rising was overcome by the Germans the terms of the Polish Question had been powerfully altered because the Home Army had been crippled (it was extinguished in the ensuing winter by a fresh Soviet offensive). This episode – its substance and its lasting emotional impact – marked the history of central Europe for the rest of the century.

In the last stages of the rising Churchill proposed that Warsaw be supplied by the western allies by aircraft which would then land on Soviet airfields without Soviet permission, but Roosevelt recoiled from giving offence to Stalin so blatantly. His messages to Stalin during the rising were less insistent than Churchill's, for although there were many Poles in the United States, Roosevelt did not have Churchill's quasi-chivalrous involvement with the cause of Polish independence, or his growing concern about postwar Europe centrally dominated by the Soviet Union – nor did he have to cope with the harrowing importunities of the Poles in London. After the rising Churchill fell back on a policy of pressing Stalin to find places for London Poles in a Lublin government, but by this time such an amalgamation was little more than a face-saver and when six London Poles did join the Lubliners they were only tokens of the imperatives of inter-allied diplomacy and irrelevant to the future of Poland. Stalin was in control and what went for Poland would go for the rest of central and eastern Europe too, once the Soviet army got there. When, in Moscow in October 1944, he and Churchill discussed east–west relations in eastern Europe and expressed their respective interests in a table of mathematical ratios, Poland was not in the list. There was nothing to be done about it.

Events – that is to say, armies – moved quickly in the last months of war. Before the Warsaw rising in August 1944 Soviet forces had taken the Lithuanian capital of Vilna (Vilnius) and Poland up to the Vistula. The rest of Poland was conquered by the end of the year and Soviet forces entered Hungary and Germany in January, Romania in February. According to General Chuikov's later reminiscences Berlin could have been taken in February if Stalin had not held back his armies for fear of upsetting the discussions going on at Yalta where Churchill was still badgering Stalin to let Poland be truly independent. Stalin sidestepped questions about postwar elections by raising the frontier question and proposing the Western Neisse river as a western frontier, to which Roosevelt and Churchill objected that it would consign an unmanageable number of Germans to the new Poland (Stalin riposted that all these Germans had run away). Stalin accepted the Curzon line in the east and, vaguely, postwar elections open to all anti-Nazi parties but without defining such parties or setting a date. He also accepted in principle an enlargement of the Lublin government by adding some London Poles. In the next month, with Yalta behind him and Berlin in his sights, Stalin sanctioned the kidnapping of a number of anti-communist Poles who were abducted from Poland to Moscow where they were all imprisoned and some of them died. In July 1945 the United States and Great Britain recognized the Lublin government. Elections were indefinitely postponed.

Shortly after Yalta the western allies crossed the Rhine. Although Stalin was in control of eastern Europe (except Greece where the British, with Stalin's acquiescence, defeated a communist bid for power at the end of 1944)[5] the fate of Germany itself was still uncertain with either side apparently capable of getting to Ber-

5.   Stalin's refusal to help the Greek communists was compounded by their own divisions and hesitations. Some favoured the bid for power, others had doubts about it.

lin first. To Churchill's outraged dismay and Stalin's amazement Eisenhower called off the race in the belief that allied agreements governing their respective zones of military operation obliged him to do so: Berlin capitulated to Soviet forces on 2 May. In the same frame of mind the Americans allowed a Soviet army to take Prague a week later in spite of an offer by the local Soviet commander for a joint operation. In June the three main allied armies withdrew to their pre-established zones of occupation in Germany (formalized in November 1944), leaving Berlin as a city under tripartite governance but within the Soviet zone and Stalin master of the three great capitals of central Europe: Vienna, Prague, Berlin.

Both sides in the Second World War had schemes for rearranging central Europe. Hitler himself cared little about the details of postwar planning but some of his colleagues – notably Alfred Rosenberg, a Baltic German – occupied themselves with blueprints and programmes which were an amalgam of vicious racism and economic planning: a perverted version of *Mitteleuropa*. Germany would constitute the dominant core of a Europe whose central *Grossraum* was the space where Germans lived – and so variable as Germans might be moved about. Among and beyond the German population were respectable non-German Nordics, non-Nordic helots and non-men. (How the Italians fitted in was left unclear, particularly to the Italians.) Economically the whole area was to constitute an autarkic centre with tributaries, a clearing system, cheap energy and a greatly improved transport system. On the fringe of the *Grossraum* would be settlements of peasant-soldiers, three and a half million of them, whose main function would be to overawe the landless and stateless poor. The racist part of the programme required extensive removals of peoples and also annihilations. Besides the elimination of Jews and gypsies, the Slavs were to be reduced by thirty million. Rosenberg carved the Soviet Union up on paper into four parts after allotting detached slices to Finland and Romania. From this exercise in map-making (compare the labours of the Congress of Vienna in 1814–15) would emerge Muscovy, the Ukraine, the Ostland (roughly the Baltic zone) and the Caucasus, all of them ruled by German Commissars, two of whom were actually chosen and appointed after the invasion of the Soviet Union in 1941.

On the anti-German side postwar planning entailed drawing new, mainly Polish, frontiers and moving people in order to make the frontiers more credible and permanent, but the major movements of people were occasioned not by planning but by the war itself. Germans fled westward from all over eastern and central Europe, including the Soviet Union, and they were killed in great numbers as they fled. The Germans had set horrible examples, not least in their prisoner-of-war camps where more than half their prisoners died; but they also paid for what was done as Germans perished, or simply disappeared with sinister implications, as they tried to escape through Russian, Polish, Czech and other lands where the German armies' deliberate and wholesale destruction of towns, villages and countryside had made Germans infamous. At least ten million Germans were uprooted or killed in the war's last stages. The allied decision to move Germans westward to make room for a Poland which was itself shifted westward was one ingredient in this huge human catastrophe. Central Europe ended the war in chaos.

CHAPTER SIX
Stalin's Empire in Europe

For the Soviet Union the end of the war was triumphant but grim. Devastation had been terrible. In the first six months alone losses of territory, livestock and minerals ranged between one half and three quarters. They were followed in the next year by further huge losses as the Germans overran the Don region and the northern Caucasus and reached the Volga. In one city (Leningrad) in a single winter 630,000 people were killed or starved or froze to death. By the end of the war 20–25 million were dead, as many more homeless, 4–5 million houses in ruins. Even when all lost territory had been recovered the first harvest was only half of what it had been in 1940. Livestock was even more drastically reduced – 23 million pigs had dwindled to 3 million – and rail tracks, bridges and rolling stock were comprehensively wrecked. Exports covered one tenth of imports. Some fighting continued, notably in the Ukraine and Lithuania, for about ten years after 1945. Never in modern history had victory been so bitterly bought.

German power was eliminated, the *Anschluss* dissolved and the Reich partitioned first into four zones of occupation and then into two separate states. Central and eastern Europe were almost entirely in the Soviet grip, but the anti-German alliance disintegrated as soon as its purpose was achieved and the allies became not only estranged but openly hostile; and the Americans had the atom bomb. This hostility split Europe into two parts. If this was equilibrium of a sort, it was very different from the *Gleichgewicht* of a past age: it was rigid and made the more unyielding by the injection of doctrinal prejudices into power politics. Although nuclear weapons, once acquired by both sides, imposed a kind of stability, the temper of the confrontation was sharpened by the vituperation with which the protagonists of private capitalism and state communism assailed one another and which surpassed even the polemics between fascists and democrats and recalled the absurder excesses of Roman Catholics and Protestants. In effect Europe was partitioned with a *modus vivendi* based on an extraordinarily impenetrable degree of often wilful non-comprehension.

The first test and first open failure of relations between the erstwhile allies concerned Germany, which they had proposed to occupy in separate zones but regulate – particularly in economic matters – in concert. At Yalta they had agreed that Germany must be disarmed and denazified. They had also fixed tentatively a sum of $20 billion for reparations, half of it to be paid to the Soviet Union and Poland, but at Potsdam they failed to confirm this provision and the western occupiers became quickly aware that any substantial reparation payments ran counter to their declared aim of making Germany pay for all necessary imports out of current production. There was little current production and what there was would be diminished by reparations, whether in cash or in the form of dismantled hardware. The Soviet occupiers made haste to remove what they could – even whole factories – from their zone in order to help rehabilitate Soviet industry, while the western occupiers adopted the opposite policy of reviving the German economy in order to lessen its dependence on themselves for food and other necessities. Stalin lost whatever hope he may have had of controlling all Germany but neither he nor any of his successors lost their fear of Germany.

Between Germany and the Soviet Union Stalin consolidated his military control and turned it into total political and economic control. This subjugation of *Mitteleuropa* was dictated by his fears and distrust of his former allies and by his urgent economic needs. Before the war ended he had recognized his limitations by conceding to Great Britain the deciding voice in Greece, even to the extent of refusing to lift a finger to help the Greek communists, and it is difficult to believe that his bid for a share in the conquered Italian colonies was more than a bargaining counter: Africa was way beyond the Soviet reach in 1945. He may have hoped that the French and Italian communist parties would share power in their countries or at least become considerable nuisances there; that they might take power for themselves was wholly unrealistic. His one sure asset was his armies' control in those places where his armies were. This asset Stalin was prepared to defend, even by measures which were bound to outrage his wartime allies. Once the war was won Soviet security took priority over the maintenance of the alliance which had had the priority only so long as Germany was undefeated.

Stalin re-arranged the map of central and eastern Europe[1] and placed almost all of it under obedient communist rule. For the Soviet Union he took Bessarabia and northern Bukovina from Romania, Sub-Carpathian Ruthenia from Czechoslovakia (thus giving the Soviet Union a frontier with Hungary) and a large slice of Poland including the cities of Lvov and Vilna. He required Poland to give Teschen back to Czechoslovakia, Hungary to cede Transylvania to Romania, and Romania to surrender southern Dobruja to Bulgaria. Although, contrary to some expectations, central and eastern European states were not incorporated into the Soviet Union as Soviet Republics (like, for example, the Ukraine in Europe or Kazakhstan in Asia), they became neutered sovereign states under the name of Socialist Republics or People's Democracies. With this status they were not only politically subordinate, which is the fate of any minor state within the penumbra of a greater one. They were also obliged to adopt patterns, political and economic, which obtained in the Soviet Union: that is to say, rule by the Communist Party whose general secretary was the effective head of the government, and a tightly centralized 'command' economy in which first regions and then plants were instructed what to produce and how much, and prices were fixed by order. Stalin forced the satellites (and Finland) to reject participation in the Marshall Plan. Their trade was largely restricted to bilateral exchanges with the Soviet Union and the nature and quantity of their economic output was regulated with the prime purpose of serving the Soviet Union's recovery. From 1948 these states were permitted no political life or debate. Postwar aspirations and initiatives were snuffed out, where necessary by a ruthless police under ultimate Soviet control. Stalin's policies magnified anti-Russian feelings which were deep-seated and added anti-communist feelings which were newer. How far he underestimated

1.   Central Europe comprises for the purposes of these chapters Poland, Czechoslovakia, Hungary and East Germany, with the proviso that East Germany's potential reunification with West Germany made it always a special case. Stalin's empire in eastern Europe comprised Romania and Bulgaria, with Albania for a while, but let Yugoslavia slip and never included Greece.

these feelings and how far he accepted them as inevitable it is impossible to judge. He acted as he did because he believed his system to be necessary for the defence of the Soviet Union against a western coalition and because he was a ruthless and unimaginative tyrant and an ageing one. He left to his successors the business of securing the defence of the Soviet Union by less auto-destructive means.

The instruments of Stalinist rule over the satellites were communist trusties, most of whom were imports from the Soviet Union and represented parties which before the war had been feeble. Since they were in no position to win elections, elections were rigged or abolished. For a short time other parties were tolerated provided they collaborated with the communists and gave the régime an aura of respectable plurality without seriously impeding communist control, but the communist dominance was quickly turned into a communist monopoly, a change of policy evident as early as 1947. In that year the Bulgarian Agrarian leader Nicola Petkov was executed; in Romania the Peasant Party was dissolved, its leader Ion Maniu arraigned and the king forced to abdicate; in Hungary the Smallholders' leaders Bela Kovacs and Zoltan Tildy were respectively abducted and forced out of the presidency; in Poland Stanislaw Mikolayczyk, having done too well in the elections in 1946 (for which Churchill had pressed so hard), felt obliged to flee the country; in Czechoslovakia President Benes survived into 1948 but was manoeuvred into a false position and had to resign, and his chief non-communist colleague, Jan Masaryk, fell to his death out of a window or, more probably, was pushed. These non-communist victims were followed by communists who, in the light of Moscow's tussle with Tito, were suspected of being less than wholly subservient to the Soviet Union.

Yugoslavia was the first country in western Europe to reject Soviet domination and the last to reject communism. It was from the start different and a great part of the difference could be summed up in the word 'Tito'. Josip Broz, later Tito, was a communist from boyhood, half Croat, half Slovene and born a Hungarian subject, who inherited King Alexander's commitment to a broad Yugoslav federation and had attained national and international eminence by his success in raising an army of a million men and women and winning battles. This army and his chief lieutenants were drawn from all Yugoslavia's major and minor nationalities. His enemies, besides Italians and Germans, were Croat fascists and Serb nationalist royalists. In Croatia Ante

Pavelic set up a separate kingdom – separate, but hardly independent since it relied on Italian tutelage and adopted as king an
Italian prince (who, however, wisely stayed in Italy). Particularly
vicious atrocities were perpetrated by the militantly nationalist
and religious Croat *ustachi* against Serbs and others. Russian aid
to Tito in these trials was sparse and late. Stalin was angered
by the establishment at Jajce in 1943 of a provisional Yugoslav
government under Tito's presidency and a Russian delegation to
Tito's headquarters was less concerned to help than to keep an
eye on him. The war casualties of Tito's partisan army were among
the most severe in Europe, but victory was complete and euphoric.
Tito aimed for the closest association with the Soviet Union and for
a comprehensive Balkan federation including Romania, Bulgaria,
Albania and even Hungary. His circumstances, particularly his
independent wartime road to power and the detachment which
Yugoslavia owed to having no frontier with the Soviet Union,
jarred in Moscow and soon after the war Stalin tried to engineer
a palace revolution in Belgrade and the substitution of leaders
more pliant than Tito who, although dismayed at the prospect
of a breach with Moscow, insisted on doing things his own way
and rejected Stalin's view that Soviet measures could and must be
applied in every communist state. An acrimonious debate ended
not in the overthrow of Tito but in the eviction of Yugoslavia from
the communist fraternity. The severity with which Tito then treated
Stalin's adherents in Yugoslavia suggested that they had come near
to success. In the event, however, Tito's position and prestige
were enhanced and he outlived Stalin by twenty-seven years.
Khrushchev and Brezhnev both tried to lure Yugoslavia back into
the fold but failed to do more than get back on speaking terms.

The breach between Moscow and Belgrade cracked the myth of
a communist monolith in Europe. It also dented in Stalin's eyes
the presumed reliability and integrity of communist parties and led
Stalin to initiate purges in the satellites' communist leadership. In a
series of trials in 1949–51 communists as well as non-communists
were charged with treasonable complicity with Tito and with western Powers. By these trials – which were reminiscent of the prewar
trials in the Soviet Union by which Stalin killed off his rivals there
– the postwar communist elites in the satellites were purged of
communists whom the Stalinist police considered to be less than
totally reliable. Rule by and through communist parties needed to
be reinforced by eternal vigilance and eternal suspiciousness. The
reasoning behind so unpromising a form of management was the

assumption that the Soviet Union and its associated states were in a state of war with the United States and its allies in Europe.

Stalin's quasi-imperial system was an overall failure and the outstanding cause of this failure was failure in the Soviet Union itself. In the satellites Communist Parties took and kept control for a generation or more. There was some economic growth in some places, as high as 10 per cent a year in the more favoured areas in the 1950s, but a combination of repression and depression created uncontainable strains and hatreds which were the more intolerable from the fact that the imperial Power had itself nothing better to offer. The Soviet Union made some headway towards recovery within the framework of a succession of five-year plans: some prewar levels were regained by 1950. But Stalin was too much a prisoner of his past and his prejudices to do more than tinker with an inherently unsound economic system. Each five year plan was a conglomeration of production targets, devised at the centre, inflexible, geared to the country's needs but not to its practical capacities. In fulfilling these targets, or getting as close to them as possible, managers drove their ageing machinery but would not risk and could not afford new equipment. Shortcomings, stigmatized as crimes, were concealed; misdirection was compounded by misrepresentation; corruption became almost a necessity for survival. Agriculture, controlled (since 1935) by political bosses who were frequently ignorant as well as corrupt, was subjected to increasingly complicated regulations. Prices and therefore incentives were kept low. Collective farms, of which there had been four million before the war averaging 1000 acres, were steadily enlarged and reduced in number and were hard pressed to earn a dividend after paying taxes and insurance and buying necessary seeds and equipment. On state farms, which were the main source of grains, potatoes and industrial crops such as cotton and flax, peasants worked for meagre wages and a meagre portion of the product. Taxes on the produce of private plots – whose average size was one acre – rose. During the forty years between the end of the war and the advent of Gorbachev strenuous, if sporadic, attempts were made to solve this basic problem, but the strenuousness of the efforts only served to illuminate the failures. They set the tone for the sense of hopelessness which pervaded Soviet society and spread to the satellites.

The death of Stalin in 1953 weakened government. Collective leadership was a mere euphemism to disguise mutual distrust. Beria was killed by his colleagues – a prudent, if gruesome, step reminiscent of the practices of Ottoman sultans. Malenkov was supplanted by Khrushchev, whose reign was hectic, short and never secure. Malenkov tried to ease the life of the consumer by decreeing excessively steep cuts in retail prices, but there was little of the new investment needed to make production possible at the prices decreed. Khrushchev publicly admitted that agricultural workers were getting too little, taxation of private produce was too heavy and decisions at the centre often wrong. There was a flurry of changes: peasants' compulsory deliveries were reduced in volume and increased in price, charges for tractor and other services were reduced, there were further amalgamations of collective farms, twenty-five million acres of virgin land (the acreage was later doubled) were brought under cultivation, workers were moved in vast numbers and volunteers enrolled. But these changes, ambitious and to some extent sensible, were uncoordinated, confusing and vitiated by the persistent vice of entrusting agricultural policy to remote or ill-informed politicians and party officials. Peasants continued to leave the land at the rate of a million a year or more. Even in years favoured by the weather targets were not met. Khrushchev so far acknowledged the desperate straits of the people by introducing shorter hours, better holidays, better pensions, more secondary education and more housing, but he shied away from the sweeping reforms needed to pay for these things and to eradicate layers of ignorance and incompetence. He let in some fresh air and some humanity, but intellectually he was not up to his formidable tasks and he plunged into spectacular failures at home and abroad, of which the most sensational was his attempt to establish a Soviet nuclear base in Cuba. Never in complete control of the Communist Party, Khrushchev never tried to downgrade it (as Gorbachev did) and was unable to survive his mistakes. Although personally he appeared in a more amiable light than other Soviet leaders, he made no friends for the Soviet Union; and although he effected some reconciliation with Tito's Yugoslavia he did not tackle the problem of the satellites. In Hungary in 1956 he dithered. In Poland in the same year he had to tolerate the return to power of Wladislas Gomulka who was an enemy of the Soviet Union and warned Khrushchev that if he sent Soviet troops into Poland Polish troops would fight them. He tried unsuccessfully to secure western recognition of East Germany, to convert east Berlin into a free city without foreign troops, and to establish better relations with West Germany. He was criticized by the Chinese for feebleness in relation to the United States and by the time of his fall Sino-Soviet relations had descended into the acute hostility in which they remained for more than twenty years. Here was a grim cautionary tale. In order to get anywhere Khrushchev needed to initiate much more radical changes than he or anybody else believed to be practicable or, possibly, could envisage.

Khrushchev was succeeded by a pall of conservative greyness. An economic spurt in the 1950s and early 1960s was reversed; output and employment declined; social services were skimped; drink, drugs, crime and corruption flourished. The period was not without its achievements, of which the most prominent was the creation of a navy of global proportions, but the Soviet Union remained isolated in world affairs and its external record was on balance heavily in debt – the split with China, fiasco in Cuba, retreat from Egypt. Neither Khrushchev nor any of his successors before Gorbachev gave thought to real retrenchment. The arms race was pursued with a vigorous unconcern for its cost or its strategic appositeness. The Cuban failure was treated as a blunder in a particular instance, not as a warning against foreign adventures which were on the contrary multiplied. Soviet leaders understood too little about economics to become adequately scared, with the result that for another twenty years they chased more of everything from Ethiopia to Vietnam to Afghanistan to outer space. In this period, with the Americans too fighting disastrously in Vietnam and American arms expenditure rocketing, the Superpowers crippled themselves and inflated their cold war to its most dangerous degree.

In the satellite block the first visible stirrings occurred in Berlin and other German cities in 1953, a few weeks after Stalin's death and several years before the more serious upheavals in Poland and Hungary. The disorders in East Germany were suppressed by the unhesitating use of force, but by 1956 hesitation and even forbearance were already evident. In 1968 a similar dilemma confronted the Kremlin in Czechoslovakia. The peoples of these three countries were gradually reasserting their independence and their separate identities in a process which stretched painfully from Stalin's death to the wondrous year of 1989, shortly after Gorbachev's elevation to supremacy in Moscow.

Poland in 1945 was quit of the Germans and occupied by the Russians. It was as comprehensively subjugated by the Soviet Union as it had been by the Tsar in 1813. It lost in territory half of what had been Polish in 1939, subject only to some compensation at German expense to the west. The communist party formed in 1918 had been distrusted by Stalin before the war and dissolved by the Comintern in 1938. Its more eminent leaders had been killed. Wladislaw Gomulka, survivor of these disasters and no Muscovite at heart, emerged in Poland during the war with a small partisan force which was, however, much smaller than the anti-communist army controlled by the London Poles until its destruction by the Russians in 1944. In popular terms the Polish communists were a marginal group in a country where the agrarians, Roman Catholics and socialists commanded many more votes. Gomulka was distrusted by the Russians because he was a Pole and by the Poles because he was, as a communist, branded as a Russian tool. In Poland's immediate postwar politics he outmanoeuvred the socialist Stanislaw Mikolayczyk and was then discarded in 1948 by the Russians. Poland, although desperately ravaged by both Germans and Russians, and although forced by the Soviet Union to reject Marshall aid, achieved a creditable economic revival and standard of living under a hybrid system in which major enterprises were nationalized but most of the land was not: one of Gomulka's offences in Russian eyes was his refusal to nationalize the land. This was, however, a false start. The economy, along with every other aspect of national life – administration, education, social services, the arts – became increasingly inflexible and politicized. Production targets set by a first Five Year Plan beginning in 1950 were impossibly high, required the recruitment into industry of large numbers of unqualified persons, and led to failures, concealment and speculation which led in their turn to delation, shortages, rationing, price rises, despair and drink. In 1956, following workers' demonstrations in Poznan and elsewhere, Khrushchev paid a surprise visit to Warsaw, saw and was scared by what was happening, and restored the disgraced Gomulka in the hope of stemming the country's domestic ills and establishing a tolerable *modus vivendi* between the Soviet Union and its largest and least friendly neighbour. Thus, a mere three years after Stalin's death, the Kremlin was tacitly admitting that Russo-Polish relations were a matter for management, not dictation. The economic situation continued to deteriorate until it precipitated in 1970 a second outburst which became the undoing first of Gomulka and then of the communist régime.

In Hungary in 1956 simultaneous protest was quelled by force which bought a longer period of superficial calm. In the last months of the war Hungarians formed a multi-party alliance designed to swing the country away from the German side to something acceptable to the Soviet Union. The largest of these parties was the Smallholders' Party, the local variant of the agrarian interest: it got more than half the votes in elections in 1945. The communist party was small, having been all but annihilated after Bela Kun's defeat after the First World War; and the social democrat party was not much bigger. Non-communist parties were squeezed out or absorbed by the communist party into an enlarged party called the Workers Party, and the communist leadership was itself purged after Moscow's brush with Tito in 1948 when Matyas Rakosi, as general secretary of the party, obediently ensured the disgrace and execution of Laszlo Rajk. Stalin's death permitted some cautious airing of new ideas by the Prime Minister Imre Nagy and others, but Rakosi and the hardliners prevailed for a few years. In 1956 serious disorders, coinciding with those in Poland, exposed the contradictions in the Soviet position and Moscow had difficulty in deciding both on its course of action and on whom to trust in Budapest. The Kremlin seemed anxious to avoid the use of force but then used it fiercely. It sacrificed Rakosi but baulked at replacing him by Nagy whose attitudes went much beyond what the Kremlin felt obliged at this date to concede. The new secretary, Erno Gero, was a compromise choice but he proved susceptible to increasing popular clamour and demonstrations in favour of Nagy. The Kremlin despatched two of its most senior figures, Anastas Mikoyan and Michael Suslov, to Budapest to reconnoitre, recommend and act. Janos Kadar was put in Gero's place, but the new government, which included anti-communist leaders from the Smallholders' Party, persisted in unacceptably radical demands: a multi-party system, total Russian withdrawal, secession from the Warsaw Pact, a neutral Hungary. There was fierce fighting and lynching. The Russian forces, which had started to leave the country, came back. Kadar deserted Nagy who appealed vainly for foreign help. The Russians put the clock back and kept it ticking for another thirty-three years.

This outcome, reaffirmed in Czechoslovakia in 1968, condemned the satellites to tackle their economic problems without radical political change or any dilution of their subordination to the Soviet Union, characterized above all by membership of the Warsaw Pact. This straitjacket remained in place until economic crisis in the Soviet Union itself forced the Soviet régime to attempt, after 1985 and the advent of Gorbachev, a reform of its own economic and political system and the abandonment of the Stalinist methods of control over central and eastern Europe. In the prolonged interval of hopeless fiddling with the economy Kadar provided the assurances required by the Soviet Union while new leaders – Jeno Fock as Prime Minister and Nezsö Nyers as Finance Minister – probed the acceptable limits of change. Central controls were further relaxed, small businesses were revived and there was some improvement in domestic production and the balance of foreign trade. Although self-sufficient in basic foods, Hungary depended on the Soviet Union for oil which it bought at specially advantageous prices. In the 1970s these prices were raised with the worldwide rise in oil prices, and increasingly costly imports from the west which had boosted the performance of the 1960s reversed the balance of payments and left Hungary with a substantial foreign debt. Debate on economic policy was open and lively and merged once more with demands for political and cultural freedom. While it was clear that the communist régime had failed to give Hungary an independent or prosperous economy, there was no general agreement about how to enter the hazardous world economy which alone could supply the capital and technology needed. Any drive to earn the foreign exchange to pay for these things was frustrated by adverse terms of trade with the west and by the inevitable consequences of starving the home market by earmarking domestic product for foreign trade.

This problem was not peculiar to Hungary. In Czechoslovakia an economy of no mean promise was distorted by subordination to Soviet needs and Soviet doctrines and by maladroit direction as the economy was managed as a department of the communist party. Foremost in central Europe Czechoslovakia had possessed a manufacturing base and manufacturing skills which could be rehabilitated after the war, but it was denied Marshall aid by order of the Kremlin and an industrial economy famous for its relatively small goods (shoes, for example) was switched to heavy industry – steelmaking and armaments – to serve the whole communist block. Older enterprises were destroyed and skills were lost; Czechoslovakia's reserves were syphoned away; trade with the west was lost; by the end of the 1960s growth had sunk to zero. In 1968 the ineffective rule of Antonin Novotny was brought to an end by the promotion of the Slovak communist chief Alexander Dubcek, whom the Kremlin at first welcomed or at least tolerated. In Czechoslovakia, as elsewhere in the block, economic problems were pressing, chiefly owing to an over-elaborate economic structure in the hands of mediocrities. Attempts to reform the system over the past ten years had proved ineffective, but since they entailed a degree of economic liberalization they had nurtured the thirst for liberalization in other fields such as censorship and political freedom. The Kremlin had tolerated economic reforms in Hungary after 1956 because they seemed not to go too far. Nevertheless, all reform was suspect. Reformers were classified as plotters intent on perverting socialist economies into capitalist market economies ruled by the profit motive and class selfishness. Dubcek overstepped the Soviet Union's limit of tolerance when his economic reforms looked like raising political issues such as the end of the one-party state, parliamentary elections and perhaps the right to secede from the Warsaw Pact. Moscow was alarmed too by the decline of communist authority, even in the police. It tried to bludgeon Dubcek and then resorted to the extreme measure of armed invasion. Dubcek was demoted by steps, back into private life via the post of ambassador in Turkey, and Czechoslovakia was relegated to rule through politically reliable communist functionaries.

The decision of the Soviet Union to use force against Czechoslovakia was taken in the knowledge that there would be no fighting, for the Czechs had declared their intention not to resist. It was therefore no true test of the extent of Soviet resolve to crush opposition within the block. But Brezhnev felt a need to rationalize Soviet actions. To justify the use of force against a sovereign state he invoked, or invented, the right of the Soviet Union to take action in order to defend socialism – a doctrine later echoed by Ronald Reagan when he made war on Nicaragua ostensibly in order to defend democracy. But this casuistry was less to the point than the pragmatic calculation of the pros and cons of armed intervention in a particular case. If sovereignty could be construed as limited sovereignty, what were the limits? For Brezhnev and his doctrine the test came in Poland in May 1970. Strikes and riots against inadequate wages, food shortages and rising prices threatened to turn into civil war. Gomulka was forced to resign. He was replaced by Edward Gierek. With a freshening breeze of openness and humanity, relaxed controls over industry, lower taxes and higher wages and investment Gierek won time but could not do anything with it in the face of popular opposition to economic reforms including freer (and therefore higher) prices and the mounting cost of imports and foreign debt. More riots in 1976 caused deaths and further retreat by Gierek who had no way of salvaging the economy without making life even worse than it already was for the great majority of Poles. Attempts to boost exports beggared the home market, aggravated shortages and rekindled protest and violence. The election in 1978 of the first Polish pope in the history of Christendom and his visit to Poland next year raised the temperature and strengthened resolve, and in 1980 workers' movements staged demonstrations and strikes, beginning in the Lenin shipyard in Gdansk, which were openly political. The government, having decided not to meet force with force, was obliged to negotiate with Lech Walesa's trade union Solidarity and similar movements in Szczecin and elsewhere. They exacted substantial concessions, including the right to strike, the right to form trade unions independent of the state, a relaxation of censorship, participation in the discussion of economic policies, higher wages and pensions, better working conditions and housing, an extra day off a week, maternity leave, appointments and promotions without regard to party membership, regular broadcasts of Roman Catholic church services: a mixture of industrial, social and religious demands. Much of this impressive catalogue was vague or unattainable without an economic miracle, but the totality and its embodiment in a formal document were revolutionary. The government's defeat and a heart attack removed Gierek and left the communist leadership divided and perplexed. Stanislaw Kania, Gierek's successor as first secretary, and General Wojciech Jaruzelski, his defence minister, represented those who accepted the necessity to negotiate with Solidarity, but they were constrained to do so within the limits set by Moscow and without the ultimate sanction of Soviet intervention. The limits, apparently if imprecisely accepted by Solidarity, were the preservation of Poland's communist system and its membership of the Soviet block: these were, for the time being, the minimal requirements of the Brezhnev doctrine. More significant, however, was the Kremlin's decision not to intervene. Widespread fears of a Soviet invasion were belied and therewith Stalinist dominion came to an end. In the following year Jaruzelski took over the government and although he became also head of the party this appointment could not conceal the fact that the army had replaced the party – a severe affront to orthodox communist doctrine which execrated the assumption of power by the military as Bonapartism. Jaruzelski imposed martial law but was unable to stem either the rout of the party or the collapse of the economy.

Much of the revolt against communist rule and Soviet domination in central Europe was economic. Middle-class dissidents might rebel against their loss of freedom and political rights, but the more effective popular revolt was a modern version of the old bread riot exacerbated by the coldly furious resentment of people pushed around for too long. Central and eastern Europe felt not only enslaved by the Soviet Union but impoverished too in the most elementary manner, and this concatenation of grievances produced collaboration between intellectuals and workers uncharacteristic of European protest movements (except to some degree in Spain in the 1930s).

Stalin had created an empire which was oppressive beyond endurance. The terms of trade imposed on the satellites after the Second World War were unfair to the point of exploitation. Trade was channelled to Soviet advantage; industries were kept short of capital. Although this phase was short-lived as the Kremlin came to weigh against the advantages of asset-stripping the disadvantages of impoverishing the satellites and exciting their hatred, the impression of Moscow's cynical selfishness remained. Stalin's instinctive reaction to the Marshall Plan had been to close the door against western funds and contacts, but this anti-western *cordon sanitaire* was relaxed in the 1950s when, for example, imports of American grain were permitted. In the 1960s, when the Soviet Union itself flirted with economic liberalization (between the dismissal of Khrushchev in 1964 and the challenge of Dubcek in 1968), the Kremlin made some attempt to allay the satellites' major economic grievances. The main instrument was Comecon – the Council of Mutual Economic Assistance – which had been created in 1949 primarily in response to the Marshall Plan and as a sop to the satellites forbidden to take advantage of it. For years Comecon was an insignificant showpiece, a somnolent, pseudo-intellectual organization in a couple of offices in Moscow. Stalin had little use for multinational bodies, preferring to deal with each satellite separately, but after his death and more particularly after the creation of the European Economic Community in 1957 some attempt was made to make the block economically more coherent and so politically more dependable. Trade within the block had been developing fast in the 1950s, if from low levels, but wider international trade was meagre and declining. Investment was high but unbalanced by an emphasis on heavy industry, largely for military purposes, and Soviet domination was more apparent than a Soviet contribution. Agriculture languished. Five year plans were altered in mid-course or abandoned. Joint enterprises, multilateral and bilateral, were adopted – for example in transport, communications, banking, pipelines – but with disappointing results. In the 1960s Comecon acquired the paraphernalia of committees, including a bureau for developing international contacts. It was also enlarged. Originally a group of six, it extended associate membership to China, North Korea and Vietnam and full membership to the last two and to Outer Mongolia. Albania defected and after 1956 Yugoslavia oscillated between associate status and absence. But achievements were small. Within the block Comecon's function was to coordinate; it lacked the EEC's authority to initiate and promote. With the wider world it established some contacts but the more important of these were restricted by the refusal of the western allies (and Japan) to trade goods which had or could have strategic value: a list of such goods was first drawn up in 1950 by a Coordinating Committee (COCOM). To the outsider eastern Europe was a block but its member states had none of the advantages of concerted politicies or effective common institutions. There was no international vision or organization and no joint bargaining. Yet the west, particularly those Europeans who had traded with eastern Europe in the past or had invested in its principal resources, was interested in renewing economic links.

Western attitudes to economic relations with the communist block were ambivalent and confused. The resolve not to supply strategically useful materials or knowledge was paramount (although the assessment was often contentious, the Americans taking the most restrictive line which often irritated Europeans who regarded some of the obstacles to their trade imposed by the COCOM list as exaggerated, plain silly or ruses to help American exporters at the expense of Europeans). Many western Europeans were pained by the split in the continent and regarded commercial contacts as a first step towards a desirable political normality. To Americans and, hardly less so to the British, central and eastern Europe were even more remote and detached than they had been a generation earlier, when Neville Chamberlain described Czechoslovakia as a distant country about which the British knew nothing. But on the continental mainland distances, geographical and cultural, seemed smaller and economic recovery added a new motive for piercing the Iron Curtain. First the French and then the West Germans began to look east as they had done in the past – for markets. At the back of the French mind may have been recollections of the old Franco-Russian alliance but in France as well as in West Germany the main thrust was economic and towards the satellites rather than towards the Soviet Union itself.

Again, however, there were limits quite apart from the COCOM list. Little trade could be done without loans and credits, and the creditworthiness of the satellites was low.

In the 1970s the mood changed sufficiently to stimulate a flow of credit, mainly to Poland which was avid for capital goods and to Hungary which imported more consumer goods, but in their quest for new channels the satellites ran over-enthusiastically into debts which, with the onset of the oil crisis of the 1970s and the related recession, they could not repay or even service. The more business in goods or licences, the larger the credits and the debts, until by the end of the decade eastern debts to the west (half of them owed by Poland and the Soviet Union) were so large that trade was once more cut to a trickle. Worldwide recession cramped the new east–west style. But there had been change: the chief obstacles were now at least as much financial as political or ideological. Politically the west had grown accustomed to Soviet dominion of eastern Europe and, while disliking it, contrived to see some good in it since the sharpness of the division of the continent created a *modus vivendi* between the hostile alliances in a situation of uncertainty and apprehensiveness. Economically, however, the west's relations with eastern Europe were neutered because the satellites were economic drop-outs.

Yet the satellites were not without economic resources and most people in central and eastern Europe were much better off than most people in Asia or Africa. Poland, Czechoslovakia and Hungary all experienced economic miracles in the sense that they greatly increased their economic output, but these miracles of endeavour were also miracles of distortion. The growth was without profit.[2] Poland's large agricultural sector increased in the 1970s and 1980s with some, if inadequate, investment but failed to feed the population or to contribute to GNP commensurately with its share of the workforce: agriculture employed over a third of the workforce but produced only a fifth of the national income. Four fifths of agricultural land were in private hands. There was a continuous drift of workers from the land to the towns. Quantitatively Poland was also one of the world's leading industrial states, although less well equipped than Czechoslovakia

2.   These three countries covered after the Second World War 120,000, 50,000 and 36,000 square miles and contained by the end of the 1980s 38, 16 and 11 million people.

or eastern Germany. Its resources included coal, lignite, natural gas and a variety of other minerals of which sulphur, zinc and lead were the most prominent. Investment in manufacturing industry was heavy from the 1960s mainly in engineering and building equipment where output increased rapidly but productivity did not. Foreign trade was insignificant and mainly with the Soviet Union, Czechoslovakia and eastern Germany. Foreign borrowing was high and burdensome. Poland was trying to enhance its manufacturing sector by doing what advanced industrial countries were already doing. It succeeded in expanding its industry but could not compete successfully with the world's established industrial economies. It was paying to do what others did better. It became a land of shortages of food and consumer goods, high and rising prices, unrequited endeavour and crippling external debt.

Czechoslovakia was a stronger competitor in the world. Its agriculture and industry were the most technically advanced and productive in central Europe. Its resources and skills were backed by outstanding educational and administrative systems. In the Caroline University in Prague, founded in 1348, it possessed one of the oldest universities in Europe; it had played a distinguished part in the educational renaissance of the seventeenth century and had introduced compulsory education in the eighteenth. It inherited from the Habsburg empire the habits and techniques of well-ordered administration. Manufacturing industry, responsible for more than two thirds of GNP, rose in the postwar decades in response to modernization and to the demands of the Soviet Union. But these demands distorted it by an overemphasis on heavy industry and armaments. Czechoslovakia had the highest income per head in central Europe and the most flourishing import and export trade – mostly but not exclusively with the communist block. Its mineral resources included coal, lignite, copper and other ores. The historic lands in the west covered rather more than half of this long, thin country which, at the Slovak end, was more like impoverished eastern Europe than modern central Europe. Like western Europe after the war Czechoslovakia had a ravaged economy with a sound base which needed repair rather than radical restructure.

Hungary's mineral resources were sparser and its domestic market smaller. Apart from bauxite, these resources were either modest or of poor quality. Its agricultural land on the other hand was rich and well favoured by climate and communications. One fifth of it was in private hands. Postwar mechanization boosted output, some of which was exported. Manufacturing and mining industry was developed after the war and overtook agriculture's contribution to GNP. The principal products were machinery and, at a later stage, consumer goods. But, like its neighbours, Hungary's economy was neither efficiently managed, adequately capitalized nor competitive enough to earn foreign revenue. From the late 1960s Hungary led the way in central Europe in recognizing the limitations of central planning and in preparing to abandon rather than modify central controls. Targets were abolished; enterprises were allowed some latitude in setting prices, fixing wages and levels of investment. Credit levels, subsidies and import permits remained under central control, and worldwide recession in the 1970s blunted the effect of reforms. Productivity and profits remained low and foreign debt multiplied. Hungary was a showcase for cautious experimentation within limits tolerated by Moscow but until the late 1980s these limits, which forbade any erosion of the communist monopoly of power or any secession from the Warsaw Pact, prevented reform beyond the level of tinkering.

In eastern Europe[3] the pattern was similar, the privations more severe. In Romania the indices of economic progress and the miseries were in specially stark contrast. A considerable proportion of the national product was invested in an attempt to make Romania a major industrial state on the basis of its petrochemical, metallurgical and hydroelectric enterprises and its abundant raw materials – coal, oil, gas, copper and iron ore, matched by cereals, wines, livestock and horticulture. Industrial development depended on imports of Soviet oil at prices well below world prices. The poor paid with their labour and savings and received nothing in return, while the ruthless megalomaniac Nicolae Ceausescu (a home-grown communist who came to power on the death in 1963 of Georghe Georghiu-Dej) stripped the country of its assets in order to build palaces and other ostentatious edifices and to repay the national debt. Similarly in Bulgaria manufacturing output was boosted in the postwar decades by more than 50 per cent but without finding

3.   Postwar Yugoslavia and Romania covered 100,000 and 90,000 square miles, each with a population of 23 million by 1990. Bulgaria had 43,000 square miles and 9 million people, slightly less of each than Greece. Albania with 2.5 million people was the area's smallest and poorest country.

markets for the product. Agriculture, of which four fifths were in the hands of the state or cooperatives, experienced the same misshapen development.

Yugoslavia exceptionally could not blame its economic plight on the Soviet Union. Its principal problems were semi-submerged nationalisms and its place in political limbo. It possessed plentiful, but relatively inaccessible, mineral resources including lignite, natural gas, bauxite, iron ore, manganese and lead; hydroelectric power; and well-endowed farming lands, fisheries and forests. Industry, notably engineering and metallurgy, was very rapidly expanded after the war, as too were agriculture (cereals, tobacco, sunflower seed), tourism and remittances from emigrant workers, but cash and credit were hard to come by, much of the industrial product was substandard, and over-centralized controls created nonsensical bottlenecks. A first Five Year Plan on the Soviet model was quickly dismantled in the 1950s, partly because it was impossibly cumbersome and partly in order to entice western aid. Centralization was attacked both by nationalists in the several republics and, on very different grounds, by technocrats and managers. Forced to institute reforms Tito was tentative. The mechanisms of central control were loosened by devolving authority to the republics and to factory committees which were accorded the right to allocate investment and profits, but one result was excessive fragmentation. Social programmes – housing, health, education, public utilities – were sufficiently successful to engender optimism but too much was initiated too quickly and the economy became overstrained. Managers who had responsibilities thrust upon them were frequently unequal to them, either in competence or in integrity. There were whiffs of democratic choice which shackled executive decision without leading to much democracy in the right place, and there was enough debate to cause perplexity without increasing efficiency. A second bout of experimentation in the 1960s further loosened controls, particularly over prices, but the take-off which was expected to follow postwar repair and investment did not materialize as inflation and external deficits supervened. From the late 1960s Yugoslavia enjoyed neither growth nor stability and a marked improvement in the standard of living began to seep away. The poorer republics, Montenegro and Macedonia, fared the worst, while the more successful became the more disaffected as they persuaded themselves that they could do better on their own. Particularism was encouraged by economic disappointments, the more strongly in the rising generation which lacked the bonds of wartime camaraderie. In Croatia in 1972 Tito took the extreme step of removing all the younger leaders of the communist party who were agitating for more autonomy or secession; he also stamped on nationalists in Serbia, Slovenia and Macedonia. But when Tito died in 1980, and increasingly in the years that followed, the Yugoslav federation was the least coherent state in central or eastern Europe.

In the years after the Second World War central and eastern Europe did not always stagnate. Half concealed behind the Iron Curtain they gave the west a misleading impression of dull sameness, but their fate was in one sense worse than stagnation since substantial economic activity was linked not to growth and modernization but to shortages, distress and disappointment. Starting from well behind western Europe they fell further behind. After being exploited by Soviet vengeance, cupidity and need they were more lastingly damaged by the economic and administrative blunders of ruling cliques which were unintelligent about economics and perverse or corrupt in administration. The result was economic distortion: large quantities of substandard goods alongside reduced output of food, the consequences of the rigid regulation characteristic of minority government and communist doctrine. National output was increased with little or no benefit to the nation. Foreign debt piled up. Living became a hopeless grind except for the favoured, often corrupt few. And this course in anti-development was accompanied by a vast amount of senseless movement. Urbanization produced social as well as economic traumas as people flocked to cities where they found too little work, overstrained public utilities and gravely inadequate social services. The gypsies of central and eastern Europe, an element all but unknown in the west, added to the movement and took it across frontiers: Czechoslovakia, for example, received a million nomads from Hungary and Romania.

The quickening of crisis came from the Soviet Union when the death of Brezhnev in 1982, quickly followed by the deaths of his two successors Yuri Andropov and Konstantin Chernenko in 1984 and 1985, brought Mikhail Gorbachev to the post of general secretary of the Communist Party and effective head of government. In relation to the satellites Gorbachev's prime aim was disengagement. The Stalinist system was expensive and nearly useless. A military technology vastly different from that of 1945 had greatly reduced the satellites' value as a buffer zone, since any missile attack on the Soviet Union would go far above them, not across their territory. There was still some point in keeping forces in central Europe to confront Nato forces and as bargaining counters in disarmament discussions, but it no longer made sense to envisage military intervention in the affairs of the satellites themselves. This anachronism was made manifest before Gorbachev's succession by the course of events in Poland when popular threats to the authority of the ruling party unseated the party and created a political vacuum which was temporarily filled by Polish, not Soviet, military rule. Gorbachev explicitly renounced the use of Soviet force throughout the block and in 1989 went further when he counselled the East German communists not to use their own forces in defence of their own political monopoly.

In economic affairs Gorbachev wanted the satellites to restructure their economies and, so far as might be therefore necessary, their societies on the new Soviet model, but at the same time he wanted to shift responsibility in each state on to that state's leadership. These leaders, however, were not in Gorbachev's position or of his mind. While he had come to power through the death of his predecessors and with the intention of reversing their policies, the satellites' rulers were yesterday's men, the authors or guardians of policies which they did not want to change.

There were, however, pressures. The satellites were in a quandary. Economic failure had so debased the quality of their products that they were regarded as substandard not only in the west but in the Soviet Union too. Moreover the west, having burnt its fingers in the 1970s, was most reluctant to extend new credits, while Gorbachev's drive for value for money was diverting from the satellites many Soviet primary products which had been exported to the satellites but could more profitably be sold at rising prices elsewhere – prices which, for the satellites, would rise very steeply indeed if Moscow were to succeed in creating a realistically priced and convertible rouble. As in the Soviet Union, so in the satellites, reform was an economic necessity which required social, political and administrative changes of daunting proportions; such changes meant popular sacrifices in the form of higher prices and more work for the same or lower pay; but such sacrifices required a degree of trust between government and governed which did not exist. Thus in Poland at the end of 1987 the government presented a programme of reforms which, upon being submitted to a popular referendum, was rejected, leaving the government to choose between letting the economy go on mouldering and imposing harsh measures on a rebellious people. The revolution had produced no winners and no new focus of responsibility. Military rule under martial law was as monopolistic as the one-party state and as economically incapable. The economy got worse: during the 1980s real wages sank by a fifth and the annual rate of inflation exceeded 100 per cent. The workers had exacted concessions without winning power for themselves. The government refused to legalize Solidarity until Jaruzelski, overriding communist and military opposition, felt obliged in 1989 to strike a deal with it which included elections for the Senate and the lower house (the Sejm), a multi-party system and a freer press and broadcasting – subject only to a guaranteed majority for communists in the Sejm. In the ensuing elections the communists were routed. Solidarity won 99 out of 100 seats in the Senate and the maximum permitted in the Sejm, 161 out of 460. Solidarity, which had grown from a trade union to a political movement to a parliamentary party, was propelled not entirely willingly or harmoniously into government and one of its leaders, Tadeusz Mozawiecki, became Prime Minister. Jaruzelski, having resigned his party post, was elected President by the Sejm. The party changed its name. But political changes brought no automatic economic relief and only disappointing foreign aid: the United States offered one tenth of what Walesa sought from it. The new government, drawing on the popular backing which its predecessor conspicuously lacked, applied shock treatment: wage freezes, abolition of subsidies and price controls. Jaruzelski resigned the presidency in 1990. Walesa and Mazowiecki both contested it, thus advertising a split in Solidarity. Walesa defeated Mazowiecki and an unexpected intruder who had spent the past twenty years in north and south America making a million.

In Hungary the rejection in 1988 of Janos Kadar, who had been in power for thirty-two years, attested the impact of Gorbachev, for Kadar had been a modest reformer before the advent of Gorbachev but thereafter hesitant. He was succeeded as general secretary of the party by Karolyi Grosz who lasted less than a year, during which colleagues, including his Prime Minister Miklos Nemeth and his Economics Minister Imre Poszgay, pressed for radical political as well as economic reforms and in effect split the party. The rehabilitation and reburial of Imre Nagy, murdered in 1958, sparked massive demonstrations and turned Hungary into a democratic state in which the communist party (which changed its name) would be one among many. More than two dozen parties were formed ahead of elections in 1990 which were won by the centre-right. The communist rump won 10 per cent of the vote.

In Czechoslovakia the equivalent revolution came last in central Europe but fast. Gorbachev, visiting Prague in 1987, showed that he did not care for the régime but was not inclined openly to force the pace of change. The régime seemed for a while to be holding back the tide, but in a flash flood of barely three weeks at the end of 1989 the communists were swept out of office. In the interval small groups of young people, writing and talking and communicating with one another, developed an overwhelming popular movement which took to the streets and, under the aegis of the loosely coordinated Civic Forum in the historic lands and of associated groups in Slovakia, formulated precise demands for the removal of communist power, free press and television and the release of political prisoners. The Forum's leader, Vaclav Havel, became president of the republic by popular propulsion and Alexander Dubcek, reappearing after 21 years, was made chairman of the parliament. Elections in 1990 confirmed and legitimized this revolution, although the communists (who uniquely throughout this area did not change their name) did surprisingly well, as too did a variety of nationalists. The Soviet Union promised to withdraw its 70,000 troops in stages up to 1991 – likewise its 50,000 troops in Hungary.

Collapse in East Germany, which preceded that in Czechoslovakia, was the strangest and in European terms the most momentous. It was precipitated by the mass desertion of its people. This exodus began when Hungary, in a gesture with no special regard for German issues, removed barriers on the Austro-Hungarian border. East Germans on holiday in Hungary found that they had an open road through Austria to West Germany, where they had automatic rights of access and citizenship. They took the road at a rate initially of several thousands a day. The exodus was swollen a few months later when Hungary, abrogating an agreement with East Germany, virtually constituted itself a transit zone for a mass migration. East Germans, already aware of political developments in neighbouring countries (largely through watching West German television) staged huge demonstrations in Berlin and other cities and under these pressures new escape routes were fashioned through Czechoslovakia, from Poland through East Germany in special trains, and eventually directly from East to West Germany. With the breaching of frontiers the Berlin wall became an irrelevance and was demolished; the city was reunited as men and women from both sides of it were allowed to pass freely from one side to the other; the reunification of Germany itself was catapulted onto the international agenda; and peoples in both halves of Europe were forced to ask themselves the question which they would have preferred to postpone: What did they think about Germany, German power and the German mood? As elsewhere Gorbachev played a significant role. Erich Honecker seemed determined to hold on to power and to what he regarded as a cause, if necessary by force. His position, however, was in one crucial respect the weakest among communist bosses since the state of which he was president was a Soviet creation and not a national entity. In national terms East Germany was not a state but a splinter. The source of its government's authority and legitimacy was not German but Soviet. When Gorbachev arrived in Berlin in October 1989 he remarked publicly on the dangers of being left behind by history and privately made it clear that the régime could hope for no help from Soviet troops. He may have gone further, thwarting a contemplated use of East German troops by encouraging the removal of Honecker. Honecker's successor as general secretary of the Socialist Unity Party, Egon Krenz, a younger but not much less tarnished member of the party's inner core, was sidetracked by somewhat more flexible communists and soon replaced by Gregor Gysi as the party changed its name and prepared to try to salvage part of its power in the unfamiliar contest of local elections. These elections, in which West German politicians played a prominent part, gave power to the right on a promise of unification and one-for-one currency swap at the earliest possible moment. Nearly half the votes were cast for the centre right, less than a quarter for the social democrats and 16 per cent for the communists.

In eastern Europe Todor Zhivkov, who had ruled Bulgaria – traditionally the most Russophil country in Europe – even longer than Kadar ruled Hungary, beat a retreat which was hastened by his persecution of the Turkish Muslims (or Pomaks) who fled the country in large numbers upon being required to change their names; and partly by an international conference of environment-alists which became the occasion for violent demonstrations and police brutality in response. Zhivkov's successor Petar Mladenov set out to give the communist party, which changed its name to socialist, a fair enough face to survive in a multi-party system and succeeded well enough to win about half the votes in elections in 1990 which dismayed the opposition but were adjuged by foreign observers to have been a reasonably fair reflection of the popular will. Mladenov himself, however, was compelled by popular clamour to resign, and the protracted search for a successor revealed a country which, having rounded up a set of incompetent and corrupt rulers, had no clear idea of what to put in their place. In Romania Nicolae Ceausescu, more a personal tyrant than a party boss and the least pro-Soviet leader in the communist block, paid the grimmest price. Riots in Brasov in 1987, repeated in Timisoara in 1989, were the prelude to a revolt in which the army deserted the dictator who, with his wife, was seized, summarily tried and shot. A National Salvation Front, formed by communists hostile to Ceausescu, claimed the role of transitional government and went on to win elections which were judged to be far from perfect but short of outrageous. Albania, isolated since breaking with the Soviet Union in 1969 and ruled by Ramiz Alia after the death in 1985 of the demigod Enver Hoxha, alone maintained the strictest communist position into, but not beyond, 1990.

Yugoslavia, although no part of the Stalinist empire, was by 1989 beset by similar economic disorders, compounded by nationalist dissensions. Inflation was out of control, the standard of living back to where it had been thirty years earlier. In 1989 the federal government introduced desperate measures – a convertible currency, commercial banks, a stock exchange – which brought inflation down to zero but caused the gravest privations and accentuated tensions between the republics. The Serbs were trying to extend the borders of the Serbian republic while the Slovenes and Croats were threatening to secede. The Serbian claim to incorporate the autonomous districts of Kosovo and Vojvodina provoked strikes and violence by the Albanians of Kosovo, who proclaimed the territory a republic independent of Serbia. Elected President of Serbia in 1989 Slobodan Milosevic declared both districts to be integral parts of Serbia but, however appealing his nationalism, was increasingly vulnerable as a communist. Slovenes and Croats denounced Serbian actions. Slovenia, in the far north west, a republic with only 1.5 million people, never an independent state but endowed with a distinct language, produced a quarter of all the federation's foreign earnings, contributed handsomely to the well-being of the other republics and resented both the economic incompetence of the federal government and the assertiveness of the Serbs. It declared itself in favour of a multi-party system and created an opposition (Demos) which won elections (but not the presidency of the Slovene republic) and threatened to secede. The Slovene section of the federal communist party seceded from the party and changed its name. Croatia, like Slovenia, had been part of the Austro-Hungarian sphere and not the Ottoman, but unlike Slovenia it could boast of a spell of independence in the Middle Ages and a modest degree of autonomy in the nineteenth century. It had a population of four and a half million which, however, included half a million Serbs and excluded a million Croats in Bosnia. Croats shared a language with Serbs but wrote it in a different script. It was a contributor to the economies of other republics and complained the more about this state of affairs as the Yugoslav economy declined. After the adoption of a multi-party system, Franjo Tudjman, a communist turned nationalist, won a parliamentary majority and the presidency in a campaign accompanied by ominous threats against Serbs living in Croatia and claims for the rectification of the frontier with Bosnia. The federal communist party endorsed a multi-party system against the wishes of its Serbian section. Both state and party were disintegrating.

The principal factors in the overthrow of the Stalinist empire in central and eastern Europe were Gorbachev and economic disaster. Gorbachev saw that the system did not work. It was an expensive millstone round Moscow's neck and it lacked even the strategic rationale which had been its justification in the 1940s. Gorbachev's disenchantment with the system was not concealed from those who operated it. They could see that they were no longer in favour and had become proconsuls in a defunct empire. But they could look for no support from their fellow citizens since, besides grossly abusing their powers and destroying basic freedoms, they had allowed whole economies to moulder and economic growth to collapse from as much as 10 per cent a year in some parts of the satellite empire to zero or nearly zero practically everywhere. Hence tensions, demonstrations and riots, repression (often extremely brutal), and revolution. Yet, with the sorry exception of Romania, these revolutions were all but bloodless, an outcome almost inconceivable in any other continent. They were also swift. And not the least astonishing of their features was the emergence of Gorbachev, President of the USSR, as a popular hero as crowds chanted his name and appeared to regard the United States and other western democracies as comparatively irrelevant.

These changes were great but not easily definable. Two were clear: the end of the Soviet empire and the reunification of Germany, a reversal therefore in the balance of power in central Europe which had swung away from Germany to Russia in the 1940s. Within the area changes were vaguer and probably transitional. Communist parties were dethroned and communism discredited, more so in central than eastern Europe. Social democrats had to struggle to evade a general contamination of the left and preserve their distinction from communists calling themselves socialists. The first *epigonoi* included more or less liberal persons from the professional and intellectual classes, a small sector and one likely to be squeezed, leaving the battles of the future to be fought between a disgraced and divided left and a resurgent right. The law of the pendulum suggested a right-wing backlash in the offing, particularly where ecclesiastical influences were strong: Roman Catholic in Poland, Slovakia and Croatia, Orthodox in the Balkans. Parliamentary democracy was a widespread aspiration but one with a future hardly more assured than its past. Whether national rivalries would be reinvigorated depended on an unknown quantity – the extent to which younger people shared the atavistic animosities of their elders. What did not change with revolution was the gathering economic calamity.

What Gorbachev had unleashed he could not control. Leaving the satellites to fend for themselves under non-communist régimes was a necessary and sensible abandonment of empire with consequences for the balance of power in central and eastern Europe which could be foreseen only vaguely. In so far as the Soviet Union was abandoning untenable positions it was abandoning not power but pretensions. In one area, however – East Germany – the consequences were more precisely visible. Formalities apart, the two Germanies were immediately reunited, the west absorbing the east so that East Germany ceased to exist as a state and West Germany became larger. Gorbachev tried to detach the new Germany from Nato but he had no more chance of doing so than he had of preventing reunification. He secured, however, undertakings that no German units committed to Nato nor Nato units stationed in West Germany would be stationed in the former East Germany, that the withdrawal of Soviet forces might extend to 1994, that Germany's own forces would be reduced in that period by nearly a half, and that Germany would reaffirm its commitment neither to make nor acquire nuclear, biological nor chemical weapons. Germany also abandoned any claim to East Prussia. Helped by German statesmanship the Soviet Union retreated in good order and in 1990 the two states signed a twenty-year treaty which marked the end of a phase stretching back to 1941.

CHAPTER SEVEN

The American Response

While it lasted Stalin's empire was the determining factor in the United States' European policies. When it ended those policies were rendered obsolete. Stalin's empire-building was an aspect or reflection of the confrontation between east and west which had been submerged by the war against Germany. It aggravated that confrontation and brought the United States politically and militarily back to Europe. The term 'Cold War' was invented to describe the resulting state of affairs.

The Cold War was not an episode with a beginning and an end. Still less was it a war in any accepted sense, although hostility was intrinsic to it. It was not primarily about territory or frontiers. The hostility was at work before the war ended and centred on Germany. Both sides conducted raids into Germany to seize persons, papers or apparatus which might be useful for scientific research into new weapons or for intelligence, and both were anxious to secure control of Germany – or as much of Germany as possible. Germany, which had brought them together, became the focus for their postwar mistrust and, in the blockade of Berlin in 1948–49, the scene of the nearest approach to open warfare between them.

Stalin had hoped that out of the war's chaos would come communist control over all Germany. He was quickly disillusioned. Two conferences in 1947 of the foreign ministers of the four occupying Powers failed to agree on terms for a German settlement or peace treaty. Germany became divided. Western and eastern occupiers went their separate ways, preserving only in the city of Berlin the semblance of their wartime collaboration. The Americans and British wished to revive their zones of occupation in order to escape the costs of financing and supplying them. France, after harking back to its policy of 1918 of shackling Germany by partitioning it, had to fall in with American wishes. The three zones were united, turned into a single state and reanimated through financial reform (a new mark exchangeable for old marks at rates varying with the nature of the obligations redeemed) and American capital. In four years west Germany's industrial output more than doubled and its GDP rose by two thirds. When the western occupiers extended the new mark to the western sectors of Berlin the Soviet authorities, alarmed by this political consolidation and economic invigoration of the old enemy, countered with a blockade designed to make the western position in the city intolerable. This position depended on access from the west through the Soviet zone which enveloped the city on all sides. The western occupiers, faced with a choice between asserting their right of access overland, if necessary by force, or abandoning their position in Berlin, did neither. Avoiding the hazards of driving their way across a hundred miles of hostile territory they organized an airlift which kept them and the Berliners in their sectors supplied with necessities for ten months. The Soviet Union gave way. The western position in Berlin was maintained. The division of Germany was affirmed and so too was the development of a separate west German state as an ally of the western Powers.

The duel over Berlin froze the German question as between the Superpowers but it did not end the Cold War. On the contrary the Cold War spread, partly in response to other events contemporaneous with the Berlin blockade and airlift and partly because it was by its very nature geographically limitless. Simultaneously with the conflict over Berlin Stalin purged non-communists, and insufficiently reliable communists, from all the satellite governments under his control in central and eastern Europe. This process, which accompanied Moscow's breach with Tito's Yugoslavia and was most startlingly marked by the overthrow of Eduard Benes' multi-party government in Czechoslovakia, was regarded in the west as not only ruthless but reckless: it intensified fears as well as revulsion. In the same period Mao's victory in China (1949) and the outbreak of war in Korea (1950) wafted the Cold War into Asia, the Soviet Union graduated into the nuclear arms race (1949) and western opposition was formalized by the North Atlantic Treaty (1949). These moves in and beyond Europe fuelled a conflict which was inherently expansive for a variety of reasons: because neither Superpower was a European Power and no more; because both conducted their conflict in ideological language, not geographical; and because both gravely exaggerated the adversary's intentions and capacities. The United States credited the Soviet Union with a determination to make the whole world communist and failed to see that any plan to conquer or subvert even the rest of Europe would be a self-defeating absurdity. In 1945 the Soviet Union lacked the strength to extend its power in Europe beyond areas already occupied by its armies, and subsequent ventures – in Cuba, Ethiopia, Afghanistan – so far from increasing its world power were predictable disasters from the Soviet point of view. On the Soviet side equally extravagant assumptions ruled. Stalin regarded his wartime allies as aggressive capitalist states intent on the extermination of Soviet communism and the Soviet state, but he failed to see that however much they hated communism they had no intention of going to war with the Soviet Union or even of doing anything practical to remove its control over its satellites. Thus the presumptions of both Superpowers were not only ideological but to a considerable degree mythical. They were, however, not therefore insignificant and the Cold War which they shaped dominated the conduct of world affairs for four decades.

Besides the propaganda based on these fears and prejudices the Cold War was waged through the nuclear threat and the development of ever more penetrating and accurate ways of delivering nuclear weapons on to their targets. The two American bombs dropped from aircraft on Japan in 1945 were countered by a Soviet test in the same class in 1949, four years behind. In 1951 President Truman endorsed the construction of an H-bomb or fusion bomb, nicknamed the Super. Truman's choice was between managing Superpower relations in the new world of the fission bomb or escalating world politics in an expanding nuclear world. The escalation might have happened anyway, but the initiative in 1951 lay with the United States and the decision reflected the temper of the times. The first American test of an H-bomb took place in 1952, the first Soviet equivalent in 1953, one year behind. In 1957 the Soviet Union successfully hoisted a rocket into space. Aircraft were superseded by ballistic missiles and the weaponry of the Cold War was further elaborated as nuclear weapons of shorter and shorter range were invented and deployed. This arms race acquired an enormous hold over the popular imagination and was accompanied by debates as ridiculous as the debates among medieval churchmen over how many angels might stand on the point of a pin. Which side had more of what became an obsessive question swamping the more pertinent question, what either side might intend to do with what it had. With time, however, the conviction grew that war in Europe between the Superpowers was a remote possibility. The conviction was grounded in the rough, but effective, equivalence of the Superpowers' long-range missiles and the gradual awareness of the inappropriateness of nuclear weapons for any conceivable military purpose (general devastation not being a military purpose).

The use, or usefulness, of nuclear weapons was mooted in the United States a year after the successful conclusion of the Berlin airlift when North Korea made a bid to overrun South Korea with the endorsement (but probably not on the initiative) of the Soviet Union. The United States intervened to stem this extension of communism which was not only unpalatable in itself but also dangerous in the context of the emergence, as it was at the time supposed, of a vast Sino-Soviet world communist Power. Six months after American intervention China too intervened in Korea to defend itself against the extension of the war by the United States to overthrow Mao's regime. The Korean War was a local war in a peripheral country which assumed universal significance. Coming hard on the heels of the fight over Berlin and Mao's capture of Beijing it raised the question, seriously and lengthily pondered by two American presidents – Truman and Eisenhower – whether to use nuclear weapons. It played a major part in changing American containment of the Soviet Union from economic containment to military containment. It launched the massive rearmament of the postwar period: American military expenditure quadrupled during the Korean War, diminished during Eisenhower's presidency but then rebounded. It created an urgent American determination to rearm West Germany, a proposal which sent shivers down European spines. It created distrust between the United States and its European allies and confusion about how far Europeans might expediently try to influence American policies in Asia. It marked the beginning of pronounced American activity in eastern Asia which spread from Korea to China's offshore islands to South East Asia and lasted for more than twenty years. By the time an armistice was reached in Korea the attempt of the French to retain their rule in Vietnam (financed from 1950 by the United States) against the communist nationalism of the Vietminh was collapsing at Dien Bien Phu (1954) and the United States, spurred on by its anti-communist ideology, was sliding into French shoes. When from 1960 the Vietminh carried the war to the south against the regime supported there by the United States, Washington ordered naval forces to bombard Hanoi and other targets in the north (1964) and landed ground forces on the mainland (1965) where, in spite of huge numbers and increasingly frightful weapons, they were first checked by the Tet offensive of 1968 and then forced to retreat, abandoning their Vietnamese associates (1973).

It was perhaps fortunate for the peace of the rest of the world that the United States' principal communist bugbear in Asia in the 1960s was not the Soviet Union but China, with which the Soviet Union had quarrelled in 1960. In Europe there was a lull from the 1950s when, following the death of Stalin in 1953, first Malenkov and then Khrushchev toyed with new policies. In Stalin's last years Soviet foreign policies were markedly cautious. When he died nobody knew what difference, if any, his death would bring. Riots in East Germany and elsewhere in the satellite empire were met by Moscow with concessions; there was a truce in Korea and an international conference in Geneva about Vietnam; and a peace treaty with Austria neutralized that country at the centre of Europe. On succeeding Malenkov, Khrushchev went to Belgrade to try to patch up Moscow's quarrel with Tito and in 1955 he set out for India, Burma and Afghanistan equipped with promises of economic aid and denunciations of western imperialism. Khrushchev's ebullience was at first ambivalent, confined to capitalizing in the Middle East on the abrupt withdrawal of American finance for the Aswan dam in Egypt, and to casting around for ways to take advantage of decolonization in Africa. But the ebullience turned to a more manic mood when he tried in 1962 to win friends and nuclear weapon sites in Cuba – an escapade which, together with American involvements in Asia, made the Cold War worldwide in fact as well as potentially, and eventually intolerably expensive. By the mid-1960s Stalin's successors had done as much as Stalin himself to consolidate the Euro-American alliance which in the decade 1955–65 came to look like a fact of nature, as immovable as any major natural phenomenon.

Yet this great alliance which overshadowed much of world affairs throughout the second half of the century came into being at comparatively short notice and against the grain of both European and American traditions. Europe's habits of independence were overborne by fear of Soviet aggressiveness and the conviction that only American power could block it. These judgements created the need for the Euro-American alliance which came into existence because the United States shared them. The United States sharply reversed its attitudes to Europe in consequence of revising its wartime attitudes to the Soviet Union. If Soviet designs had been less feared there could have been no need for the alliance and if American might had been less awesome there would have been no point in it. The abatement of either would weaken the alliance.

As long as the war with Germany lasted President Roosevelt had managed to sidestep the incompatibility of Stalinism with the political and human values of the western democracies. He viewed the Soviet Union from a long way away and he viewed it primarily as a state with which other states had to deal. Roosevelt was a patrician professional politician with a pragmatic approach to public affairs and an aversion to the emotional popular strands in the American body politic which focused on the sins of Soviet society rather than on the problems of co-existing with the Soviet state. He was, as his repeated re-election showed, a trusted leader but he was not representative of the popular emotions which, the United States being a singularly open democracy, play a considerable part in influencing its statecraft. Roosevelt, therefore, who died four weeks before the war in Europe ended, bequeathed to his successors the makings of a policy towards the Soviet Union which was never likely to be made.

In the first postwar years Great Britain contrived to blandish the United States into a dominant role in European affairs as the leader of an anti-Soviet alliance. In both London and Washington the mood was mixed. Some on the British side had reservations about a leading American role in Europe; some on the American side were convinced of the necessity for a forward policy. The clinching factor was the behaviour of the Soviet Union itself in central and eastern Europe. This behaviour caused the United States to reverse its determination to withdraw once more from Europe and, the more so after the outbreak of the Korean War, to rearm vigorously after a few years of rapid demobilization. It created the hostility between the Nato allies and the Soviet Union which remained virtually unquestionable for forty years. Without Stalin there would have been no Nato and without Stalin's successors Nato's history would have been very different from what it was. Few individuals have had so marked an impact as Stalin on the face of Europe from the Urals to the Atlantic.

Next to Stalin the creation of the alliance was the work of Great Britain. The country which had once called in the New World to redress the balance of the Old upset by Napoleon had no hesitation in doing the same again. On the European side – which in the years 1945–49 meant Great Britain far more than any other state – the alliance was an insurance and a lifeline. These were years of dismaying uncertainty. Confidence, as well as material well-being, was in short supply among statesmen who, better than an euphoric populace, were appalled and perplexed by postwar shortages and dislocations. Although Europe admired the astonishing achievements of the Soviet Union against Germany these achievements could not expunge a more grisly view of Russia which included Tsarist autocracy and cruelty, Stalin's slaughter of ten million peasants, his rigged treason trials and terrible labour camps, and the rampages of his armies in Europe in the closing stages of the Second World War. The United States, friendly, generous and liberal, was at the opposite end of the political spectrum. While some might argue about the contest between communism and capitalism, many more saw a simpler contrast between tyranny and freedom. So Europe's principal concern was to make and keep the closest alliance with the United States, to be secured by American nuclear weapons, American money and a continuing American conviction that in the Superpower conflict Europe was more important than any other part of the world.

But the end was clearer than the means, for the Euro-American alliance was as uncharacteristic as it was crucial. Americans had roots in Europe which had a sentimental pull, but politically American attitudes to Europe were coloured by disappointment and disapproval, of which the leading states in western Europe were the principal butts. The peace-making in 1919 had not gone as the American president intended. Woodrow Wilson felt let down by Lloyd George and Clemenceau who had treated his plans for a new and better world order as distracting moonshine. Throughout the interwar interlude France was in American eyes a stubborn and chauvinist obstacle to peace and goodwill in Europe, more benighted than Germany. In addition, both France and Great Britain were imperial Powers which had extended their empires by the war and operated closed economic systems which – British imperial preferences in particular – impeded the free trade to which the United States had become converted. Between the wars Americans liked to think that politically they could wash their hands of Europe, although they never completely did so: as early as 1924, for example, they were sponsoring the Dawes Plan for the settlement of war reparations (Dawes was an American general). In the 1930s the new Germany joined this rogues' gallery by reason of its aggressive temper and, if only secondarily, its brutality. Although soft on German economic penetration of central and south eastern Europe and on German claims to change frontiers in the name of ethnic self-determination, the United States became increasingly alert to Hitler's disdain of international conventions and shocked by Nazi abuses of decency, so that when a second world war become seemingly inescapable the United States was vastly more sympathetic to Great Britain than to Germany, even if it did not join the fighting until Hitler forced it to do so by himself declaring war on the United States in support of Japan.

Between the wars the United States had sought wealth rather than conquest, except in Central America where it was perennially ready to put the boot in. While to Europeans the United States seemed culpably isolationist, Americans themselves felt isolated. At the Paris conference in 1919 American proposals for making the world safer had been received with inadequate enthusiasm and pared away by unbecoming nationalist indifference to American faith in a League of Nations, leaving Americans with the feeling that their sensible intentions had been rebuffed. They concentrated, therefore, with a clear conscience, on making the most of their great and growing economic advantages. Prosperity was attainable without having to fight anybody for it and they had the added comfort of believing, again sensibly, that the pursuit of American economic interests could happily coincide with what was economically good for the rest of the world. But Americans were not guileless. They saw the world as a peaceful, but not necessarily amicable or honourable, battlefield between three major economic forces: the United States, the British empire and a Schachtian (economically aggressive) Germany. They contested British economic power and feared a possible Anglo-German diarchy. Some Americans were in favour of encouraging the Germany of Schacht and Hitler in the hope, ostensibly, that Germany might be pushed into over-exertion and collapse – a delusion so naive as to suggest an element of political partiality. With Great Britain they sparred. They found in Chamberlain a disdainful prime minister whom they in turn distrusted. Chamberlain in peacetime was as hostile to American intervention in European affairs as Churchill in wartime longed for it.

The war began the transformation of American attitudes, but how deeply and how permanently remained at the war's end a conundrum. In spite of ingrained prejudices against entanglements, epitomized in Roosevelt's casual but significant remark at

Yalta about Americans in Europe all going home in two years after the end of the war, the United States proved biddable and settled down to prolonged encampment in Europe with only sporadic and tactical threats to go away. Initially this involvement had a strong flavour of benevolence – the Marshall Plan its main outward sign – with an associated political purpose to counter communism and neutralism. But the impulse to help was accompanied by an equally powerful impulse to thwart and to use western Europe to deploy not only sympathy but arms (eventually against enemies such as Libya as well as the Soviet Union). Having overrated Stalin's human qualities during the war Americans overrated his military capacities after it and, even when they possessed a monopoly of nuclear weapons, were fidgety about an entirely implausible Soviet advance beyond Germany and about the effectiveness of western communist parties. (Although this latter fear was superficially more plausible, no communist party achieved anything of note on its own account except in Tito's Yugoslavia.) This obsession with Soviet power and communist influence was supplemented by the fiercely emotional and ideological anti-communism which, from Senator Joseph McCarthy to President Ronald Reagan, pervaded the United States to an extent unknown in Western Europe. When in the 1980s Europeans developed an almost vituperative contempt for the genial but stupid Reagan they were expressing their view that he talked dangerous nonsense about the Soviet Union. (That he talked nonsense about other things did not bother Europeans so much.) To fear of the Soviet Union was added, on the American side especially, a hatred which gave the alliance an extra tenacity.

This tenacity weakened only when the policies which it dictated threatened to become ruinously expensive and the advent of Gorbachev in 1985 offered an occasion for some retreat from the politics and costs of confrontation. Gorbachev was not the first anti-Stalinist portent but others (Khrushchev, Kosygin) had been marginal and fleeting: they seemed nicer human beings but not necessarily less dangerous Soviet leaders. Western distrust was rooted in the destruction of even a semblance of multi-party government in central and eastern Europe, in the Soviet blockade of Berlin in 1948 and in the emergence of the Soviet Union as a nuclear Power. The sheer growth of Soviet military might seemed to sanctify the nuclear arms race by which the United States aimed to contain, deter and even perhaps ruin the Soviet Union. Since the first Soviet nuclear explosion occurred in the year in which

Mao Tsedong's capture of Beijing seemed to have created a hugely expanded communist realm under Soviet leadership, and since war broke out in Korea only one year later, Soviet evil intentions were so axiomatic that the proposition that the war had been instigated by Moscow was as universally believed in the west as had been the proposition that the victims of Katyn had been killed by Germans: the climate of opinion made true what was in fact false. It propelled the United States into rearming Germany; converting the containment of the Soviet Union into the containment of communism, including Chinese (but not Yugoslav) communism; and supporting anti-communists such as Synghman Rhee, Ferdinand Marcos and a clutch of Latin-American detrimentals, however unattractive they might be in most other respects. The enemy was now worldwide and the fight had become global: not European.

In the same year, 1950, an American policy paper assumed, for the sake of argument but also with the intent to impress its closed circle of readers, that the Soviet Union was likely to start a war either by aggression or by miscalculation; that such a war would be, or quickly become, a nuclear war; that a surprise first strike by the Soviet Union would be fatal; and that the overriding task of American planners was therefore to prevent surprise. Soviet aggressiveness was in part a planning contingency, but in the view of the policy paper it was also a practical possibility. Since an early warning system might well prevent total surprise without preventing total destruction, the only safe defence was powerful deterrence. While on the one hand the Korean War dictated a reinforcement of conventional forces in Europe, the Superpower arms race even more insistently required the expansion of the nuclear deterrent. To the former all members of the newly created Euro-American alliance would contribute men, the United States most of the money. The latter was a distinct and exclusively American responsibility. The combination was from the start alarmingly costly but the needs overrode the costs and they were reinforced at intervals throughout the coming decades. The death of Stalin in 1953, for example, raised hopes of climactic change and three years later the relatively emollient Khrushchev denounced Stalin and many of his works at a supposedly secret Congress of the Communist Party of the Soviet Union and preached peaceful co-existence (which appeared to mean a state of no-war between the Superpowers accompanied, however, by undiminished endeavours to catch up with the United States in new arms and by new ventures). But in the same year, the Soviet Union used force to suppress protest in Hungary and the hopes hovering fitfully about the horizon in the mid and late 1950s were further dampened by the collapse of the summit meeting of 1960 upon the disclosure of American spying over Soviet territory with U-2 aircraft (one of which was shot down); by an unproductive meeting between Khrushchev and the newly elected President John F. Kennedy; by Khrushchev's assent to the building of a wall through Berlin to keep East Germans from migrating to the west (2.5 million from a population of 17 million had already done so); and above all by Khrushchev's attempt to install nuclear missiles in Cuba. Signs of change in economic policies when A. N. Kosygin was prime minister evaporated. A Partial Test Ban treaty in 1963 and a Nuclear Non-Proliferation treaty in 1968 (which the Superpowers never implemented as regards themselves) were feeble sparks of hope compared with the expansion of Soviet naval and world power in the same decade. In the 1970s the Soviet Union put large forces into Ethiopia and invaded Afghanistan in the space of less than three years (1977, 1979). The course of events seemed to justify those western pessimists who maintained that significant change in the Soviet Union was inherently impossible.

American power was at all times greater than Soviet Power. American military might was solidly based on unrivalled productive capacity. In 1945 neither the one nor the other was in question. The American economy and the American armoury seemed not only relatively far superior to those of every other state but even absolute. The United States was so rich that it could do anything, even go to the moon. This was no great surprise since – quite apart from the prognoses of Choiseul in the eighteenth century and de Tocqueville in the nineteenth – the rise of the United States to a unique economic eminence had been a phenomenon observed by all from the beginning of the twentieth century and the economic wonder of the interwar period had been the great leap forward of American manufacturing industry.

The United States possessed essential resources in raw materials, capital and labour; it cherished and relished education, research and invention; and it developed in pioneering style the more humdrum managerial and organizational skills. But what distinguished the American economy between the wars and where it most clearly outpaced its rivals were plentiful investment and a zest for the new. Before the war of 1914–18 the United States' principal competitors were Great Britain, Germany and France, but even before 1914 American industrial production was moving to exceed the combined output of these three. In trade, three quarters of American exports and imports were into or out of Europe, and three quarters of that three quarters were with Great Britain, Germany and France. In the supply of capital for the world the United States was displacing Great Britain. The first Great War was an adventitious aid (so too was the second). The prosperity of Europe, based on trade and industry and the combination of the two, was offset by a comparative lack of raw materials (except in Russia where they were considerable but very imperfectly exploited). Nevertheless this weakness was a minor one until the First World War crippled Europe's economies. Postwar recovery, although impressive, did not reverse the gap between them and the United States which the war had widened. This widening accelerated. Europe lost permanently its prewar share of world trade and failed to resume its dominance of international capital markets. In the Great Depression Europe's industrial production fell by nearly 30 per cent and trade by 60 per cent. The unquantifiable collapse of morale was also one which, once more, turned to American advantage. The Second World War redoubled this advantage as the United States, uniquely, fought but remained out of range of enemy action. When that war ended few doubted that American prosperity and power were in a class of their own. So was American self-confidence.

Nevertheless, there came about an arms race which was widely believed to be a race on roughly equal terms. It takes two to make a race and the Superpower arms race began when the Soviet Union followed the United States into the nuclear elite. The United States, faced with the need to respond, had a number of choices and adopted them all. They were principally three: to improve the means of delivering existing weapons, the most notable success being the B-52 bomber which came into service in 1955 (the Soviet Union had no aircraft capable of carrying bombs to the United States and returning); secondly, to develop more powerful nuclear weapons, notably the fusion or thermonuclear bomb; and thirdly, to diversify the nuclear armoury, notably through the introduction of tactical or battlefield weapons. Since these last weapons could not be deployed against the Soviet Union without stationing American forces in Europe, they had a direct impact on Euro-American strategy. Less directly, other aspects of nuclear strategy did so too. The emphasis on nuclear weapons downgraded conventional weapons and reduced American conventional forces in Europe to the status of a political symbol, so making them irremovable without a political upheaval. The primacy of American long-range strategic weapons carried with it doubts whether the United States would ever use such devastating terror in defence of Europe, and these doubts were redoubled when the United States became vulnerable to similar Soviet attack from intercontinental missiles and so might be required to save Europe by putting its own people at risk. The deployment of tactical weapons in the European theatre posed the question in whose hands they should be. The alliance was inescapably bedevilled by these problems of the credibility of nuclear weapons, the allocation of responsibilities over their use, the greater exposure of the European allies and the uncertain role of non-nuclear forces. Yet throughout the Cold War no differences over these questions were allowed to disrupt the alliance, even in the case of France which withdrew from active military participation but remained a member. This was a measure of the allies' common hostility to the Soviet Union, recalling the steadfastness of the anti-German alliance of 1941–45 so long as it had a common enemy.

The first allied plan, adopted in Lisbon in 1952, envisaged a land force of 96 divisions, of which 50 were to be in the central sector, and an air force of 9000 aircraft. This was a plan to fight a losing non-nuclear war in Europe, much of which would be overrun by the enemy while American long-range bombers retaliated against Soviet cities and industry. It assumed that the American nuclear armoury had failed to deter war. It was an expression of no confidence in the capacity of the deterrent to deter, not however because of its nature but because of its size at this point. The Lisbon targets were never reached and were abandoned as soon as nuclear weapons became more plentiful and variegated, and strategy preponderantly nuclear. Dependence on nuclear weapons meant not second thoughts about their usefulness but more of them.

In the United States a new administration ended in 1954 the Democrats' tenure of the White House which had been uninterrupted since 1932. The new men were worried by the costs of modern armaments and the arms race and by the flaws in the prevailing nuclear strategy whose credibility was suspect. President Eisenhower was a thrifty man and his Secretary of State, John Foster Dulles, was intellectually offended by the gap between the power of nuclear weapons and their value in practice. For Eisenhower the beauty (if any) of nuclear weapons was not their fearful destructiveness but the economies which they promised by comparison with an equivalent non-nuclear deployment. For

Dulles nuclear weapons were rhetorically rather than militarily useful; they provided a new kind of sabre-rattling, so frightening that talking about them would suffice to cow opposition. For both statesmen nuclear weapons were a fact of life and not, as in the 1940s, a monstrosity to be kept in a closed Pandora's box and talked about with bated breath. Time alone was effecting this change and it was accelerated by the unexpectedly rapid advance of the Soviet Union towards parity with the United States or worse, an advance dramatized in 1957 when the Soviet Union became the first to put a satellite (sputnik) into space. This threat was all the more disturbing for Americans who regarded Russians as unfettered by humane or moral inhibitions.

Dulles toyed with the idea of brandishing nuclear weapons at Moscow and demanding a Soviet retreat from central Europe, but this was going hazardously far and was quickly abandoned as unrealistic. Dulles had stubbed his toe on the uncomfortable fact that the threat to use nuclear weapons was a bluff and that every increase in their destructiveness increased the element of bluff and therefore the risk of the bluff being called. His threats of massive and indiscriminate retaliation broke the credibility barrier and obliged the Republican administration to recognize that there was no safe or sensible alternative to the Democrats' sounder, if frustrating, policy of containment.

The rise and decline of massive retaliation prompted new thoughts along two different roads. The one accepted the probability of an outbreak of war and sought means to control and then stop it: this was the concept of limited war. The other continued to concentrate on deterrence while looking for ways to make it more persuasive.

A limited war between Superpowers presupposed a war in which the protagonists would refrain from using nuclear weapons for an incalculable period, short or very short, during which they would have second thoughts and go into reverse. But anybody who had second thoughts in such a situation must have done little thinking in the first place. The notion of limited war between the Superpowers was muddled thinking of an alarmingly dangerous kind. Fortunately the notion died quickly. The alternative was to make deterrence more credible. The instrument to hand was tactical nuclear weapons which, with shorter ranges and far less destructive power, would give Nato a capacity for more various and above all less fantastic response to a threat. This was the policy of flexible response. Nato's Lisbon plan had been replaced in 1957 by another (thirty divisions instead of fifty in the central sector) whose targets were once again not reached; and in 1967 it formally adopted the policy of flexible response. Massive retaliation was deterrence in its purest form; it entailed surviving a first strike and then hitting back devastatingly with American strategic weapons. Flexible response improved on massive retaliation by importing into the calculations weapons so much less appalling that the enemy must suppose their use to be likely: weapons for use rather than for ostentation. It gave Nato a role in deterrence since tactical weapons, unlike the American strategic force, must be incorporated in Nato forces. Nevertheless flexible response was hardly more credible than massive retaliation. Flexible response supposed that a war in Europe might begin without nuclear weapons and would remain non-nuclear until the non-nuclear forces shouted for help, and that the nuclear combat would then remain at the tactical level. It meant postponing the introduction of each category of nuclear weapon in the hope that at some point before the last the aggressor would prefer retreat to escalation. This theory was not demonstrably absurd but it was very difficult to envisage a war proceeding in this way. Furthermore, since tactical weapons were a link in a chain, their credibility depended on the credibility of the weakest link in the chain, so that they were no more credible than – as much a bluff as – strategic weapons. Bluff is not nothing. It is itself a weapon; but all bluff is subject to a law of accelerating attrition.

In the last resort all nuclear strategies fall foul of a para-dox. Nuclear weapons are prized not for fighting a war but for preventing it. Where earlier armouries were partly deterrent but mainly belligerent, nuclear weapons are overwhelmingly, if not entirely, deterrent. They are never to be used but their existence ensures that the occasion to use them will never arise. They are unusable but useful, or so it was supposed. This strange state of affairs made some sense in the short term and so long as nuclear weapons were exclusively of the long-range variety: the intercon-tinental missiles of the Superpowers. But when nuclear invention spread into intermediate and short-range armouries the situation became not merely paradoxical but muddled since it was not clear whether these nuclear weapons were exclusively deterrent or not, and the shorter the range, the greater the doubts about the strategic purpose. Intermediate and battlefield weapons were assigned a role which included their use: one kind of weapon might be used to inhibit the use of the next. Yet this proposition dented the

pre-existing doctrine of pure deterrence and also the proposition
that nuclear weapons were not for use. But if they were to be
employed, they led toward the use of strategic weapons, which
use was by definition absurdly and unproductively catastrophic.

These shifts in doctrine were accompanied by attempts to give
Nato, or more particularly Nato's European members, a role at
once significant and dignified in an alliance dominated by the
nuclear arm which, after the invention of lesser nuclear weapons,
was no longer the exclusive preserve of the American Strategic Air
Command (which was not part of Nato). More generally, these
matters were a special aspect of Euro-American relations. In a first
phase, immediately after the creation of Nato, American pressure
for the admission of West Germany to the alliance had alarmed
Europeans and produced a scheme for a European Defence Community which the Americans approved, the British disdained and
the French wrecked. German admission to Nato was nevertheless
secured. It was followed by abortive plans for international nuclear
forces while Great Britain and France simultaneously developed
their separate nuclear forces. In a later phase the growth of Franco-
German entente and of the European Community (again approved
by the United States but by Great Britain only halfheartedly at best)
strengthened West German identity but not in the military field.

When in 1950 the Korean War prompted the United States to
canvass the rearmament of West Germany, no European liked
the prospect of rearming yesterday's enemy so soon, least of all
the French and other continental victims of German aggression.
A first attempt to reconcile necessity with susceptibility failed. In
order to rearm West Germany without recreating German divisions, corps and even higher formations, an integrated European
Defence Community (EDC) was proposed, but in spite of American
threats of an agonizing reappraisal of Franco-American relations if
France rejected the plan the French parliament did so when Great
Britain refused to join: British aversion to European cooperation
was strongest in matters of defence where, for the British, it was
Nato or nothing. But the Korean War also impelled France to
a reappraisal of its relations with West Germany and after the
successful inauguration of the Steel and Coal Community France
fell in with the policy of making a sovereign West Germany a full
or nearly full member of the alliance. West Germany recovered
its military status subject only to the undertaking not to make or
possess nuclear, bacteriological or chemical weapons. It became
a special case, eventually the most important European member

of the alliance but the only one debarred by treaty from becoming a nuclear Power. This ban, however politically defensible, became more anomalous as West Germany shifted from being a late comer to Nato to being the one country without which Nato could not exist.

West Germany was not the only anomalous partner in Nato. Great Britain and France differed from all the other members and from one another in being nuclear Powers of a different order. After the war the British went their own nuclear way in secret, spending huge sums on nuclear research and manufacture while at the same time offloading on to the United States the costs of giving aid to Greece and Turkey which Great Britain said it could no longer afford. In 1960, however, Great Britain recognized what had been suspected for some time: that the costs of its projected intermediate range nuclear missile *Bluestreak* were too high and the missile itself already obsolescent. Partly out of necessity and partly in the light of improvements in Anglo-American relations after their rift over Suez, Great Britain decided to buy in its place the American missile *Skybolt*, at which point the British nuclear programme ceased to be independent. Two years later this programme almost collapsed when the United States decided that it no longer needed *Skybolt* for itself. The American administration was willing to go on making some *Skybolt* missiles for Great Britain in return for a British contribution of half the development costs, but this price was judged too high and Harold Macmillan negotiated with John F. Kennedy (1962) the purchase of *Polaris* submarine missiles on relatively favourable financial terms but on condition that the British nuclear force be committed to Nato. This deal gave Great Britain a nuclear element in its armoury for so long as the Americans might continue to manufacture *Polaris* or Great Britain could afford to buy its successors. To Americans the British deterrent seemed insubstantial or worse. The sharpest of American Defence Secretaries, Robert MacNamara, described it as without credibility and dangerous. The British stuck to it in the mysterious belief that it gave them some influence over American policies.

In theory Great Britain had an alternative to this revised policy of remaining a nuclear Power at the price of dependence on the United States. The alternative was an Anglo-French programme. De Gaulle may have hoped that the British would turn to France but if he did he profoundly misread the situation. In matters of defence Great Britain looked to the Atlantic connection and not to Europe. At Macmillan's suggestion Kennedy offered de Gaulle

Polaris on the terms negotiated with Great Britain but de Gaulle –
who, on his return to power in 1958, had inherited an independent
nuclear weapons programme – refused the offer on the grounds
that it would rob this programme of its independence. De Gaulle's
wartime distrust of the United States had not diminished, and
during his years of retreat he had observed the collapse under
American pressures of the inept Anglo-French attempt to overthrow Nasser in the Suez War, a collapse imposed on London by
Washington and accepted by London without reference to Paris.
Diplomatically as well as militarily this one joint Anglo-French
venture had been a disaster.

One consequence of these events at the beginning of the 1960s
was a boost to Franco-German *rapprochement*. The enmity of these
two Powers has always been exaggerated by outsiders. Between
the Franco-Prussian War and the first Great War it had been
intense for a short time but latent most of the time. Between the
two world wars there had been a substantial, if often repressed,
current – cultural, intellectual, political – in favour of improving
Franco-German relations, and pro-German feelings in Vichy France
were by no means wholly disreputable. Konrad Adenauer was
no less keen than Frenchmen like Schuman or de Gaulle to put
an end to Franco-German animosities. He made proposals for a
Franco-German union within a year of becoming Chancellor, but
since his main aim in the 1950s was to clamp western Germany into
the Nato alliance he did little to pursue his Franco-German theme
until the 1960s and de Gaulle's return to power. The two statesmen
held much publicized meetings in 1960 and 1962 and in the latter
year de Gaulle made a sentimental tour in Germany where he was
vociferously acclaimed and responded by relaxing as much as it
was in his reserved nature to do. A Franco-German treaty in the
following year formalized these developments and inaugurated a
period of regular and increasingly closer confabulations between
the heads of the two states and their successors.

This sub-plot had, however, a limited impact, particularly in
military matters. Just as the British during the war had never been
willing to subordinate their relations with the United States to their
relations with de Gaulle, so now western Germany was careful
to avoid any move likely to give offence to Washington. For de
Gaulle, however, the Franco-German *rapprochement* was an escape
from isolation – a Franco-British *rapprochement* being in Gaullist
terms unattainable – and it contributed to his decision to put an end
to French military cooperation in Nato. A bizarre American scheme

for nuclear multilateral naval forces (1963), which would have given Germans an entry into allied nuclear units, collapsed under the weight of its inherent contradictions and in 1966 de Gaulle withdrew all French forces from the alliance while maintaining France's membership of it. This was a political gesture with some strategic inconvenience but no serious strategic weakening of any of the parties. France remained protected by the mutual nuclear deterrence which prevented either Superpower from risking war in Europe, while the United States and other Nato partners accepted French ambivalence because they preferred to have France half out than wholly out of the alliance. The effect on the Soviet Union was negligible, because the French decision marked no more than a tiff in the alliance and not a reversal of alliances. The resignation of de Gaulle in 1968 altered the tone rather than the substance of interallied dealings.

The French nuclear force, unlike the British, was an independent force, but its independence manifested and destroyed its effectiveness. It might deter an attack on France but it could barely deter an attack on West Germany, and what France needed to deter was not an attack on itself alone but any Soviet act of aggression anywhere in Western Europe. There was no French undertaking to use its nuclear weapons in response to such an attack nor much likelihood that it would. The British nuclear force evinced an equal but opposite ineffectiveness. In so far as it was British it had the same incredibility as the French; in so far as it was an addition to the alliance it added insignificantly to it. The West Germans, who were in the front line, had no nuclear force and seemed not to be alarmed by the lack. The Americans disliked the British and French forces because they eroded American control over nuclear power and strategy and were a bad example to would-be predators.

Nato's political and strategic imbroglios were no more severe than those of any alliance. For most of the time they were latent and subordinate to the common purpose. It was, however, difficult for the alliance to react smoothly to the challenges of change, of which the most prominent in the 1970s and 1980s were the introduction of intermediate nuclear weapons and the onset of bilateral Superpower negotiations on arms control and reductions.

Intermediate nuclear weapons served no strategic purpose. They appeared not because they were needed but because they had become possible. They were first deployed by the Soviet Union in the 1970s and by the early 1980s Soviet SS 20s were trained on targets in Europe, including cities, at the alarming rate of about one new launcher a week. President Carter's first reaction was to counter this trend by increasing the allies' most effective weapon, the US Navy's sea-borne nuclear armoury, but Europeans wanted something more obviously equivalent to the SS 20 and in 1979 Nato decided to place in Europe 464 Cruise weapons and 108 Pershing II missiles (the former being extremely accurate, low-flying non-ballistic weapons; the latter being ballistic weapons). This was an about-turn by the Europeans. From the 1950s the Americans had wanted to place medium-range missiles in Europe, but the Europeans had demurred. With the appearance of the SS 20 they changed their minds. Yet if the assumptions of the deterrent doctrine were correct, all these weapons were otiose. If the Superpowers' long-range deterrents kept the peace, the additional deployment of other nuclear weapons added nothing to the security of those deploying them.

The European allies who pressed Carter for Cruise and Pershing II had miscalculated the temper of their own electorates. Campaigns against nuclear weapons which had died down revived and the new weapons were introduced only after feverish debate. The protest took an anti-American flavour which was nourished by Reagan's aggressive tone and measures. Reagan reinstated the development of the B–1 bomber which had been stayed by Carter in the course of the SALT II discussions with the USSR, indulged in public vilification of the Soviet Union and in general so altered the balance between carrot and stick as to leave very little carrot showing. He escalated the war of arms as well as the war of words by pouring money into defence budgets with the apparent purpose of elevating the United States to a position of material and moral superiority, whence it might dictate the course of world affairs. Reagan's idea of negotiating was to amass in advance so much power that the other party would have no choice but to concede – a contradiction in terms, a hazardous and costly course, and probably an impossibility. In 1983 he unveiled his Strategic Defence Initiative, a defensive anti-missile umbrella which was all but universally regarded as strategically a mirage, technically impractical and economically ruinous. The allies were promised a lucrative share in the attendant research but these pickings turned out to be minuscule. The allies, while welcoming any sign of the unflagging vigour of the United States, were perturbed by the President's unbridled language and disordered thoughts. In his second term, however, these matters were eclipsed by more momentous changes: the advent of Gorbachev and real disarmament.

When Leonid Brezhnev died in 1982 he was succeeded by Yuri Andropov and then by Konstantin Chernenko, whose main contribution to history was that they both died soon after taking office. In 1985 Mikhail Gorbachev became General Secretary of the Communist Party of the Soviet Union and in 1988 President of the Soviet Union. He was resolved to introduce revolutionary changes in external policies, including defence policies.

The Soviet economy might be able to go on keeping the Soviet Union in the same military league as the United States (although that was doubtful), but it could not at the same time develop a full modern economy and maintain, let alone improve, public services, living standards and research and education. The Soviet Union was in decline. After the first postwar years of recovery economic growth had been rapid but at declining rates; the standard of living rose substantially from its devastated level but did not maintain its pace. The Soviet economy was far from catching up with western economics and comparisons were depressing. Agriculture was devouring investment with little to show for it; transport was breaking down; an energy crisis loomed; raw materials were to be had in Siberia but only at extravagant cost; the percentage of GDP absorbed by defence budgets, undisclosed and possibly by the 1980s no longer rising, was certainly uncomfortably high. Soviet economists could not fail to observe this potentially disastrous pattern, but until the advent of Gorbachev Soviet politicians lacked the will or the intelligence to do anything to change it. Gorbachev was sufficiently impressed by the approach of disaster to risk revolutionary change.

There were two broad areas where the problems might be attacked. The first, most comprehensive and most daunting, was the Soviet system itself. Revolution begins at home. Changes in the system could not remedy a lack of resources but they could improve, and greatly improve, the use made of available resources. The Soviet system was by its nature a peculiarly interlocking one in which the economic could not be disentangled from the social strands, the organizational from the behavioural. Gorbachev set out to overhaul and loosen the apparatus of central control over economic enterprise and, at the same time and necessarily so, to tackle pervasive corruption, inertia and inefficiency. Secondly, he set out to reduce Soviet commitments abroad which were more costly or more hazardous than they were worth: the Stalinist system in eastern Europe, the occupation of Afghanistan and subsidies to Vietnam, bad relations with China and above all the arms race. His motives were clear and hard-headed: he reckoned that the Soviet Union could not afford the arms race. Gorbachev's predecessors were like La Fontaine's famous frog. Under them the Soviet Union was blowing itself up until it was fit only to burst. Gorbachev on the other hand was like La Fontaine; he knew the frog would burst.

Besides revolutionary change in the Soviet Union were also specific, if tentative, approaches to arms control in the 1970s and two, more general, oscillations in strategic thinking. The 1970s were a decade of striking technical innovation, immensely increased spending and some exploration of the possibilities of a truce in the arms race. The innovations included anti-ballistic missile (ABM) systems designed to enable the victim of a first strike to survive and deliver a second; and the introduction of ever more ingenious and indefeasible weapons such as missiles with multiple but independently targeted warheads (MIRVs), missiles launched from submarines and missiles with vastly improved accuracy. Negotiations on arms control produced a first Strategic Arms Limitation Treaty (SALT I) which was signed by the Superpowers in 1972; a second, abandoned in 1977 but resuscitated in 1979, was approved by the Foreign Relations Committee of the US Senate but refused ratification by the Senate itself and killed in 1981 after Reagan succeeded Carter as president. The 1970s saw also the gradual, if far from universal, appreciation of two strange consequences of the nuclear revolution: the usefulness of not keeping secrets, and the unimportance of matching like with like weapons.

A strategy based on aggression required secrecy. The less one adversary knew about the other's strengths and deployment, the greater the latter's chances of dealing a stunning blow. But a strategy of deterrence required the opposite, since maximum deterrence was to be achieved when the adversary had certain knowledge of the dangers he faced. Consequently reconnaissance aircraft which revealed the enemy's awful strength added to the deterrent, and the supercession of aircraft by intelligence satellites of greater and greater penetration and accuracy made assurance doubly sure. For two or three decades the deterrent was reinforced by photographic technology until Reagan's half-baked Strategic Defence Initiative threatened to cancel this benign invention by removing the mutuality from deterrence and so destabilizing the strategic equation. If 'Star Wars' meant anything – and the Soviet Union could not safely assume that it did not – the Soviet Union had to think seriously about making a pre-emptive strike before it was too late and its own deterrent was negated.

Deterrence had a second novel characteristic. A state which relied for its security on being able to fight and defeat an enemy needed more and better weapons than the enemy: its armoury must match and exceed the enemy's in quantity and quality. But a deterrent weapon is not set against the enemy's deterrent weapon but against his cities and peoples and their defences. What constitutes deterrence is the ability to hit targets, not the ability to match weaponry. To talk therefore of modernizing nuclear weapons is to reveal a melancholy failure to understand the difference between battle weapons and deterrent weapons.

The long-range ballistic armouries of the Superpowers were so obviously superabundant that it was comparatively easy, given the political will, to reduce them. The reduction of long-range armouries by the elimination of superfluous numbers did not impinge on strategy, so long as the armouries remained in existence at levels which did not impair their deterrent credibility.[1] At Geneva in 1985 Reagan and Gorbachev agreed in principle to halve their long-range armouries. A few months later Gorbachev proposed the total abolition by the end of the century of all nuclear weapons of all categories, including the French and British. This was a reversion to grandiose simplistic improbabilities. The next year, at Reykjavik, Gorbachev advanced and Reagan agreed to dramatic proposals which contradicted engagements given by Reagan to his allies (who were not consulted), undermined Nato's basic strategy and were inconsistent with his own previous pronouncements. His flimsy grasp of strategic problems led him from earnest bombast to naive pliability.

The issue was not strategic weapons but their lesser brethren: first, intermediate-range forces (INF) which were themselves divided into two sub-categories of long- and short-range intermediate weapons, the former with ranges over 1000 kilometres and the latter with ranges between 1000 and 500 kilometres; and secondly, tactical or battlefield weapons with even shorter carrying power,

---

1.   In so far as they were not credible at all, this was so on grounds altogether distinct from their numbers – the feeling that they could not be used because to use them would be suicidal or superlatively immoral.

mostly artillery but including also bombs carried by aircraft. The reduction of INF was more complex than the reduction of long-range weapons for three reasons: the parties involved were not two but many; reduction came to mean total elimination; and elimination presented a challenge to Nato's fundamental doctrine of flexible response which rested upon the possession of a series of weapons of graded malignity.

The arguments about INF turned particularly on the longer-range weapons in this category: the SS 20s which the Soviet Union had begun to deploy in 1977 to replace its SS 4s and SS 5s, and the Cruise and Pershing IIs which Nato resolved in 1979 to deploy in response. Deployment of the Nato weapons began in 1983 after the Soviet Union had failed to foment enough dissension in the western camp to prevent it. On coming to power Gorbachev sensed that he could not force the withdrawal of Cruise and Pershing II without offering the withdrawal of all SS 20s in Europe. He seized on an earlier remark by Reagan who had proposed, whether seriously or rhetorically, total elimination – the zero option – and at Reykjavik they all but adopted the zero option for INF. But Gorbachev, overreaching himself, tried to secure also the abandonment of 'Star Wars' to which Reagan was immovably addicted. The agreement, therefore, fell through, but Gorbachev reconciled himself to the continuation of 'Star Wars' – perhaps he was content to leave it to the Americans themselves to whittle it away – and he renewed proposals for an INF agreement and extended the zero option from long- to short-range INF (these being mainly, on the American side, obsolete Pershing Is in store in the United States and, on the Soviet side, the SS 12 and 23). The outcome was an agreement on INF signed in Washington in December 1987.

This agreement provided for the destruction of specific numbers of launchers and missiles by the end of 1991 – more than had been proposed at Reykjavik. In order to get the INF treaty Gorbachev accepted on-site inspections and agreed to destroy Soviet inter-mediate weapons in Asia too in return for the destruction of similar American weapons on the American continent, including Alaska. Europeans applauded but were privately unhappy because the elimination of INF blew a large hole in flexible response which required that reductions in any category should be short of zero and leave that category in existence. With the removal of INF what had been a ladder became a chain with two extremes but no connecting link.

The conclusion of the INF agreement pointed to the next

category, battlefield weapons with ranges below 500 kilometres. The application of the zero option to intermediate weapons transformed battlefield nuclear weapons from being a rung in a nuclear ladder into an alternative to non-nuclear battlefield weapons and so much more likely to be fired than to serve as a cog in deterrence. By limiting Nato's nuclear forces to this category the INF treaty also limited nuclear war in Europe to nuclear war in Germany. The West Germans naturally disliked a situation in which Nato's nuclear weapons were all sited on their soil and trained on other (East) German targets. They proposed – at first on the political left but then too on the right, which regarded this development as a recipe for electoral disaster – to remove this threat by removing nuclear battlefield weapons as well as intermediate nuclear weapons. Since some of the former, of which Nato was deploying about 4000, could hit Soviet territory Gorbachev too was keen to ensure their complete elimination. Nato's continental members rallied mostly to the increasingly urgent German demand for east–west discussions on this subject, whereas the Americans wanted first to strengthen the category before engaging in discussions which might lead to a third zero and Thatcher, after some fluctuation, took the extreme view that Nato should never even consider a third (battlefield) zero. Within the alliance debate was focused on the Lance missile, of which Nato had 88 in service and which were due to go out of service in 1995. The Americans and British described the development of a new weapon to replace Lance as modernization, implying no new departure. The Germans, however, dissented and insisted that no such new weapon should be adopted or developed by Nato until east–west talks had been initiated and had failed. Gorbachev pressed his advantage by announcing that there would be no modernization of Soviet battlefield weapons and that the Soviet Union would not engage in talks about the reduction of non-nuclear forces in Europe if Nato went ahead with a replacement for Lance. This threat was all the more compelling since Nato, relying more heavily than its adversaries on nuclear weapons, was markedly inferior to them in non-nuclear weapons and correspondingly keener to proceed with their negotiated reduction. The modernization of Lance was quickly and quietly abandoned.

The main aims of the second Reagan administration and its successor under George Bush were not easily reconcilable. Both were determined to pursue disarmament and the detente between the Superpowers which Gorbachev's advent was making possible and in 1990 Bush concluded with Gorbachev a first agreement for reduction – as distinct from limitations – in the strategic nuclear weaponry of the Superpowers. Both American presidents were no less determined to retain a more-than-token presence in Europe, but also to cut costs which were excessively burdensome and, in American eyes at least, unfairly apportioned among the allies. Unprecedented deficits in the United States' balance of payments combined with public opinion to require some adjustment and the resulting debate on both sides of the Atlantic revived the image of the alliance as a two-pillar edifice and so emphasized the distinction between its two geographical parts. The continental Europeans had fewer inherent objections to this way of seeing things than had the British, for whom the two-pillar pattern was an embarrassment since they did not clearly know to which pillar they belonged. Nato had been created in a different configuration, and the British feared that in a two-pillar alliance the two pillars would drift apart and the whole edifice would collapse. They did not want to be distanced from the United States or lumped in with the continental Europeans, particularly at a time when the Thatcher government was making Great Britain unpopular with these countries in the context of the European Community. The Thatcher government was ill-prepared for this dilemma. Reagan, whose conception of politics barely rose above the personal level and who had found in Thatcher a politician with whom he could converse at ease and who leaned over backwards to pander to his foibles, had been well content with a special and narrow Anglo-American relationship. Bush, however, reverted to the more characteristic outlook of Truman, Eisenhower and other Americans who sought to encourage European integration. In this tradition a closer European Community, so far from undermining the Euro-American association, could provide it with a sound new basis appropriate to the changing relations between the Superpowers.

The trends were disturbing the original conception of the alliance. Both the premises on which it had been constructed were weakening. The Gorbachev factor in European affairs and in the Soviet Union itself were melting fears of Soviet designs; and the travails of the American economy, greatly aggravated by Reagan's presidency, were calling in question the American capacity to pay for the alliance and popular American willingness to do so. With both superpowers becoming depreciated Europe had less to fear from the one, less need of the other and less likelihood of being blanketed by either.

Nato as the counterpart of the Warsaw Pact was losing its enemy, for the dissolution of the Pact was inherent in the revolutions of 1989 and the Pact ceased to function even before it ceased formally to exist. The two alliances agreed in 1990 on considerable reductions in their non-nuclear forces. Secondly, Nato as part of the Euro-American military alliance against the Soviet Union was half-way to limbo as the prospect of a war between the Superpowers receded to vanishing point: in this respect Nato might survive as a contingency planning group against the possibility of a new Cold War one day. In its third manifestation – as the symbol of American involvement in European affairs – Nato would survive until replaced by something broader and no less positive, for although Gorbachev acknowledged the United States as a European Power, this American involvement needed to be defined and expressed in new instruments – defining the United States as, with others, a participant in and guarantor of peace and security throughout Europe after the Cold War and establishing formal pan-European engagements to supercede western ones. For this last purpose the European Conference on Security and Cooperation (ECSC) might be the appropriate medium. A first ECSC, comprising the United States and Canada as well as nearly every European state, had been convoked at Helsinki in 1972 to agree upon measures to diminish the risks of war in Europe, to promote commercial and cultural exchanges and to define civil and political rights and monitor their exercise. It reached a variety of agreements, normative rather than contractually binding, and it developed into a series of recurrent conferences but without the status or institutions of a fully fledged international organization. Although it was little more than a forum it might be used to fashion a peace settlement which would complete the unfinished treaty-making after the Second World War and establish a framework for international relations in Europe after the Cold War and the depreciation of the Superpowers.

CHAPTER EIGHT
The Depreciation of the Superpowers

The cooling of the arms race was part good sense and part necessity. The necessity lay in the decreasing net capabilities of both Superpowers. This decrease smudged the world picture in which these Superpowers had been clearly distinguishable from all other states. For a generation after 1945 Europe gave the appearance of two back-to-back domains, each an appanage of the Superpowers. The Superpowers were nearly omnipotent; they possessed nuclear weapons; they were two; and they were profoundly, all but irreversibly, antagonistic. The danger of another and greater war was presumed to be acute. Throughout this period each side spoke of the other with extreme distrust and even hatred and both sides prepared for a war which, however, fewer and fewer people expected to occur. This was a period of unprecedented unreality in international affairs. It was dominated by ingenious, erudite and scholarly debate about the size and capabilities of the Superpowers' rival armouries. But in reality the Superpower regime made Europe unusually stable. Forty years are a long time in the international politics and for forty years all major shifts in Europe were postponed.

During the 1980s this picture of Superpower dominance became discredited. It persisted only as a blueprint to which nobody any longer paid much attention. 'Superpower' was no longer equated with nuclear weapons. A dozen or two dozen states acquired these weapons or the capacity to make them, but neither Japan nor Germany had any. The original two Superpowers were shown to be far from all-powerful. Although still militarily in a class of their own, they were nevertheless depreciated – and the one so much more so than the other that the old picture of these two Superpowers pulling all the strings was made to look grotesque.

The depreciation of the Soviet Union, at first muted and perceived only by specialists, was exposed by the Russians themselves. It was, if not a bombshell, at least a political earthquake. The Soviet Union had been the single largest factor in European affairs since the Soviet capture of Vienna, Prague and Berlin in 1945. In central and eastern Europe the Soviet presence, in western Europe the fear of Soviet power and intentions, provided the axioms on which policies were constructed. The Gorbachev revolution was a declaration that the Soviet Union was an almighty failure. Gorbachev's predecessors may have sensed this truth but, if they did, they could think of nothing better to do than await the reckoning: *après nous le déluge*. They did nothing to avert the deluge. The significance of Gorbachev was that he announced the coming of the deluge and proposed to prevent it. Were he to succeed the Soviet Union would be a more wholesome place and also stronger. That it should be wholesome was evidently desirable; that it should also be stronger was not universally welcome to its adversaries.

The modern history of Russia is a steady expansion. The most serious checks to this expansion were caused by the Crimean War and by defeat and revolution in 1917 and the ensuing civil war. Russia has become the biggest state in the world – not necessarily a source of strength – and embraces a variety of peoples, of whom a quarter are not Slavs. Of the non-Slavs the largest block, about a fifth of the whole, are Muslims – mostly Turks in Asia and Azerbaijan plus a smaller group of Iranian Tadzhiks. The remainder, about twenty million or one in ten of the total population, are in the three Baltic republics, Moldavia, Georgia and Armenia. The problem of minorities – or, as they are officially denominated in the Soviet Union, nationalities – is endemic and has been manifest in the Baltic, Moldavian, Caucasian and Asian republics. It was not, however, the problem which forced the leadership of the Union to take the dangerous step of putting Gorbachev in charge. That precipitant was the twin failure of the economy and the political system. The Union's commitments exceeded either its resources or its ability to manage its resources or, most probably, both. The failures engendered corruption, petty tyranny and disintegration on a scale not only shocking but potentially catastrophic. Those who faced and measured the economic failings concluded that they could not be remedied without radical political and administrative reform. Lids had to be taken off kettles, with a multiplication of the proverbial risks. Reform entailed ructions within the ruling

apparatus, turbulence among non-Russian peoples and the open-
ing of windows of vulnerability to west and east. The licence to
criticize the Communist Party, ebulliently embraced in big cities
and peripheral republics alike, might challenge the party's rule,
initiate something like anarchy, stimulate a conservative backlash
and ruin any prospect of economic improvement.

To the west were the satellites and beyond them the Nato
alliance. To the east was China, traditionally and recently hostile.
Beyond again, the Soviet Union had friends in neither direction. It
lacked the classic resource of being able to make or threaten trouble
for its adversaries at their back door. Stalin did not know how to
make friends. Even in the satellite block he made no friends, only
subalterns. His subjugation of central and eastern Europe was
effective only so long as these parts of Europe were passive and
Moscow could keep them so. If and when central or eastern Europe
should become recalcitrant Moscow's external problems must be
severely aggravated. The Soviet Union enjoyed the minimum of
goodwill within the satellites and had none of the economic carrots
and sticks with which the United States might beguile or belabour
its neighbours.

Stalin had conquered the three Baltic states of Estonia, Latvia
and Lithuania; Bessarabia, northern Bukovina and Ruthenia; and
parts of Finland, east Prussia and Slovakia (and also southern
Sakhalin and the northern Kuriles off eastern Asia). None of these
accretions became a source of strength against a possible encircle-
ment of the Soviet Union by a coalition of European, American
or Asian enemies. Largely irrelevant in an age of ballistic missiles
which pass them by, these territories figured chiefly as zones of
potential discontent and controversy. Huge armaments made the
Soviet Union militarily the greatest European Power and a World
Power, but great only in the tally of weaponry and vulnerable if the
assembling and maintenance of these forces overstrain the Soviet
economy and mortgage the future. With no friends and – as Reagan
used fondly and correctly to stress – with more powerful enemies
than any state had ever had, the Soviet Union kept on adding
to the strains (in Afghanistan, for example, and by its ruinous
subventions to Vietnam) in a desperate effort to keep abreast. The
effort had been predicated upon fear of the United States and it
failed. Gorbachev's policy was to abandon the effort, or much of
it, in the hope that the fear, or much of it, was misplaced. He would
disarm, unilaterally if need be; he would allow the satellites to step
out of line to some (undisclosed) extent, and even, if need be, to

step further out of line than he would wish; the Warsaw Pact was expendable; foreign adventures would be curtailed or abandoned; diplomacy would have to fill the gap left by the renunciation of forces and bravado. All this as a contribution to the all–engrossing business of making ends meet, reforming the Soviet economy and political system, and keeping the Soviet Union, or most of it, intact. While observers could not tell how far he might succeed or how long he might be allowed to go on trying, they could assume that if his policies failed or were reversed the Soviet Union would be a paper tiger. To that extent the west was in a no-lose situation. The follies and crimes of decades could not be retrieved in a handful of years. A new style of government might bring more freedom but could not quickly satisfy demands for more and cheaper goods and better pay: the quality of life and the standard of living are only loosely linked. Given also ethnic and religious grievances in all corners of the Soviet Union, the hazards of Gorbachev's course were very great. The gaping crack between formidable armed forces and precarious political and economic coherence was laid bare.

The Soviet Union is a Power in decline, absolutely and relatively. Decline is not irreversible, nor does the decline of a neighbour make him easier to live with or necessarily less aggressive. The consequences are veiled but certain facts are clear. Like other Powers in decline, the Soviet Union has a choice between acknowledging the facts or kicking against the pricks. The Slav population is static, the non-Slav still growing. Agriculture has been nothing short of a disaster. Vast sums, equal to about one third of all annual investment, have been thrown at the problem and yet the Soviet Union is obliged to import food in what are called good years as well as bad. The obvious corrective of freeing (a euphemism for increasing) prices and encouraging private cultivators – a small but comparatively efficient minority – to produce for the market at a decent profit is political dynamite, since townspeople accustomed for years to cheap food will be outraged. In industry Stalin and his successors continued in peacetime some of the back-breaking economic miracles of the war years, but the effort and investment were focused on a narrow and mainly military sector and the rate of industrial growth was not sustained. So far from catching up the Soviet Union fell back. The causes may be diagnosed: an inefficient and corrupt administrative system, blinkered policies contrived by a selfish, stupid and scared ruling class, bad planning, an industrial labour force becoming inadequate in numbers and skills, a dearth of capital, the perennially inflated cost of maintaining the pace of modernization in weaponry and civilian technology, and an energy crisis which has been dispelled neither by a large nuclear programme nor by having dug deeper into the earth than anybody else in order to extract steam. To remain a major Power the Soviet Union had to escape not only from the crippling economies of the Cold War but also from the isolation which had denied it access to capital markets and new technology. This is a long haul, for which even the most inspiring leader must have solid popular and political support and military acquiescence; and even success would make the Soviet Union only one among several, never again one of two.

There can be no Russian empire in Europe. The notion that there could be sprang from two things: the Soviet Union's triumphs against Hitler's Germany and rapid acquisition of nuclear weapons and, secondly, a vaguer feeling that it was Russia's turn to attempt what Spain, France and Germany had tried in the past. But nuclear weapons did more to negate aggressive imperialism in Europe than to facilitate it, even before these weapons ceased to be a monopoly of the Superpowers; and neither Stalin's Russia nor the Tsars' stands in the line of the conqueror of the sixteenth to twentieth centuries. What Spain and France achieved and Germany nearly achieved is out of the Soviet reach. Spain, in the far south west of the continent, sustained for a time a continental empire only because, and so long as, it commanded bases in the Netherlands and Italy and the wealth of the New World. The French monarchy, more central and far older and more coherent than Spain's, became Europe's most spectacular western empire but failed, nevertheless, to dominate the German lands beyond the Rhine; and when, succeeding to its great designs, Napoleon overcame the Germans he was defeated by England and Russia. Prussia/Germany, most central and most industrialized of all aspirants to hegemony, was tripped up by having to face two ways – the other face of centrality – and, in spite of coming close to great victories in 1918 and 1941, failed to extend its power beyond its borders for more than three or four years at a time. Russia, as peripheral as Spain but without Spain's outposts, the least coherent of major modern states and the poorest in terms of the balance of resources against ambitions, has failed to incorporate or rule foreign lands in Europe in peacetime – except on its Polish and Finnish fringes in the nineteenth century and then by agreement with other Powers. Empire over Europe, whether pursued by Russians or anybody else, is a mirage and now so obviously so that it is hard to believe that any government could be foolhardy enough to attempt to create it.

There is nothing about the Soviet empire to make one suppose that it can escape the fate of all empires: dissolution. Some time its Muslim people will secede. The sizeable Russian populations of these republics will either withdraw into Russian lands or become alien pockets in central Asia, not unlike the erstwhile pockets of Germans in *Mitteleuropa*. Turks here and elsewhere may begin to dream of a new Turkish empire. The Baltic and Caucasian republics pose a more immediate and harsher problem since their loss, besides entailing a grievous loss of face as well as territory, would require a major re-ordering of military defence installations – and, in the case of Lithuania, a border dispute with Ukraine. In countering these centrifugal trends Gorbachev has to devise a looser federal structure which will satisfy non-Russians and keep them in the Union without leaving the Union a merely hollow shell. The crucial question, however, is whether the Slavs of the Union will hold together or whether the western provinces – Ukraine and White Russia (Byelorussia), both of them independently members of the UN – will once more make a bid for separation from Great Russia (which now includes Siberia). Gorbachev's testing ground is the Russian heartland, old Muscovy, and its kin; and the test is what he himself has diagnosed – economic and political reform, a better life and government less incompetent and less corrupt. He grasped the inseparability of the economic, social and political strands and expressed it in his campaign for *perestroika* – fundamental reorganization. This reorganization entails decentralization, devolution of responsibility and decision-taking, flexibility in costing and price-fixing; a hefty hacking away of bureaucratic tangles, mediocre management, corruption and poor communication between one region and one administrative level and another; cures for managerial ignorance and a low level and narrow range of popular education. His dilemma lies in balancing the urgency of these interlocking changes against their inevitable hardships, notably in higher prices (many rents, for example, have not been altered for more than half a century) and loss of office in the bureaucracy. No pace could be right: after the failures and distortions of a lifetime change must be either too slow or too quick for one body of people or another. Veiled battles during 1986–87, as new faces came to the fore and new laws were enacted, gave the pace-setters led by Gorbachev himself the advantage, but neither completely nor finally.

One of the Soviet Union's perennial disappointing harvests did not help. The record of Gorbachev's first years was familiar and inadequate: industrial output growing but the rate of growth falling, investment down, productivity down, exports down, only foreign debt up. The spirit was good, popular support at first emphatic, but the outcome uncertain as continuing economic decline pointed to national catastrophe, popular disillusion and political dissension. Gorbachev lost much of his popularity and his momentum. Failure to deliver economic betterment created impatience; threats to thousands of party placemen created fear and resentment. Rival plans for economic reform fuelled political dissension without producing an economic policy. Intertwined with the problem of what to do about the economy was the problem of how to keep the Union together. This problem had two dimensions: how to keep dissident republics whose dissidence was largely nationalist within the Union, and how to apportion power between a Union government and republican governments which wanted more power for themselves within the Union. For the Baltic republics secession was a practical possibility; for the central Asian republics it was emotionally compulsive but entailed daunting perils; the Caucasian republics came somewhere between these two groups, while for the Slav republics the threat of secession was a weapon in the fight for wider autonomy as Boris Yeltsin and others sought to convert the Soviet Union into an association of states linked by treaty rather than republics linked by a constitution.

Gorbachev began by shifting authority from the organs of the Communist Party to those of the state. Elections were held in 1989 for a Congress of People's Deputies of the Soviet Union (2020 members) and a Supreme Soviet (750 members), and the Congress by a majority of 59 per cent elected Gorbachev president of the USSR for five years and gave him extensive but not untrammelled powers. (Later elections to the presidential office were to be by direct popular and secret ballot.) Gorbachev became also chairman of a new presidential council and a new defence council, but this accumulation of power was offset by two limitations in particular: the Supreme Court might declare his acts unconstitutional, and the Supreme Soviet might by a two-thirds' majority override a presidential veto of new legislation. His principal radical adversary, Boris Yeltsin, secured election to the presidency of the Russian republic, thus establishing an independent power base, independent of the crumbling Communist Party. At its 28th Congress in 1990 the party's radical wing constituted itself a distinct party or faction, while at the other extreme conservatives, led by Yegor Ligachev, failed to capture the principal party posts. Gorbachev, who remained the party's General Secretary, emerged from the Congress with tactical victories in a forum of diminishing relevance. The party's politburo, which had ruled the Soviet Union for so long, ceased to be the centre of power in the state and was no longer sure of its authority over the constituent republican parties which began to declare themselves above the All-Union party. But Gorbachev, although he side-lined the party, failed to establish an alternative central authority. He was obliged to sacrifice the Council of Ministers (whose economic programme under the cautious Nikolai Ryzhkov was not only controversial but overtaken by events) and replace it by a Federal Council to include the chiefs of all the republics, a Security Council for (broadly) external and internal security, and a cabinet of experts rather than ministers. Confusion reigned.

The depreciation of the Soviet Union is an unalloyed good because the USSR has been a source of fear without being a source of assistance or assurance. American super power is different. The United States may be envied or disliked but it is not feared, at any rate not in Europe. Central Americans may take a bitterer view of the United States, but for Europeans the United States has been a source of bounty and strength. The Marshall Plan and the Berlin blockade were episodes which made a mark out of all proportion to their duration. The American alliance was embraced by western Europe with great relief and little dissent and when hostility to the United States began to develop the issues – the Vietnam War, American softness on Asian and Latin American dictators, double standards in the Middle East in favour of Israel – were non-European. They had only a marginal impact on Euro-American relations and were shrugged off as aberrations by an over-burdened but essentially decent and intelligent friend. The historical importance of Nixon and Reagan was their contribution to the destruction of this frame of mind – and of the belief that in the United States the holders of high office habitually told the truth. Like the Austrians against the Ottoman Turks, the Americans adopted the role of defenders of civilization against the barbarians. Many Europeans, particularly among the more self-consciously cultured classes, resented this posture and tended in revenge to compare the best of European with the worst in American culture – its superficialities, crassness and propensity to religious extravagance closer kin to Muslim and

Jewish fundamentalism than to anything still surviving in Europe; and as Truman's Cold War developed into Reagan's Jihad the difference in mood became more pronounced.

Structures are less pliant than moods. The alliance was a markedly unequal one. This imbalance was taken for granted and did not at first seriously worry the European allies. Its benefits more than outweighed the embarrassment, since overmastering American military strength was the alliance's essential precondition and overmastering American economic strength paid for it. The United States was accepted as a very senior partner whose particular wishes, judgements and prejudices would have to be accommodated. If there were doubts on this score they were dispelled as early as 1956 when the United States aborted the grotesque Anglo-French attempt to overthrow Nasser in collusion with Israel and did so with no attempt at tact or delicacy. Thirty years later the United States carried out its own similar attack on Libya from bases in Europe, in the knowledge that it would encounter widespread European disapproval, and in the belief (which proved correct) that such strains and storms would leave the alliance intact. Yet there was change in the air. At Suez Europeans were taught a lesson: junior partners must consult the wishes of the senior partner and must not count on any *post hoc* indulgence. Over Libya the Americans demonstrated their opposite right as senior partner to act independently with little or no consultation, but perhaps they too learned a lesson: that it would be unwise to do it again. If that were a valid reading of the situation the terms of the partnership were shifting.

By the 1980s western Europe had ceased to believe that it could not defend itself, although it had shivers about the cost of doing so. An American alliance was still highly desirable but perhaps no longer crucial. Nor, given changing American moods and declining American solvency, could it be depended upon indefinitely. Western Europe's assessment of the Soviet menace was milder, its confidence in its own economic strength robuster. To abrogate the Nato alliance or allow it to wither untimely might be a lamentable failure in statesmanship, but it would not be a disaster except upon one disputed premise.

For security against Soviet aggression western Europe needed an insurance policy. This need persisted even though the risk insured might appear from time to time to diminish: the risk could not be reduced to zero. For nearly half a century the insurance was a dual one. It consisted, first, in the American long-range deterrent under exclusive American control and, secondly, in Nato. The first of these factors was, for Europeans, an act of faith since it rested on the assumption that the American deterrent would have this effect if it were uncoupled from the Nato alliance. On the more hazardous view the American deterrent worked for Europe only because of the explicit American commitment contained in Nato. The argument turned on whether, in Soviet eyes, the United States was committed to the defence of western Europe by its treaty obligations or by its own national interest. It could be powerfully argued that, alliance or no alliance, the United States would in no circumstances willingly permit Soviet aggression against western or Mediterranean Europe without retaliating, and that this conclusion was as evident in Moscow as anywhere else. The logic of this argument was that western Europe was protected from Soviet attack by the United States. But in matters of defence logic is not enough and states seek to make assurance doubly sure. Hence the continuing value of Nato as a contractual American commitment independent of the United States' assessment of its own interests. Such arguments cannot be tested. Nor is there any way of showing that a purely European alliance (equipped with nuclear weapons, as it most probably would be) would be an adequate deterrent. Such a deterrent would be slighter than the American long-range missile force and it might suffice, but nobody can prove that it would.

Nato has had two great virtues for Europe. American membership and the stationing in Europe of powerful American forces (more than mere tokens) have kept the European allies safe and feeling safe; and the Americans have carried a large share of the costs of deploying the allied forces and an even larger share of the costs of developing future weapons. It is impossible that the sharing of current costs will not have to be drastically revised to European detriment, not so much because the European share has been shamefully low but rather because the American economy can no longer afford the drain on its balance of payments; and it is improbable that the United States will maintain for much longer its visible military presence in Europe on anything like the scale of recent decades. It follows that the terms of the alliance have to be seriously discussed and perhaps dramatically altered. Not to acknowledge that the alliance which fitted the first postwar generation does not fit the next is stupid. Only ostriches can get away with being ostriches.

The Nato pattern of alliance was an opportune paradox. It was an

exceptionally close association between exceptionally unequal partners. But this pattern was automatically challenged when western
Europe began to develop a distinct and coherent international
identity. It was also bound to be upset by any significant reduction
of the American military presence in Europe, not only on account
of the symbolic force of that presence but also and more concretely
because departing Americans would take their most effective military and intelligence equipment away with them. They could not
turn it over to their allies because it was by definition too secret.
Its removal would represent not a reallocation of responsibilities
among partners but a denuding of the European theatre – and this
denuding would reinforce the Europeans' tendency to look after
themselves. From being a cluster of junior associates they would
become, willy nilly, a more distinct element whose association
with the United States would look more and more like an alliance
between two roughly equivalent states in the manner of alliances
between major states in past centuries. At the European end this
cluster or alliance would be similar to but not coterminous with the
European Community, since the European members of Nato and
the members of the Community were not the same. The forming
of a European economic and political block and, on the other
hand, the reappraisal of the purposes and the financing of the
Euro-American military alliance create awkwardnesses: over Euro-
American relations in general, of which Nato was the major symbol; over the antithesis, particularly in commercial competition,
between the European Community and the United States; and over
western European defence policies. These separate issues criss-
crossed. In Great Britain the champions of the Anglo-American
special relationship refused to contemplate the possibility that Nato
had run most of its course and treated the European Community
as a dangerous disturber of sacrosanct priorities. Although they
probably constituted no more than a sizeable and diminishing
minority in the world of politics and a negligible minority in the
worlds of economics and finance they had the power to delay,
damagingly, the readjustment of the alliance and the development
of the Community. The obstacles to readjustment were real. In
western Europe, including Great Britain, the most formidable was
not financial or political but psychological – the habits of thought
which went with the existence and persistence of the several sovereignties which, however attenuated in practice, still demarcated
Europe's constitutional framework and, more concretely, with the
reliance on American nuclear weapons for security. The removal of

American forces, in part or entirely, would require something new, which was difficult to visualize. France possessed an independent nuclear force, Great Britain a dependent one, West Germany was committed to having none. Spectacularly substantial disarmament was hardly conceivable; in practical terms disarmament meant gradual reductions in armouries, beginning with weapons which were unwanted because excessive or obsolete. Even assuming the Soviet Union to be deterred by the independent American long-range deterrent, or to have renounced for the time being the appetite for exercising power by territorial acquisition, Europeans would still want weapons enough (and a little more) to outface the Soviet Union. Since none of them contemplated aggression against the Soviet Union they did not need armouries on the Soviet, let alone the American, scale: defence might be secured by much less than an aggressor's power. But the range was likely to include nuclear weapons, first because some of them already possessed such weapons; secondly, because the Soviet Union had them; and thirdly, because nuclear weapons could not be disinvented and were unlikely to be totally discarded. (Non-nuclear zones do not make much sense. First mooted soon after the end of the Second World War by, among others, Adam Rapacki and Anthony Eden, they designated areas from which nuclear weapons would be banned, but with the immense increase in the range of ballistic weapons a prohibition on their emplacement in a given area became of small account. A nuclear-free zone is a yearning to be quit of war but not a way of preventing or side-stepping one.)

To these shifts in Euro-American strategic relations were added shifts in economic relations and in the perception of American economic power. Bluntly, western Europe had come up and the United States had gone down – against expectations a great deal, in hard fact less so but enough to allow western Europe to think in terms of equal competition with the United States in world trade and, more generally, to doubt the United States's previously unassailable role in economic affairs.

Just as the United States was the inescapable and irreplaceable chief of the Nato alliance, so was it the necessary leader in any international economic system and in 1944 it had taken the lead at Bretton Woods in devising and imposing such a system. But within a short time of getting into its stride the system unravelled. It failed to weather rough waters and its failure belittled the United States which had shaped it and was supposed to be able to operate it.

Immediately after the war the United States was in an economic class of its own. Its wealth enabled it to do whatever it wished to do – or so it seemed. So extreme a view had to be an exaggeration and the exaggeration began to be uncovered by repulse and stalemate in Korea and, more strikingly, by failure and retreat in Vietnam: failure to match power to purpose. The more fundamental fallacy became apparent with the rise of the Japanese economy which served notice on the Americans that their economy was no longer unique but faced a potentially hurtful challenger: failure to maintain uniquely dominant power. This was a surprise, the economic equivalent of the shocks to American military confidence administered by the first Soviet nuclear explosion and the sputnik.

In 1950 the GNP of the United States was more than three times that of the Soviet Union, more than ten times that of Japan, and between eight and five times that of each of the three leading countries of western Europe. But by 1980 this hegemony, although still there, had been reduced to less astronomic proportions: not much more than twice that of the Soviet Union or Japan, only three to four times that of West Germany or France, six times that of Great Britain; and the Community's combined GNP had passed the American. When the size of populations is taken into account the American lead over the Soviet Union had slipped slightly from a factor of 3 plus to 3 minus; compared with Japan a lead of almost 7 to 1 had been all but eliminated; and both West Germany and France showed higher GNP per head of population. Each of these last two countries had also a higher GNP per head than either Japan or the Soviet Union. The most striking change was in Japan, whose share of gross world production doubled between the end of occupation (1952) and 1960 and doubled again between 1960 and 1980. Measured by productive aggregates the United States was still the world's leading economic Power and, since its dominance was reduced not by any major loss of resources or output but by its own profligacy, it was inherently capable of retaining a substantial, if lower, lead. The condition was that it decided to live in the world of the 1980s and 1990s and not that of a generation gone by. The principal difference between the American economy and its principal rival – Japan – was that the American was overstretched and the Japanese was not. But this was not a fact of nature. It was a consequence of human decisions.

Two things in particular eroded confidence in the American determination to adjust: the failure of the Bretton Woods system and the performance of the Reagan presidency.

Bretton Woods was a symbol and promise of American superpower. It proclaimed the need for an international economic order. This order would emanate from American economic power. The war of 1914–18 had killed the old economic order regulated by Great Britain[1] and the Great Depression killed hopes of reviving it. The United States was among those countries which scurried into protectionism – the Smoot-Hawley tariffs of 1930 preceded the formalization of Great Britain's espousal of imperial preferences in 1932 – but the United States also led the way back towards free trade. Roosevelt's principal advisers, including Cordell Hull and Henry Morgenthau as Secretaries of State and of the Treasury, were implacable free traders and much of Roosevelt's own enthusiasm for a United Nations to replace the League of Nations came from his commitment to internationalism in economic matters. At Bretton Woods in 1944, before the war ended, the spadework for a new order, financial and commercial, was laid: on the one hand an International Monetary Fund (IMF) and International Bank for Reconstruction and Development (the World Bank) and, on the other, an International Trade Organization (ITO). The guiding principles were, first, fixed but variable exchange rates to eliminate the bugbear of uncertainty in money markets and, secondly, the abolition of preferences and the reduction of tariffs and other commercial obstacles in order to maximize the flow internationally of goods, money and services. The hopes were stability, growth, controlled inflation and therewith rising living standards made possible by the growth which would itself be encouraged by stability. This vision was liberal in the sense of demanding non-discriminatory trade practices and freely convertible currencies and it sought to create new international institutions within which a dominant and regulatory American role would be performed and monitored.

Within this system the dollar was defined in terms of gold; all other currencies in terms of the dollar. For the United States the system was a gold system; for everybody else it was a dollar system. The rest of the developed world (i.e. states with international purchasing power) wanted to acquire dollars and the United States provided dollars, but it did so in such undisciplined profusion that it drowned the system and destroyed the value of the dollar

1.   Great Britain's abdication of its role can be precisely dated: August 1914 when the right to convert sterling into gold was suspended and investment in sterling outside the British empire was forbidden.

in terms of gold. Dollars were disbursed abroad not merely for imported goods and materials but also to cover the costs of military and other establishments overseas: not merely commercially but also for reasons of policy. This latter item created the problem, for although US trade was in surplus, payments overall were in deficit on account of the outflow of funds to finance, in effect, over-ambitious defence and foreign policies. An incipient crisis at the end of the 1960s was averted by raising interest rates in the United States so that European and Japanese money flowed in, but the dollar – once so scarce and valued – had lost its value because the foreigners in whose hands the dollars accumulated did not want so many of them: there was a glut of dollars – the Eurodollar glut, or glut of dollars in European accounts. The dollar's value was reduced and the United States, which had been operating as a world bank, was doing so with a currency whose quoted exchange value was no longer credible. And, further, just as European economies had collapsed when American funds ceased to be available in 1928–29, so the American economy could collapse if Japanese and other foreign funds ceased to flow into the United States in the 1980s or 1990s.

In 1971, in response to growing speculation against the dollar, Nixon was forced to suspend the convertibility of the dollar into gold at the prescribed price, thus acknowledging that the dollar was over-valued. By this date the gold reserves of the United States had halved since the birth of Nato. The exchange value of the dollar fell at once by 10 per cent, ultimately by 30 per cent. A few months later the leading industrial states concluded the Smithsonian agreement which set new exchange rates. Thus the dollar was devalued in terms both of gold and of foreign currencies, but within another two years this revised version of Bretton Woods disintegrated as all the world's main currencies were unpegged from the dollar and allowed to float. The resulting instability was immediately compounded by a quadrupling of the price of oil in the space of three months (the immediate cause of this calamity being the war in the Middle East in 1973) and similar increases in the prices of other raw materials. These perturbations were a setback for the idea that the United States possessed the skills and the resources needed for managing an orderly world economy.

Nixon's devaluation of the dollar in terms of gold was effected without warning or foreign consultation and caused worldwide shock and uncertainty. The gold–dollar standard on which the postwar international economic system rested was removed and nothing was put in its place. The United States could neither on its own run an international economic order nor get other countries to do what it thought necessary for the running of such an order. The alternative to the devaluation of the dollar was revaluation upwards of other currencies, notably the currencies of the countries with the largest trading surpluses with the United States, but there was no way by which the United States could compel these countries to revalue, even though a devaluation of the dollar was a nasty blow to Japanese and German exporters. The sovereign state's only response to imbalance was to readjust its own currency; it could not force others to revalue theirs'.

Given the special position of the United States in world economic affairs, the American devaluation was not only a currency adjustment but also an abdication of the world role. But there was no other country which could assume that role. Suggestions for a dual American-Japanese role ignored the fact that the United States and Japan were distinct and competing economies without any of the common institutions or authorities, or the experience of close cooperation, which would be needed to sustain it. An American-Japanese entente, although distantly conceivable, was not a present practicality. There was therefore a vacuum and world economic affairs were henceforward handled by short-term arrangements and by long-distance telephone calls between the world's chief central banks and finance ministers. The new dollar rates which took the place of the gold–dollar standard did not hold firm, currency markets became unstable, and faith in the dollar continued to decline. The new dollar standard was a quasi-standard which worked, so far as it did, because there was no alternative. The dollar was still king but a wayward and undependable king in a world no longer attuned to monarchy.

The Bretton Woods system was much more than a currency stabilization system. It was an economic system which incorporated a monetary system, and the disintegration of the gold–dollar monetary system was the strongest blow yet to a would-be economic order which was also an American dream. The Bretton Woods system incarnated the American phase of free trade, which was a sequel to the earlier and much longer phase dominated by Great Britain. In each phase the world's strongest trader sought to impose an order which was a projection of its own economic power and interests, but which was neither so well suited to lesser economies nor at all well suited to the weakest economies. The case for world free trade was the maximization of economic exchange and activity among unequal economies. The working of free trade required, primarily as a matter of justice, some recognition and adjustment of these inequalities and, as a practical matter, a powerful regulator to preserve the system from centrifugal forces. The world might benefit from freer trade but there was no natural world economy. There were a small number of powerful, and a large number of relatively powerless, economies. Before the Second World War the powerful were the United States, the British empire and perhaps a Schachtian Germany or (had it succeeded) a Nazi New Order; after that war the United States, Japan and perhaps the European Community. If it was in the interest of the strongest of these economies to superimpose a free trade order on the world, it was incumbent on that economy to regulate and adjust that order. That is what, by the 1970s, the United States was shown to be failing to do. The confession of this failure weakened the United States.

Bretton Woods was always something of a gamble. It was an essay in international collaboration inaugurated at a time when the discrepancies between the parties to it were extreme but at the same time imperfectly acknowledged. The United States alone had benefited economically from the war. American agriculture was rescued from years of depression and doubled its output; American industry received incomparable boosts in research, invention and capital. All other belligerent economies, victors as well as vanquished, had lost enormously. Because of its essential liberal character (in the economic sense of liberal) the Bretton Woods system benefited the strong and so tended to widen the gap between the United States and the rest: it dealt the United States better cards. Keynes, its principal opponent until he felt beaten into accepting and commending it, spoke for a country which had been forced to sell its overseas assets, had lost its foreign markets and was bankrupt in the sense that it could not pay its debts. The principal organ of the new system, the International Monetary Fund, lacked adequate resources to succour the needy as was quickly demonstrated by the hasty improvization of the Marshall Plan for supplying Europe with money, a task which should by current theory have been undertaken by organs created at Bretton Woods.

There was in the 1970s scant sympathy for the United States in Europe or anywhere else. In 1971, and again in the renewed instability of the 1980s, Europeans blamed the United States for printing and exporting dollars to balance its overseas commitments instead of curbing its own spending and raising taxes – that is to say, for refusing to raise money from its own people so long as it could get it from foreigners (who were, however, unpredictable lenders and could be enticed to lend money only by more money in the shape of higher rates of interest on their loans). Japanese leaders were equally critical, particularly when Americans argued that the dislocations were the fault of Japan for being too successful and showing too little international responsibility. The Reagan years aggravated the problem. They were a period of conspicuous over-stretching, flavoured by Reagan's paramount concern with 'walking tall', his determination to increase military spending and at the same time to cut taxes (and social disbursements), and his blithe sallies into escalating the Superpower conflict into space with his 'Star Wars', big and expensive nonsense from a clouded mind. The Reagan presidency suggested that the United States lacked the skills or perhaps the determination to manage its own economy. Reagan's understanding of economics was not great and he did not seem to bother to enlarge it. His main promise on entering the White House was to balance the budget. He presided, however, over the accumulation of budget deficits which would have been unthinkable a few years earlier. He held two simple views: that taxes should be cut and defence spending increased. The gap would be bridged because cuts in taxes would foster businesses and so enlarge the tax base and tax yields: that is to say, economic growth, induced by low taxes but tight money, would fill the gap. This did not happen and the deficits grew not only in total but also as a percentage of GNP. By 1982 the growth strategy had failed and was reversed. Money was made looser by lowering interest rates; monetary targets were relaxed. This was a short-term expedient designed to inject growth into the economy before once more tightening monetary controls and still avoiding tax increases. In the longer term deficit financing was preferred to tax increases. Growth continued but so did the gap. The magic equalizer was the value of the dollar which was allowed to soar, curbing consumer imports and pulling in foreign money. But the value of the dollar lacked substance and credibility and a spectacular rise in 1985 was followed by an even more spectacular fall. To some extent the fall was managed by government interventions. Governments, foreign as well as that of the United States, were scared of an uncontrolled fall and contrived to manipulate it. But the fall removed the factor which had for a time allowed the administration to pursue its mixture of loose fiscal and tight monetary policies.

When Reagan left office in 1989 half of the population of the United States were worse off than they had been eight years earlier in spite of the fact that the domestic economy grew in those years at an average annual rate of 2½ per cent. Personal savings virtually ceased; whereas in the 1970s domestic savings financed investment at an average rate of 7 per cent, in the 1980s investment fell to 6 per cent and the greater part of it came from borrowing abroad; the rate of investment in manufacture was below Japan's and of several Europeans'; huge deficits on the budget and on external account (the latter rising to over $12 billion a month)[2] were papered over by importing foreign money at high interest rates which steeply overvalued the dollar, crippled exports, destroyed foreign capital assets and amassed an external debt costing $50 billion a year in interest alone. The industrial future was clouded by a sharp decline in higher education in science and technology – the number of American doctorates in these fields fell below those awarded in Japan (a country with half the population of the United States and equal educational standards), while nearly half of American PhD's were foreign students who went back home when they got their degrees. Domestically the net effect of Reagan's eight years in office was to favour the rich and the elderly. Overall the burden of personal taxation remained virtually unaltered and although corporate profit taxes were reduced corporate profits fell. Measured by such indicators as infant mortality and housing standards, inner cities decayed to points approaching some of the black spots of the Third World. Employment slumped at the beginning of Reagan's first term and then recovered, but a high proportion of new jobs was in service industries or government, not in production. Unrestrained defence expenditure engendered a great deal of corruption in the soliciting and placing of contracts. Government seemed to be out of control as a variety of official agencies and semi-official groups engaged in policies which were concealed from Congress, the public and even perhaps the President and were sometimes illegal and almost always unsuccessful, whilst at a

2.   The deficit on external account was a small proportion – less than 4 per cent – of GDP but a serious worry so long as it had to be covered by high-cost foreign funds. Every three months the United States raises large sums of money by offering new Treasury Bonds for sale. By the end of the 1980s the total sought in this way was about $30 billion and a quarter of it came from Japan.

more personal level an unwonted number of cabinet members and senior officials became so immersed in corruption as to leave scant time for their proper duties. The Irangate affair, which involved raising money for one purpose in order to divert it to another and illegal one, was only the most blatant example of many such activities, clandestine, unconstitutional and bungled. The outside world, which had noted little but the economic opulence and military might, became aware of the fact that this hugely rich country was failing to look after its poor, balance its books or ensure seemly government.

The debit side of this economic performance was accentuated because, for all Reagan's rhetoric, there was so little to show for external policies which had turned the United States into the world's biggest debtor. In Central America the United States proved incapable of getting its way in Nicaragua in spite of resorting to war by proxy and to covert operations in breach of international law (which were condemned by the International Court of Justice); in the smallest Central American republic, El Salvador, which Reagan had promised on his first election to the presidency to set to rights, all the efforts of the United States, open and concealed, to install an acceptably moderate right-wing regime failed and opened the way for the extreme and brutal right; and in Panama the United States, after turning a blind eye to the deplorable drug-running activities of General Manuel Noriega and even paying him large retainers for some ten years, tried first to bribe him to leave the country, then to remove him by conspiring with his enemies, and resorted finally to military invasion to capture or kill him. Even regionally, let alone globally, the United States was finding it hard to turn power into results. A prodigious expenditure of money to promote stability and democracy in the American continent achieved neither.

What the United States lost in these years was not so much power as respect. Respect for American leadership, which had been high in the days of Truman and Eisenhower and had risen during Kennedy's brief presidency, slumped with the crudities of Nixon, the futilities of Ford and the inadequacies of Carter, to reach unparalleled depths with Reagan, perhaps the least intelligent leader in American history. Nixon was regarded, to put it mildly, as less than honest, Carter as sadly less than efficient and Reagan as a comprehensive defective, and these judgements – although tinged with Europe's ever latent anti-Americanism – were not wide of the mark. By the end of Reagan's presidency Great

Britain was the only member of the alliance (apart perhaps from Turkey) with a government staunch enough to ignore his failings or resist the temptation to exploit them. Spain, which had joined Nato in 1972, was insisting that American aircraft be removed from bases in Spain by 1991. Portugal was seeking revision of the agreement permitting the use of the Azores as an American base. Greece, which had never forgiven the United States for liking and helping the colonels who took power in 1967 and abused it for seven years, was exacting a high price for extending beyond 1988 the leases of naval and air bases. The Danish government came within a few votes of defeat over the question of admitting to Danish harbours Nato vessels carrying nuclear weapons. There were proposals for reanimating the Western European Union as a semi-independent alternative to Nato: the Netherlands proposed sending a joint WEU[3] force to the Gulf War but Great Britain, France and Italy vetoed a move which might be construed as a vote of waning confidence in Nato. Even Great Britain was moved to formal expostulation when the United States invaded without warning the Commonwealth state of Grenada, and although Margaret Thatcher allowed American forces based in Great Britain to be used for an attack on Libya she had to face unusually strong criticism for her collaboration in a clearly unlawful action.

But the military pre-eminence of the United States remained, the economic base was not beyond repair, and the fact that the United States was relatively no longer the Power that it had been did not take it out of the first rank or demote it from the top place in that rank. In the mid-1980s it had 16 per cent of world trade against Japan's 7 per cent (and the Community's 30 per cent).[4] If the United States was riding for a fall, the fall was some way off. The United States faced none of the disasters which threatened the USSR – economic collapse, disintegration – and the gap between them was widening as the ever increasing costliness of new technology hit the USSR harder than the United States. In the military

3.   Western European Union (WEU) was formed by the Treaty of Brussels in 1948. Its members were Great Britain, France and the three Benelux countries which had already concluded an economic union among themselves. West Germany and Italy joined WEU in 1952, following the collapse of proposals for a European Defence Community (EDC).

4.   See *International Trade Statistics Yearbook, 1985* (United Nations, 1987).

field the United States had relatively little need for allies, in Europe or elsewhere. It needed to curb its own unnecessary extravagance because it had been building a giant's military power on less than a giant's economic resources. It might press on or trim sail, but if it pressed on, it must lose its freedom of action in the world and perhaps, like earlier empires, plunge into terrible trouble. European empires had collapsed upon similar miscalculations. In the seventeenth century the Count-Duke of Olivares, judging that war was the best way to assert and maintain the greatness of Spain against France, committed Spain to extravagant military exertions which failed and from which it never recovered. In the next century over-ambitious and over-expensive external policies were one of the principal causes of the French Revolution. By the nineteenth century statesmen were becoming more alive to the economic requirements of national flamboyance: the British empire was accumulated in the face of persistent doubts about its cost and abandoned when it became apparent that the resources for holding it no longer existed. In the mid-twentieth century de Gaulle extricated France from North Africa because he had the sense and strength of character to pull out before he was thrown out. The same question confronted American statesmanship later in the century: what could the country afford, given that power is the resultant of the equation between resources and commitments? So long as military power was the prime factor in the American world view, American external policies would be fashioned in response to the Soviet Union's actions and presumed intentions, but as soon as economic consideration and competition assumed an equal prominence American external policies would be fashioned, not solely in response to the ailing and over-rated power of the Soviet Union, but in response to the economic strength of, certainly, Japan and, perhaps, the European Community.

The economic constraints have become the more pressing. The United States has to come to terms with its incapacity to do without international support in economic affairs. In military matters alliance means agreements with third parties against the USSR, but in economic matters the cooperation required is not against an adversary but with it. The United States cannot manage single-handed the world's economy but it needs that economy to be managed. So, too, does Japan. The big questions such as the terms of international trade, global investment and Third World debt can be tackled only by these two Megapowers in association. Such an association is not a military alliance, for which neither has a need, but it implies a deeper mutual accord without which each Power imperils its own prosperity. The most evident mark of the American rise to world power in the course of the present century has been the displacement of the European Powers. The touchstone of its continuing eminence into the next century will be its capacity to handle a competitive partnership with Japan in which the competition has to be tempered to the need for partnership.

But the Japanese may see things differently. Japan's tradition in international behaviour is thin and predicting Japan's behaviour is correspondingly hazardous. In spite of the ending of the shogunate in 1867 Japan has remained throughout the succeeding century a cultural enclave, aloof and idiosyncratic. Great Britain in its heyday gloried in insular isolation but British isolation was an open door compared with Japan's intellectual self-sufficiency. Japanese power is aggressive without being military, a novel and puzzling stance and one which, if successfully maintained, will mark a decisive change in the conduct of international affairs. The acknowledged Superpowers of the late twentieth century based their powers on weaponry which they cannot now afford and which they never could use. Japan, having been forced to foreswear such weaponry, has learned a new way to power but remains undecided about the need to temper its exercise by international cooperation.

Part Three
New Patterns

CHAPTER NINE
France and Germany: Recovery and Entente

Western Europe recovered from the war fast. This was a surprise. In the first couple of years after the war western Europe was thought to be in such dire straits that only massive American aid could save it from catastrophe. This was a fortunate exaggeration since American aid was thereupon provided and played an important part in recovery. It primed a recovery which, without it, would have been much more laborious.

A second surprise was the rapid repair of Franco-German relations, the very opposite of what happened after the first war. French and Germans buried the hatchet, with conviction and with momentous consequences. By 1950 these ancient enemies were together taking the first steps which led to the creation in 1957 of the European Community. Great Britain spurned the Community and then joined it without conviction.

The third major element in postwar western Europe was its alliance with the United States (and Canada) by the North Atlantic Treaty of 1949. This American involvement in Europe was predicated upon estimates of Soviet strength and European weaknesses. Both were much exaggerated, but a continuing Soviet menace and European incapacity to resist it remained fundamental and virtually uncontested propositions throughout the ensuing decade. The United States became the custodian of western and Mediterranean Europe. Europeans would have preferred to do without a custodian. They were used to managing their own affairs but for the time being they no longer believed that they could.

Of these three remarkable factors – postwar resilience, Franco-German reconciliation and American tutelage – the first was grounded in the Marshall Plan which was itself a spontaneous and unexpected turn in events, not only because it was strikingly generous but also because it was an aberration from the broad trend of American economic policy: the Bretton Woods vision (already described) of a non-discriminatory and non-preferential system based on free trade and convertible currencies. This vision was unpalatable for different reasons to the Soviet Union and to western Europe (and, later, to the Third World when it came into existence and demanded preferential treatment, which Europeans were readier to concede than were Americans, for its fledgling trade and industries). The Soviet Union distrusted the American scheme less for economic than for political and ideological reasons: it preferred its own system, autarkic or nearly so *in suo orbe*. Western Europe was not ready for the full Bretton Woods scheme. It needed emergency aid and breathing space before it could feel strong enough to participate in a postwar liberal economic order; and when subsequently it regained confidence it created in the European Community a sub-system which was internally cooperative but externally adversarial – particularly competitive with the United States.

In 1945 American plans were, in European eyes, too thorough-going and above all premature. The British, although atavistically and rationally attached to a liberal order, had abandoned it under compulsion in the 1930s and the compulsions had increased. Other Europeans were even more urgently concerned about immediate economic disabilities. The embryonic International Trade Organization was therefore so circumscribed before it was born that the Americans themselves rejected it and accepted instead what amounted to an indefinitely continuous programme of multiple tariff negotiations, swaps and cuts under the auspices of a General Agreement on Tariffs and Trade (GATT).[1] Whatever the virtues of

1.   The GATT, signed by 23 states in 1947 as an interim measure, became an effective instrument for expanding trade with a membership which increased fourfold by the 1980s. It promoted and monitored a multiplicity of tariff reductions between particular members which were then extended to all members subject to escape clauses applicable in defined circumstances. It recognized the right of members of a customs union to accord preferences to one another provided that the union's external tariff did not exceed the average of its members' several tariffs at the date of the formation of the union. It recognized, from the 1960s, the right of developing states to be exempted from reciprocity. It concentrated on trade in industrial materials and goods

the American scheme, Europeans feared that all the advantages
would flow to the United States unless a transitional regime were
introduced during which the worst of wartime damage and dislocation, which the United States had escaped, might be repaired.
Western Europeans regarded themselves as liberals but not yet.

The Marshall Plan was an implicit acceptance by the United
States of these pleas. It was designed as an exceptional and brief
derogation from the Bretton Woods scheme. The Plan, as propounded by the US Secretary of State, George C. Marshall, was an
offer to the whole of Europe of financial aid – most of it as free gifts
– over the limited period of four years 1947–51. (The timespan was
later extended in some respects. The free gifts totalled $17 billion.)
Its prime purpose was restorative, the rehabilitation of industrial,
agricultural and financial activities – particularly in West Germany.
A second purpose, which emerged as a useful implication but
not as a precondition, was to encourage European integration,
whatever that might turn out to mean. Americans found it tiresome
to have to deal separately with many different states and they also
believed that the unity which had been so fruitful in North America
must be equally beneficial for Europe, if only Europeans could be
forced or nudged out of their petty historical furrows and made
to see their field as one.

In its basic economic purpose of using American money to get
Europe back on its feet and back at work the Plan was entirely
successful. The money was generously supplied and it fell on
fruitful soil since Europeans did not lack the necessary working
and administrative skills. But in its broader purposes the Plan was
atrophied from the start. Besides the Soviet refusal to participate or
allow any of its satellites to do so, the British succeeded in killing
its supranational aspects and ensured that the organization at the
receiving end should be an intergovernmental committee and not
a supranational authority as envisaged by Americans. (This Committee – later Organization – for European Economic Cooperation
began with sixteen European members and two North American
observers. It was transformed in 1960 into the Organization for Economic Cooperation and Development in which the United States,

until the 1980's when it turned its attention to agricultural produce,
services and intellectual property – and was nearly brought to a halt by
conflict in the first of these areas between the European Community
and, on the other hand, the United States and other food-exporting
countries.

Canada and Japan were full members: OEEC became OECD.) This instinctive British reaction was mainly nationalist, an inability and unwillingness to conceive government as located anywhere outside the traditional sovereign state. It also owed something to the reluctance of an enfeebled state to grasp more than one nettle at a time. British opposition to European integration, or to any form of collaboration likely to entail integration, puzzled and irritated Americans and persisted as a discordant undertone at the American end of Anglo-American relations.

Of the three principal states in western Europe one – Great Britain – was wounded but triumphant, a second – France – had known the extremes of shame and exhilaration, and the third – West Germany – was rapidly transformed from subjugation to a leading role.

France's recovery, although greeted with less astonishment than the legendary West German recovery, was no less remarkable. France's abasement had been both material and psychological and it had long roots. France was losing ground before the first Great War. Its population was static and its workforce, rural and urban, was therefore in relative decline. It had been (with Belgium) the chief western sufferer in the first war which ravaged its industrial north east and its morale nationwide. In the 1920s monetary reform and a certain monetary affluence, coupled with economic reforms (including the beginnings of agricultural reform through the consolidation of farms into larger units) encouraged hopes which did not survive the Depression. After the shocks of the Second World War France made an abortive and expensive attempt to retrieve its overseas empire and seemed set to renew its interwar record of political and parliamentary instability, aggravated by severe inflation. The more hopeful signs were occluded but they existed: a population rising after a long period of stagnation, an accelerated move off the land which provided a new demographic basis in the towns for industrial renewal and advance.

In order to recover something like its prewar status and poise France needed to escape the worst consequences of national humiliation and division, to restructure and expand its material base, and to cut its continuing commitments to fit its emergent resources. In all these respects it achieved a high measure of success, attributable to an exceptional combination: on the one hand the preservation, in spite of the years of misfortune, mismanagement and discredit, of substantial assets in education, material resources and technical and administrative skills; and on the other hand leadership. France had in de Gaulle the one European who in the twentieth century might claim to be the peer of the famous statesmen of the previous century whose conduct of affairs was grounded in intelligent and measured pragmatism and whose love of country was not, for all its intensity, clouded by vain ambitions.

During the war de Gaulle squeezed every possible drop of advantage out of a desperately weak situation. He was on good terms with nobody of comparable status. Churchill, although less paranoid than Roosevelt about de Gaulle, was never on easy personal terms with him, was always prepared to subordinate French interests to American caprices, and treated France as a secondary element in a future Europe. De Gaulle on the other hand insisted that France was a perennially major factor and he did not shirk from abusing the United States and Great Britain when they thwarted him. Churchill was slow, Roosevelt slower, to admit that de Gaulle was the dominant figure among the anti-German or 'free' French and both tried to avoid recognizing the French Committee of National Liberation in Algiers unless they could use it to circumscribe de Gaulle. They failed to see that de Gaulle's too evident distrust of them, which they resented, had ample grounds in their own dealings with Darlan, Pétain's right-hand admiral, and with General Giraud, by whom they wanted to supplant de Gaulle. So long as the war lasted de Gaulle was a big fish in a small pond, the sort of big man who brings out the worst in other big men, in the sort of small pond which is not drying up but is about to bubble and teem. In all these matters Churchill and Roosevelt were shortsighted, unlike lesser colleagues (Eden for example) who were not merely emotionally pro-French but more realistic and sensible about the future role of France in Europe. The mistrust between these allies lived on after them.

De Gaulle, far more than Roosevelt and more even than Churchill, was intent during the war on its aftermath. Of the problems ahead the first was national unity. It was threatened at two levels. There was, first, the open sore of hatred between Vichy and the Resistance, between collaborators who were regarded as no better than traitors and those who rejected the surrender of 1940 and were regarded as no less than heroes. But, secondly, division in France was older than this rift. As the country where the French Revolution had occurred France had continued for a century and a half to exhibit, and even to nurture, with peculiar tenacity the cleft between left and right which had been engendered and denominated by the Revolution. Naggingly nourished by the failures of the interwar years the bitterness was once more inflamed by the collapse of 1940, the debate about where to lay the blame and the opposition to Vichy in which the main thrust of the left came (after an equivocal interval) from a Communist Party claiming to unite the heritage of 1789 with that of 1917. Yet the French Resistance to the Germans and the heirs of Vichy came to acknowledge a single leader who was not a communist or even of the left, but a nationalist general and patriot of antique hue.

In fact France had ceased to be a revolutionary country. By the twentieth century the French Revolution had become an inspiration to more people outside Europe than in it. In France itself there was more of romantic imagination than plausibility in its revolutionary repute. Although the mismanagement of the Third Republic had mirrored the mismanagement of the *ancien régime* which had precipitated the Revolution, and although the bitterness of the Vichy years reanimated the traditional animus between left and right, there was only enough in these emotions to revive a mood, not enough to create a truly revolutionary situation. Fears – or hopes – of a successful communist bid for power *à la* 1917 were ludicrously wide of the mark: popular support was too thin and in any case the army was on the wrong side. After de Gaulle had allayed the emotions they vanished for good. The 'events' of 1968, particularly the role of the students in Paris, were a belated flicker of past heroics. The notion that they heralded a revolution was wholly implausible, even at the time. The political impact of the students was, for good or ill, negligible. France was still divided between right and left but, like other western countries, the extra-parliamentary manifestations of this divide were strikes and other forms of modern industrial discontent.

This is not to deny the powerful personal role of de Gaulle – only to insist that it was played on a stage which, however fervid and strewn with litter, was not one where barricades were going to be run up. Neither in its politics nor its economics was France as old-fashioned as many outsiders were accustomed to believe. De Gaulle's task, at the time of the liberation in 1944, was to reassemble and relaunch France. His achievements were to hold the anti-Vichy forces together, damp down the vengefulness of the triumphant Resistance and thwart an Anglo-American plan to treat France as occupied territory. With his obdurate faith in France, combined with a bold but well-judged exercise of authority, he animated a spiritual revival which survived a relapse into political squabbling in the 1950s and fashioned the new self-confidence without which France could neither have pioneered the end of the old Franco-German feud nor have accepted the end of empire in Asia and Africa.

De Gaulle had to defend this authority on two fronts, domestic and international. In 1944 the Americans and British planned to treat France, as they had treated Italy a year earlier, as just another piece of recovered European real estate with regional administrators to be appointed by themselves and a new currency made and secretly printed in England, but de Gaulle pre-empted them and assumed as of right the prerogatives of government. In the same year he went to Moscow and after his visit the French communist chief, Maurice Thorez, who had spent the war there, returned to France but did not challenge de Gaulle's national pre-eminence. Within France the last stages of the war were marred by brutality, murder and summary justice (or injustice), but the situation was brought quickly under control and the rule of law imposed: the victims of indiscriminate revenge and lynch law were far fewer than those condemned by civil and military courts whose jurisdiction may have been questionable but whose sentences were not widely impugned. Yet the main task remained – to restore the country's material base and adjust French commitments at home and abroad to France's capacities.

The first half of this task – the restoration and reorientation of the economy – was guided by the modernization (or Monnet) Plan; the second by the relinquishment of empire. Both ventures succeeded so well that a generation later, and in spite of ups and downs, France was one of the world's very few independent nuclear Powers.

Divestment of empire, the negative half, was hindered by ambivalence, notably in French Indo-China where an early inclination to leave was reversed and the ill-fated attempt to stay afflicted France into the 1950s and paved the way for the even more ill-fated American attempt to effect a lodgement on the Asian mainland. But the eventual loss of French Indo-China and the abandonment by Pierre Mendès-France and de Gaulle of Tunisia and Algeria respectively freed France of material and psychological burdens which it could no longer afford. If France was slower than Great Britain to resign its empire it nevertheless made a more complete job of the readjustment, as British tribulations in Rhodesia and Ireland were to show.

The positive aspect of French recovery was economic. Economic recovery began at once and persisted in spite of political fumbling. The war had cut French output by two thirds, but within two years of the liberation in the summer of 1944 nine tenths of this downfall had been retrieved. France was on the way back to prewar levels of economic activity more than two years before the proclamation of the Marshall Plan. Politically, however, France relapsed into stagnation and even for a time into reaction. A string of unstable coalitions revived prewar despondency at home and distrust abroad. Political power shifted to the right (an ex-Vichy minister, Antoine Pinay, became Prime Minister in 1952) until the Poujadist movement split the right and so brought back the left in 1956–57. De Gaulle left politics and Paris in disgust in 1953 but returned in 1958 to serve another ten-year stint, during which he completed decolonization and furthered the entente with West Germany begun by Robert Schuman. He retired permanently in 1969 after mishandling the 'events' of 1968 and making an injudicious attempt to smuggle abolition of the Senate (which he disliked) into a project for the reform of local government.

In his last period of power de Gaulle had dominated the right and attracted votes from outside its normal ranks. After his departure Gaullism ceased to be an identifiable political force although political parties claimed its name and heritage. De Gaulle's apparent heir Jacques Chaban-Delmas was pushed aside by Valéry Giscard d'Estaing who became President but lacked de Gaulle's nearly total command of the right and also lost the working-class support which had been given to de Gaulle. These voters reverted to the socialist party which François Mitterrand was re-forming with the aim of displacing the communists as the main voice of the left. Mitterrand was a leader of considerable intelligence and equal cunning, the one quality more specially remarked by his supporters, the other by his enemies. He was also patient and although in 1978 the united left was trounced and the socialist-communist alliance broke up, in the process Mitterrand had overtaken the communists everywhere except in some urban strongholds and he went on to win presidential elections in 1981 and 1988. Once in power he stayed there. First elected to the presidency little more than a year after Margaret Thatcher began her remarkable hold on power in Great Britain, he comfortably outlasted her. When in 1989 he celebrated the second centenary of the fall of the Bastille he demonstrated that France remained wedded to the Revolution, but not to revolution. Apart from the fringe of *la vieille France* – nostalgic, snobbish, paternalistic, patchily fascist – France was from right to left a stable and prosperous country, much of its industry modernized, its agriculture slimmed, its strongly centralized administrative system in harmony with flourishing regional loyalties and proudly active provincial cities and towns. Social outcasts – victims of poverty or racial prejudice – were a blot on this civilized landscape; education, particularly in universities, was the subject of perennial criticism and occasional violent revolt; urban crime and police behaviour were ugly and getting uglier. But France had become sufficiently united and efficient to dispense with the heroics used by de Gaulle to fight his country's way back to confidence at home and prestige abroad, and it had found in the alliance with West Germany the key to a dominant share in the direction of European affairs.

Throughout the postwar decades the French economy was directed and rejuvenated by the Monnet Plan, more precisely by the sequence of five year plans (the third was a three year plan for 1958–61) by which the state exercised broad and remote control. As after 1919, so after 1945, French governments faced serious economic problems which they wanted to solve without abandoning the French tradition of pandering to the little man. Demands for large reparations in 1919 had been a way of escaping the need to tax small farmers and small businesses. The refusal in 1945 to reform the currency or cancel the accumulations of wartime paper money had the same source and fuelled inflation until Antoine Pinay put a brake on rising prices – and on everything else, the classic right-wing cure that kills. With the Monnet Plan France found a middle course, although one immediate effect was the Poujadist protest which attracted 2.5 million votes at the elections in 1956. The plan consisted of a modest Department of State which tackled selected economic sectors by laying down broad guidelines to be filled in by both private and state-owned enterprises. At the centre the planning staff's first concern was to set priorities in a progressive restoration of all sectors, but even in the selected areas the Department did not fix targets or norms. Its business was the allocation of resources when these resources were not enough for the simultaneous satisfaction of all sectors at once; and the decision which should come first. The second plan (1952–57) gave particular attention to education, research, training and marketing, and succeeding plans gradually extended beyond strictly economic areas to social policies and a welfare state, fashioned by the state and financed by employers and employed. Under this supervision the French economy grew in the 1950s by

an average 4.5 per cent a year and in the 1960s by 5.8 per cent,
a performance which astonished France's neighbours and allies
and many French men and women too. Postwar squabbles over
drafting a new constitution, the impatient withdrawal of de Gaulle,
and the instability of the governments of the new Fourth Republic
had confirmed European views that France was a hopeless case:
least of all did the rest of Europe look to France for initiatives in the
economic sphere. Yet in 1950 the French Foreign Minister Robert
Schuman made a proposal of the greatest significance. He proposed
that France and West Germany (and others) should combine their
coal and steel industries under a single international authority.

This was a first step in international planning for industry (not
trade). It pointed explicitly towards wider economic cooperation
and integration – wider in the sense of embracing more countries
and more industries. Equally explicit was its political intent: in
the first place to end Franco-German hostility and then to foster a
union among European states, extending from economic alignment
to something like a political confederation. In 1950 the recent war
was still in everybody's mind, and the memory was one of the
Schuman Plan's parents. Another was calculation: with the United
States showing a decided partiality for the rehabilitation and rearming of West Germany, France could not afford to persevere in
an anti-German course. Yet a third was a new optimism which was
spreading over western Europe: Italy, for example, joined the Coal
and Steel Community although it had no coal or iron to speak of.
The second war, like the first, created a fervent desire to prevent
another, but the means were different – not the emasculation of
the losers which Clemenceau had hoped for, but the relegation
of enmity in indissolubly shared fortunes. By these means the
postwar revulsion from war would be put to permanent advantage.
It is probably true to judge that western Europe was purged of the
causes of war between its several states from the beginning of the
twentieth century; and that it recognized this blessing and built on
it from the middle of the century. This was one of the differences
between the two halves of the continent. In eastern Europe after
1945 war became remote but not so surely eliminated, because the
main guarantee of peace was the Soviet Union's control over the
actions of its satellite states rather than the removal of their ancient
disputes and internal dissensions.

The Schuman Plan, which came into operation in 1952, and its
progeny, including the European Economic Community established by treaty in 1957, testified to the pacific and law-abiding

aspirations of the arch-enemies, France and Germany. They testified also to their new-found economic weight and thence to
renascent political capacity and ambition. Without the former
the latter were impossible or inconsequential. If the pattern of
Europe were to change, the impulse had to come from a forceful
Franco-German example.

In France, as elsewhere, the 1970s and 1980s were a test of economic nerve and skill. Inflation threatened the living standards of
individuals, the survival of businesses and the government's hand
on economic regulators. It was met by deflation with its attendant
hurt to businesses and jobs. When the medicine proved inadequate a new prime minister, Raymond Barre (1976), introduced
more comprehensive reorganization (*perestroika avant la lettre*): less
central direction of economic affairs, a drive for efficiency with
the alternative of closure. Inflation was not checked; Barre got
the balance not quite right but not disastrously wrong. The same
modified *dirigisme* was adopted by the socialist government which
took office in 1981. It was unable to prevent further rises in the
rate of inflation and unemployment, but the rises were less than
critical.

The recession which began after 1973 with the quadrupling of
the price of oil and increases in the prices of other raw materials
checked the advance of the French economy and dented French
optimism. It posed too a special problem for a country which was
in transition. Traditional activities, including agriculture, already
threatened by change, were additionally threatened by depression;
newer industries, upon which modern France was to depend, were
still neither securely established nor large enough to compete
with their German equivalents. While the former feared that the
acceleration of an integrated European economy would weaken
them yet further, the latter looked increasingly to the promised
expansion of the Community for salvation. In the 1980s these
fears and divisions found political expression as a part of France
voted for nostalgic or chauvinist conservatism (of which Le Pen's
National Front, besides being racist, was the extreme manifestation), but the greater part voted for parties of the moderate right
and left which, although uncoordinated, pinned their hopes on
a go-ahead economic expansion which required both a benign
world economy (which could not be guaranteed) and the continued
transformation of the Franco-German relationship from conflict
into partnership. France had now a higher GNP than Great Britain,
absolutely and per head of population, and it had fared better in

the difficult 1970s and 1980s, but it had not dealt with the whole of its backlog of antiquated industries, and its quasi-independent defence policy – although it absorbed only about 4 per cent of GNP – was becoming too costly to maintain alongside continuing commitments overseas and domestic social demands.

The circumstances of 1945 might have created a Franco-British axis but did not. Both countries had suffered much and survived; both ended the war in the glow of victory; both had lost or were plainly losing great empires. They were Europe's premier nationalists, with a tradition of political self-consciousness reaching back to their Hundred Years War in the Middle Ages; alone among Europeans (except the Soviet Union) both resolved soon after the war to equip themselves with nuclear weapons. Yet, as after the first war, they were soon out of step and out of sympathy with one another. Their most urgent external concerns were decolonization and the relationship with the United States. For the British decolonization, at first grudgingly acknowledged and then efficiently executed, was the end of an era and of a status. It left a gap which was not adequately filled by the new Commonwealth which, in British eyes, was the shadow and painful reminder of something altogether prouder and grander and in no sense a power base. The French were slicker and more adventurous. They would set out to make the end of empire no more than a change in appearance which would enable them to preserve influence and prestige at the cost of abandoning only formal dominion. Because they were divided among themselves they failed in Asia, but they had some success in Africa and even attracted former British colonies into the orbit of francophone West Africa. With regard to the United States French leaders of all parties looked askance at the British claim to have a special relationship and at the policy, preponderant over most of western Europe, of building American power permanently into European affairs. This was a hazardous stance since American aid was needed in Europe – financial aid for a few years, military support for longer. Nevertheless France, playing as if from strength a hand which was never as strong as it was presented, kept the Americans at arm's length and sponsored a new western Europe in which France was an indubitable leader and the United States an outsider. For this policy, anathema to the British, a close alliance with West Germany was essential. It was at first doubtful since Konrad Adenauer, whose political authority was unchallengeable within West Germany for more than a decade, began by putting all his eggs in the American basket, but a well-timed de Gaulle–Adenauer accord partially detached West Germany from total dependence on the United States and this accord was followed by a meeting of minds between Giscard d'Estaing and Helmut Schmidt, two exceptionally intelligent leaders (neither unaware of his intellectual superiority). Both developed also a disdain for Margaret Thatcher which, together with her own distrust of a European world about which she knew little, cemented the Franco-German continental entente.

Germany, unlike France, had been congenitally optimistic and successful ever since its emergence in 1870 (the jolts of the 1920s notwithstanding) and its chief postwar need therefore was to recover the position it had held in prewar Europe and the world. Whereas France – and Great Britain – had been in relative decline throughout the century and needed to restructure their economies, West Germany's need was to repair damage – heavy damage, but damage for whose repair lavish outside funds and expert domestic skills were available. The total defeat and surrender of Germany in 1945 included – as in 1918 they had not included – the undeniable defeat of its armies and their elimination from German politics for at least a generation and probably more. The governments of the Weimar Republic and Hitler's government had depended on the army. The governments of the new German Federal Republic did not. Even the recovery of *Wehrhoheit* (the right to arms) did not put the army back in its accustomed place in the governance of Germany. Rather the contrary, since the denial of *Wehrhoheit* by the Treaty of Versailles had been a major element in making Weimar governments militarist and Hitler's rise possible.

More important to its neighbours than the defeat of the German army was the exorcism of its military spirit. A direct military threat was in abeyance, but this had happened before. The testing time would be the years when Germany's status and capacity remained under the shadow of its aggressive past – humbled, even appalled, by that past; anxious for rehabilitation; dependent on others for the beginning of recovery; contemplating a future which it had not yet the power to shape. In European minds this issue was not yet decided when the Americans, upon the outbreak of the Korean War, determined to reconstruct a strong German state and arm it, but the temper of this rearmed state was decisively set and manifested by its first chancellor, Konrad Adenauer, who – rejecting the essentially adventurous, even piratical, stances of Wilhelmine and Nazi Germany – made West Germany's integration with the west the key to his policies: with the United States in Nato and, less remarked at the time but no less decisive, with France in a developing series of economic ventures. Reunification of Germany could be forgotten for the time being, if only because time would take care of it. This conscious course was as important as the Superpower confrontation in the bisecting of Europe in the first postwar generation. The pattern of Europe was not set by the United States and the Soviet Union alone.

West Germany's postwar economic recovery was steady and strong for nearly half a century. It was grounded in the division of Germany, the accompanying revaluation of the West German currency and $1.5 billion of American aid. The loss of territory to the east was more than offset by compensating advantages: the lands lost were less valuable than what was retained; refugees from the east provided an additional and peculiarly mobile labour force. So long as it was under foreign occupation West Germany had to contribute to the costs, but these were offset by inflowing funds to support the occupation and were lower (net) than a defence budget would have been. Although destruction had been terrible, some things were not destroyed: efficient administration, education, industrial skills, discipline. Investment was high enough to boost growth without inflation. The contrast with the aftermath of the first Great War was striking and present to the minds not just of historians but of people at large, half of whom lived through both periods. Germany's experience of the aftermath of defeat was far more bruising after the first war than after the second. On the earlier occasion Germany had reeled from chaos to boom to depression to tyranny. The loss of territory, population, raw materials and manufacturing industries had been compounded by violent internal upheavals and financial collapse. Public finances slipped out of control because governments were too weak to increase taxes with the result that budgetary revenue covered only a third of government expenditure and the remaining two thirds had to be borrowed. The external balance of payments was crippled by war losses, by reparations stretching indefinitely into the future and by the general shrinkage of the domestic economy and inflated manufacturing costs. In all these respects history conspicuously failed to repeat itself.

After 1945 reparations from West Germany were soon stopped. The western zones of occupation were severed from the Soviet zone and quickly converted into an independent sovereign state. It had firm government: Adenauer was chancellor from 1949 to his retirement in 1963 at the age of eighty-seven and he inherited from Bismarck and his heirs a political tradition which sanctified more stringent central direction of the economy by the state than was tolerated by liberal or *laissez faire* tenets. The urgent need for rehabilitation obliged organized labour to reduce its demands to a minimum and accept a junior role in industry. Stability, efficiency, plentiful and disciplined labour, the currency reform in 1948 (when a new mark was introduced by foreign fiat), foreign aid in capital and foreign exchange (specially valuable for the purchase of food and imported raw materials) – all these things contributed to trebling the new state's industrial output in the four years from 1948 and to raise its GNP by two thirds. The war's drain on population was quickly made good and the population stabilized around 1970 at sixty million (East Germany had seventeen million). Output per head rose; there was little unemployment and only a small redistribution of wealth. Unlike in Great Britain the middle classes did not come to feel that they were paying too much for the relief of those below them or for public services such as health, education and social betterment. There was little revolt against welfare programmes even when inflation in the 1970s collided with the economic euphoria of earlier years.

The West German economic miracle was a tribute to how Germans and their governments handled their resources, but it could not endow the country with resources which it had not got and these included oil and essential minerals. Like Great Britain therefore West Germany lived on exports. It was obliged to make and sell a surplus of manufactured goods in order to pay for necessary imports of raw materials and, additionally, to pay for yet other imports which were stimulated by the growth of the population and of its standards and expectations. It had to look outward. Its crucial markets were in western Europe where four fifths of its exports were sold, but continuing success would force it to look further afield – to eastern Europe or the Third World.

At the date of the Schuman proposals, a mere five years after the end of the war, Germany was catching up with France and, if still some distance behind, with Great Britain. It had half accepted, half chosen, to forego national integration and complete sovereignty (it might not possess the most modern weapons) in favour of closer association with neighbours than nineteenth-century statesmen would have thought proper. Towards the end of his life Adenauer became less fixated upon the United States. He seems to have concluded that the American phase in the history of Europe was a limited one, limited in time and diminishing (although by no means disappearing) in scope.

He steered clear of any 'special' relationship and, ever the realist, put more emphasis on Franco-German relations, particularly after de Gaulle's return to power in 1958: perhaps elder statesmen gravitate naturally to one another. The Franco-German agreement concluded in the year of his retirement was an earnest of a continuing and permanent partnership between the continent's two most substantial Powers and the core perhaps of an extended political and economic union.

Adenauer left office in 1963. He was difficult to shift, partly because – like Churchill – he had limited faith in his obvious successor but partly – also like Churchill – because he simply could not bring himself to go. A scandal in 1962 (the *Spiegel* affair) in which he and his defence minister, Franz Josef Strauss, were caught trifling with the truth, forced Strauss out of office in Bonn and eased out the chancellor himself a little later. Ludwig Erhard, the godfather of the economic miracle, had the misfortune to become chancellor in the shadow of a bigger man and at the moment when the miracle was paling. He held on until 1966 when the two major parties (Christian Democrats and Social Democrats) formed a Grand Coalition with Kurt Kiesinger as chancellor and Willi Brandt as foreign minister. It governed for three years. Brandt explored openings to the east. Romania was the most biddable of the Soviet satellites because its eagerness for western goods was supplemented by a positive enjoyment of being odd man out in the block. Least biddable was East Germany whose leaders – Walter Ulbricht and after him Erich Honecker – were stolid Stalinists, immovable until left high and dry by Gorbachev's disavowal of Stalinism after 1985. Brandt, who succeeded Kiesinger as chancellor in 1969 but had to resign in 1974 when a member of his office admitted to being a spy, secured treaties with the Soviet Union, Poland and East Germany – the core of his *Ostpolitik*. He recognized the post-Hitler frontiers in central Europe, with the reservation in the East German case that Germany might be reunited by peaceful means. His agreement with East Germany (1972) owed much to pressure from the Soviet Union which was hoping to tap German technology. A year after the treaty Brezhnev visited Bonn. Having established its *bona fides* with its former enemies in the west the new Germany could begin to mend fences to the east, even make gateways through them. The Germany of Adenauer and Brandt was, by the seventies, Europe's most influential state barring only one, and unlike Bismarck's Germany or Hitler's it scared nobody.

Nevertheless, when they cared to look into a misty future, Germany's neighbours wondered if West Germany might not one day be in a position to contemplate alternative policies and, whether or not reunited with East Germany, to recover the luxury of independent choice. This apprehension was stimulated in the 1980s by two things: the crumbling of communist rule in East Germany in 1989 which carried reunification with it, and a debate about the recent past which amounted at times to an attempt to exculpate the Nazis. This probing of the interwar years, primarily by historians and other *savants*, was a reaction against what was in their eyes an exaggerated ascription of guilt to Germany which saddled the new Germany with unfair blame and deprived the younger generation of proper pride. To redress this wrong revisionist writers and polemicists sought to explain away Nazi excesses, or even to justify them, by arguing that Nazi violence and atrocities were no more than a part of a pattern of twentieth-century violence which had been inaugurated by communism, and that even the campaign against the Jews had to be understood in the light of the Zionists' declared intention to support the western democracies against Germany in the event of war (hardly a surprising choice for them when it was expressed in 1939). These arguments amounted to a revival of the Nazi belief that Jews and communists were destroyers of civilization and should themselves be destroyed. A Germany which tolerated such views could not be accounted a good neighbour or acceptable ally.

In 1990 two things stand out: German power is once more paramount in Europe and West German democracy has been a success. All power is alarming if it belongs to somebody else and German power is additionally alarming because it is German: there is no evading this legacy of the last hundred years. The most reassuring item in the balance of fear and hope lies in the contrast between West Germany since the Second World War and Weimar Germany (not Nazi Germany). Weimar democracy was sickly and incomplete, not much loved by Germans, not much regretted; a failure. Its successor has already been in existence for four times as long and constitutes one of the most successful political and economic entities in the world. West Germany's present mood, largely a product of this success, scares none but the most paranoid or the most hagridden by the past. Yet moods change and it is wise to acknowledge that they do and to try to guard against changes for the worse. Not only is Germany capable of dominating a European states system; such a system is by its nature an invitation to assertiveness. The more prescient of Germany's neighbours foresaw, even before the war's end, that Germany might be defeated but could not be made to evaporate. They were the first to give thought to an alternative order in Europe in which Germany might recover its strength, retain its identity and pride, use its skills and resources, and yet do all these things in a context more conducive to cooperation than domineering. Their ideas foreshadowed the Community which became practical politics when France, initially hostile or indifferent, adopted them and took the lead in fashioning the novel experiment of a permanent association of less-than-sovereign states. The prime purpose of the European Community was to take the malignancy out of an inevitable resurgence of German power. The conversion of France to this scheme was an essential pre-condition. The conversion of Great Britain would redouble its prospects. But few in Great Britain perceived the political purpose of economic union and those who did perceive it mostly did not like it.

CHAPTER TEN
Great Britain Perplexed

Great Britain's recovery from the Second World War was even more robust than that of France or West Germany, but the recovery was not consolidated or sustained and the country's political touch became uncertain. In 1945 leadership in Europe was Great Britain's for the asking on the single condition of making a quick economic recovery. The recovery was made but the opportunity was allowed to pass through a mixture of political shortsightedness and economic mismanagement. The shortsightedness consisted in not believing that moves towards economic and political integration in western Europe were real, the mismanagement in failing to turn financial recovery into industrial modernization.

Great Britain's position at the end of the war was strange and misleading, and the British were themselves misled by it. On the one hand were victory and the British share in it, the gratifying lesson that even the bleakest odds may be outfaced by will and courage, a mood of generosity and confidence. On the other hand were grievous losses and another dent in the once formidable British dominance in world affairs. The Second World War, like the first, landed Great Britain with a dual task: to recoup war damage and to take up once more the longer-term business of converting an ageing industrial economy into a modern one. Both wars distorted the economy by focusing it on war needs and leaving others – notably the United States – free to acquire British overseas assets and accelerate their competition with British enterprises. Both wars also generated an intense desire to make Great Britain a better place for more of its people. This aspiration, which went back before the first war to Lloyd George's social insurance schemes and to assorted Victorian philanthropists, aimed to succour those at the bottom of the pile and to make society less unfair by modifying the extremes of wealth and poverty in terms of both incomes and opportunities. The construction of a welfare state added to the complexities of government and to the strains on the economy. The first postwar governments succeeded in mastering their urgent economic problems and in laying the foundations of a welfare state, but the restructuring of British industry lagged and when in the 1970s the general economic climate turned harsher those who were paying through taxes for the welfare state – more acutely aware of its cost than its benefits to them – became grudging. The costs of the health service in particular, which became the main focus of the conflict between the economically acceptable and the socially needful, were swollen beyond all expectations by increased longevity, the increased price of medicines and the new variety of treatments and cures.

The management of the war economy had been prudent. Nearly half of the daunting costs had been paid out of taxation, the other half by selling assets and by borrowing. The first postwar need was for money – to repay debts, restart the peacetime economy and replace lost assets. Recovery was imperilled when American Lend-Lease was abruptly terminated in August 1945 and again when the American loan negotiated by Keynes to fill the financial gap was not much more than half of what Keynes deemed necessary and was made conditional on the convertibility of sterling within one year. Only the impossibility of doing without the loan persuaded the British government to accept it on these terms and at the end of the prescribed year sterling collapsed and convertibility had to be abandoned. Great Britain was salvaged by two things: the Marshall Plan inaugurated in the next year, and the skilful direction which enabled Great Britain to dispense with Marshall aid halfway through its projected four-year span.

The Labour government allocated the greater part of Marshall funds to industrial investment and expansion. It kept interest rates low and wages under control. Taxes remained high but did not impede economic growth, which averaged 4 per cent a year. Unemployment was kept below the level marking 'full' employment. These achievements made it possible as well as desirable to devalue sterling to £1 = $2.80, a devaluation of nearly one third which dramatically boosted exports and the balance of payments without inflicting bothersome inflation.[1] Prewar productivity was reached

1.   Devaluation was a blessing heavily disguised. It was forced on a

by 1948, the aggregate value of foreign assets was regained, and prewar levels of personal incomes restored.

The key aims of the welfare state were two: full employment, defined first by Sir William Beveridge as an unemployment rate of no more than 8.5 per cent of the workforce but later redefined as 3 per cent; and a comprehensive insurance scheme, embracing the entire population and covering sickness, old age and unemployment. The Labour administrations of 1945–51 instituted measures to these ends, pursued the extension of public education introduced during the war by the Conservative R. A. Butler, and embarked on a programme of nationalization. The Bank of England (still a private company) and public utilities and services were brought into national ownership and under central control. So too, more controversially, were certain industries selected in fulfilment of long-standing Labour pledges which were neither completely coherent nor – particularly in the case of steel – broadly endorsed.

The British Labour Party was one of those things which made Great Britain different from the rest of Europe and puzzling to it. It had little socialist baggage and tended to deride ideas by calling them doctrines or, worse, dogma (Greek for doctrine). Ideologists were near the bottom of the Labour pile and intellectuals almost as suspect in the Labour Party as among Conservatives. Labour leaders were the conscious heirs of nineteenth-century reformers – champions of working-class underdogs – or radical parliamentarians who had in effect given the lie to the prevailing notion that Great Britain thrived on *laissez faire* with the law of the market modified only enough to differentiate it from the law of jungle. This was to ignore a vast and characteristic amount of Victorian legislation, such as Factory Acts and Health Acts, which clipped the unacceptable face of nineteenth-century capitalism and established in Great Britain a tradition of statute-by-statute reform. One effect was to marginalize socialism while reformers, who thought of themselves as doers and not thinkers, got on with the job of making things better for many people at the expense of some.

The pace of reform was subject to external accidents and to sound practices at home. Great Britain's promising postwar start was

reluctant and embarrassed government and regarded by the public as a humiliation. But it got rid of an over-valued pound, the albatross of a trading nation.

checked by the Korean War and the American splurge on strategic raw materials which caused the cost of imports to rise sharply, if temporarily. In the same years – the 1950s – governments began to remove and reduce obstacles to trade (chiefly import quotas), thereby taking away protection from key industries, stimulating competitive imports and eroding the favourable balance of payments. Imports of manufactured goods rose gradually but substantially until they accounted for nearly four fifths in value of all imports instead of one fifth, while the balance of payments became such an obsession with governments that in 1964 a new Labour administration resorted to unlawful measures to redress it: a general levy or surcharge on imports which contravened the rules of the GATT and had to be removed in response to international clamour. (The reimposition of selected quotas would have been legitimate.) When the levy was abandoned sterling, once more over-valued, was devalued to £1 = $2.40. This zigzag sequence of expedients did, however, put the balance of payments decisively into the black once more until the Vietnam War, like the Korean War, raised the world prices of raw materials, to the advantages of those who had them but the detriment of those including the British, who had to buy them.

The Industrial Revolution had given the economic palm to those countries with manufactured things out of other things which they imported, and of these countries Great Britain had been the one with the greenest palm. The Industrial Revolution made it the world's richest and so most powerful state – manufacturing goods in profusion, selling a handsome surplus abroad, exporting capital as well as goods, and therewith acquiring foreign assets. If there was one weakness in this position it was the narrowness of an economic base which consisted of coal and just a few industries. It was vulnerable, therefore, to the appearance of competitors in these prime areas and also to the development of different prime areas, or new products, or methods of production. A manufacturing economy fails when it is caught making the wrong things, or the right things in the wrong way, and in either case losing the export business which pays for its imports. In the first thirty years or so after the Second World War there was some adaptation but not enough to meet greatly accelerated competition. In the 1980s Margaret Thatcher turned to a radical transformation which misfired. Great Britain which, as Napoleon famously remarked, had been an emporium and then became the industrial centre of the world was to be turned, in Thatcher's vision, into a service area – an offshore island offering financial and other services, like the Cayman Islands but without the sun.

This faltering was uncharacteristic. The First World War and the Great Depression had destroyed Great Britain's ability to regulate and finance a world economy, and the Depression had ruined British trade, but both catastrophes also revealed an extraordinary British resilience. The toll of the war was three quarters of a million dead and twice as many injured; 40 per cent of shipping lost; foreign markets lost; heavy foreign debt. A boom in 1919–20 did not last. By 1925 the textile industry was down to one third of its prewar output, steel output was nearly halved, iron more than halved. Between the wars unemployment was never less than 10 per cent of the workforce, reached 22 per cent overall and 40–50 per cent in some areas or industries. When the coal mine owners proposed to cut wages by a quarter the miners had to accept. Determination to restore (in 1925) and maintain the exchange value of an overvalued pound restricted industrial exports and prevented the accumulation of savings, thus weakening defences against the coming Depression. Yet after the Depression the British government, learning from Keynes and his Swedish predecessor Knut Wicksell, reanimated the economy with remarkable speed by policies of cheap money (low interest rates), a dexterously increased money supply, a large building programme, statutory control of the resulting speculation, and protective duties (modified by discriminatory imperial preferences). These measures gave Great Britain an active economic role in a restricted economic sphere – the Empire and Commonwealth – and so abrogated Great Britain's world role in favour of something smaller but still considerable. The weakness of this conversion in scale lay in the fact that Great Britain remained crucially involved in the wider zone whose regulation it had vacated. The measures were also half measures since they were accompanied by meagre industrial retraining, no serious attack on monopolies or restrictive practices, no purposeful policies to replace industries in inevitable decline, and a blind eye to the poverty and ill-health which had been savagely aggravated by unemployment; and they were quickly followed by the second war, at the end of which old economic problems reappeared and pressure for expensive social reforms had become more insistent.

The scope of these problems was international. The British economy had long since ceased to be a discrete unit. The British industrial and commercial classes were well aware of this crucial fact. They knew that the question was not whether to operate worldwide but how best to do so in the more difficult circumstances created by relative economic decline. The British have not been as xenophobic as has been commonly made out. They have had on the contrary a worldwide vision, shared by few in Europe. Tsarist Russia had a wide vision because of its inescapable contacts with Asia from the days of the Mongols onwards, but the vision came in spasms and was usually unattractive. France, too, took the world for its oyster, but unlike Great Britain never subordinated its European concerns to global ones: it was obliged to give the security of its European land frontiers precedence over its colonial expansion. Great Britain was in the unique position of being committed economically to global policies which required a European peace for their best protection with, at the same time, the unique advantage of being able to put peace before security as long as the Channel was a military barrier: the Channel was a substitute for politicking in Europe. But paradoxically British globalism was not in the strict sense international, since there were few sovereign states in those parts of the globe where the British traded and imposed themselves. Great Britain's instinct to remain aloof from European affairs as a concomitant of imperial power and commerce made sense so long as Great Britain was a world Power, but after 1945 at the latest Great Britain was less a world Power than a European Power. The complicating factor was the fact that in spite of being no longer a first-class world Power the British remained critically involved in the world: loss of power was not accompanied by loss of interests round the world.

At this point the British were seduced by two will-o'-the-wisps. The first was the Commonwealth, a broad association of sovereign states – fifty in 1990 – which had evolved out of the British empire, a body of not inconsiderable substance and value but not a power centre or a reinforcement of the British position in the world because the Commonwealth was not united in its views or needs and least of all united behind British views. The Commonwealth was no longer the British Commonwealth, although the British sometimes treated it as though it ought to be. The British had managed to shed their colonies sooner than expected and with good grace and creditably little fuss (except in Rhodesia). Whether by accident or design – and there is little evidence of design – this was a happy outcome since the colonies were becoming expensive. Swift and amicable decolonization ensured a transfer of sovereignty with surprisingly little loss of contacts or opportunities. But as a whole the resulting Commonwealth was no more than ancillary to British international purposes and needs.

The second will-o'-the-wisp was the 'special relationship' with the United States. Between the wars Anglo-American relations had been poor and leaders on both sides were wont to speak rudely of each other, in private sometimes very rudely. The war changed that, but the special relationship created by the war was the personal one initiated by Churchill and welcomed by Roosevelt. Apart from this strange element the relationship, a military alliance, was more ordinary than special, although it did create on both sides a warm friendship at popular level. It was important during and for the war, but it was a threadbare base for postwar political or economic association. It was essentially emotional and, by representing the relationship as not far off an equal one, it obscured important realities: for example, that the British contribution to victory had been in material terms a minor one and, even before Pearl Harbor brought the United States into the fighting, heavily dependent financially on the United States. What endured was the ease of communication at many levels inherent in a common language and common experience and tradition, but this was no guarantee of common interests or viewpoints. Even during the war Roosevelt, an intensely personal politician, seemed to believe that he could achieve a special relationship with Stalin as well as with Churchill, although he did not envisage that he would thereby create a 'special' Soviet-American relationship. (Roosevelt never visited Great Britain during the war.) The British were resentfully aware of American determination to undo special economic arrangements such as imperial preferences and indeed the empire itself and to invade British economic preserves such as the Iranian oilfields, and they were also convinced, at that time correctly, that they knew more about affairs in and around Europe than Americans did. On the American side Churchill's influence over Roosevelt – for example, over priorities of war in Europe and the Pacific, over Mediterranean strategies, over the notion of pushing into central Europe from Italy through the Ljublyana Gap – annoyed other Americans, particularly Roosevelt's chiefs of staff, and although this British influence dwindled with the growing predominance of the American war effort, a sense remained of wily British self-interest not in line with American values. After the war distrust sharpened with the termination of cooperation in nuclear weaponry, rivalry for Middle East oil and power, and similar jostling for advantage in other economic areas such as civil aviation. This competitiveness co-existed nevertheless with a genuine mutual admiration, particularly in official circles and particularly so long as the wartime generations survived.

British leaders clung for decades to their belief that a special relationship existed, must never be compromised (Margaret Thatcher's regard for Ronald Reagan and her acquiescence in his sillier ideas and wilder actions was an extreme example of this abnegation of judgement) and, in peace as much as war, constituted a beacon for British foreign policy. But it degenerated into mutual backscratching. Mutual backscratching between individual leaders is not the same as a special relationship between states. As a state the United States has had a special relationship with one state only, Israel. The United States gave Israel aid exceeding $3 billion a year in spite of legislation forbidding aid to countries guilty of serious violations of human rights. It is hardly conceivable that it would have favoured any other country in this way.

The belief in a special relationship with the United States provided an alibi for Great Britain's reluctance to engage in more than secondary association with continental Europe and it goes far to explain why, when Great Britain did join the European Community, its contributions to the partnership were embarrassingly petulant. When, as the war ended, Churchill and other British statesmen feelingly acclaimed the idea of a United Europe, their rhetoric was either marginal and eccentric or, in Churchill's case, a disguised plea for burying Franco-German hatchets. Whatever continental Europeans might suppose, the victorious British had no thought of joining a European union of any kind. They applauded the formation of Benelux (1947) without feeling that this example had anything to do with them, and they hardly even noticed the Franco-Italian customs union formed a year later. In 1950 joining the Schuman Coal and Steel Community was never seriously considered by the British cabinet. A rationalization of continental coal and steel production was interesting only in so far as it raised the question whether this new consortium would undercut the British steel industry which the British, about to open new steel works at Margam in Wales, believed it would not. Competition, not collaboration, was the watchword so long as production was thought to be short of demand.

The British attitude to a European association began to shift in the 1960s, not so much because the British caught the exciting vision which had led six of their neighbours to concert the European Economic Community in 1957 but because they calculated after a few years' reflection that they would do better inside a community than outside. EFTA (the European Free Trade Association), the alternative sponsored by Great Britain as a way of getting free trade without economic union, was not a success. But it took Great Britain ten years to gain entry to the EEC, followed by a further period of haggling over a revision of the terms of entry, a protracted and less than wholehearted courtship.

Two British applications to join (1961, 1967) were repelled by de Gaulle, ostensibly on the grounds that the British were asking for too much special treatment, more profoundly because de Gaulle regarded Great Britain as an American cat's paw. De Gaulle's first veto, at the beginning of 1963, was caused (or justified) by the Kennedy–Macmillan meeting at Nassau, where Kennedy traded Polaris to Great Britain in return for the commitment of the British nuclear force to Nato. At Macmillan's suggestion Kennedy made a similar offer to de Gaulle who, however, rejected it because it would have made the French nuclear forces dependent on the United States. The second British application was made by a Labour government. The Labour Party and the trade unions were divided, but Harold Wilson became persuaded that life outside the EEC was becoming too difficult. The 1960s were cruel to myths: the happy notion of Great Britain as an independent offshore island like Japan was too clearly a mirage; the Commonwealth, equally clearly, was not a back-up organization for British influence in the world, and British trade with its members, white as well as black (Australia, for example, as well as Nigeria), was declining; the special relationship with the United States came under unprecedented strain during the war in Vietnam.

De Gaulle was at first still hostile, restating his original objections and adding that Great Britain's accession would do the Community more harm than good because of the poor state of the British economy (the pound was devalued in November 1967). Yet de Gaulle appeared not inflexible and he indicated to the British ambassador in Paris that the time for British accession might be ripening. Ineptly these bilateral exchanges were relayed by the British to the other five members of the Community who interpreted de Gaulle's overtures as a bid for a Franco-British takeover of the Community. Their alarm and anger aborted whatever might have been in the making.

But de Gaulle's days were numbered and his successor, Georges Pompidou, together with a new British prime minister, Edward Heath, switched the debate from broad principles to more detailed and laborious argumentation over knottier problems: safeguards for some Commonwealth products, a specially long transitional period for agriculture, special limitations on the British contribution to the common budget. For whether or not Great Britain was a special case in de Gaulle's sense, it was a special case in other respects. It was joining a largely agricultural community, far more agricultural than the British economy; it traded more extensively outside Europe than did its prospective partners; it cherished traditions of cheap food. It would incur disproportionate burdens under the rules of the Common Agricultural Policy because of its dependence on extra-European foodstuffs, and it would make a disproportionate contribution to the common budget unless it were granted lengthy periods for adaptation. Pompidou and Heath surmounted these problems and Great Britain (with Ireland and Denmark) became a member of the EEC at the beginning of 1972, but Heath then lost office (1974) and his Labour successors felt impelled to maintain that they could have done better. Wilson contrived to satisfy half his party by accepting British membership and the other half by renegotiating the terms and submitting them to a referendum which endorsed membership by a margin of two to one.

If Great Britain had joined the EEC at its birth the Community's nucleus would have been stronger in material resources and human skills (administrative, mechanical, technical); in broadening the Community's base and perhaps its vision; and in giving additional reality to a tenuous experiment. By fighting shy of this experiment and then joining as a postulant instead of a founder Great Britain arrived in critical rather than constructive mood, at a time when the original members had had more than a decade of working together, and when the world economy was about to move into recession and uncertainty. Great Britain thus missed the tide in two senses. It proved on arrival a *mauvais coucheur*, an impression accentuated in the 1980s by Thatcher who was incurably xenophobic and failed to persuade her partners that she had any use or liking for people who did not see things exactly her way. Europeans who had longed for British association in earlier years began to wonder where the balance between pros and cons lay.

Yet the British should not be judged too harshly for their failure to perceive where their best interests were. They were being asked to abandon the ideas not of a lifetime but of five centuries. The English drift away from the continent began with military disengagement at the end of the Hundred Years War. Thereafter the English

Channel was magnified from a geographical fault into a cultural and political bastion. At the Reformation English Protestantism, while less extreme than some, was more thorough: English Roman Catholics became insignificant in a sense which was never true of any equivalent religious or cultural minority in French or German lands. In the Industrial Revolution England was an early starter and for a time uniquely successful. In the spread of European imperialism England's achievement was the most resplendent and the most distracting from continental affairs. The English were not particularly hostile to Europeans – they were in fact less hostile to them than they were to one another – but they were conscious of differences which they readily construed as superiority and, sometimes discreetly but sometimes not, developed an aloofness and an ignorance which could be more irritating than open hostility. They also became richer and were inclined to ascribe this good fortune to virtue. By the twentieth century these idiosyncrasies were dissolving. Religious differences had ceased to count. The Industrial Revolution had become common property in western Europe. Great Britain's economic dominance was eroded and its empire disappeared. Communications, notably the telephone and air travel, cut the Channel down to size. Even the airs of superiority were tempered as their material base lapsed.

The 1980s were dominated by the powerful personality but less powerful intelligence of Margaret Thatcher. Thatcher was no ordinary politician. In the first place she was a woman and female heads of government were still rare, earlier examples being restricted to Bandaranaike, Gandhi and Meir. She was also exceptionally successful, politically. Beginning in 1979 she won three British general elections in a row, an unprecedented achievement. (Another woman, Vigdis Finnbogadottir won three successive presidential elections in Iceland in the same decade.) She was a politician of exceptional determination. Her talents were for fighting, fewer for anything else. She brought to British politics a crusading spirit and a sense of righteousness not seen for a long time. She disliked debate, despised consensus and regarded concession as tribute paid to virtue by vice or weakness: she was neither a true House of Commons figure nor a good performer in its debates, which she increasingly shunned. Partnership was suspect if the other partners were less than acquiescent. She was outstandingly good at tackling problems but less good at understanding what the problems were. She was a thorough nationalist except in relation to the United States, to which she was disposed to be subservient: for the discredited slogan My Country Right or Wrong she seemed to substitute, in deference especially to Ronald Reagan, the even stranger device Your Country Right or Wrong. (But she was put out by his invasion of Grenada without notice, contested his imposition of economic sanctions on the Soviet Union and Poland in 1982 and did not conceal her dismay at his erratic behaviour during his meeting with Gorbachev at Reykjavik in 1986.) She accepted the possible usefulness to Great Britain of the European Community, partly on the basis that what had been forged could not easily be unforged, but she resolutely resisted any diminution of national sovereignty, regarded national and international interests as basically antithetical, and treated Community meetings as battlegrounds where it was her business to fight her colleagues in the British interest rather than to discuss with them common interests. She had difficulty in concealing her impatience with partners or colleagues who failed to see that she was right and they were wrong, with the result that even when she was broadly right (over the Common Agricultural Policy, for example, and the British contribution to the Community's budget) she got less than her due because her tactics did more to irritate than persuade. She presented an image of Great Britain which was not amiable, intelligent or sensible. Forthright, vigorous, very hard working, courageous – she was nevertheless humourless, sometimes vindictive and increasingly wilful. She could change her position but not her mind. Her speeches were crisp and clear but she had nothing interesting to say. She was unfairly handicapped by her sex since her male colleagues lacked the guts to oppose her and her male supporters beyond the fringes of government – particularly in the press – revived the vice of toadyism.

Thatcher's limitations were most damaging in economic affairs. She inherited an unenviable state of affairs. The promise of the 1950s had not been fulfilled. France, Italy and Japan had joined the United States and Germany in successful challenges to British manufacturers and exporters. In motor cars, aviation engineering, plastics, electrical goods and equipment, electronics, computers and drugs British firms were left behind; after spending huge sums they were forced to abandon the race or sell themselves to foreigners because they had failed to win an adequate share of world markets. The longer-term problems of the economy had not been purposefully tackled for an accumulation of reasons: the timidity of politicians, the complexity of the problems, the painfulness of remedies and, paradoxically, the resilience of the economy after the war which nurtured a degree of false optimism and allowed painful measures to be postponed. The Labour Party, although ostensibly *dirigiste*, did not believe in planning and had nothing comparable with the Monnet Plan. The resumption of industrial growth by 1948 had proved both an achievement and a trap. It allowed people to sidestep the fact that much of the industrial infrastructure, devoted to old enterprises and old methods, was rusting.

Regeneration required a degree of courage verging on insensitivity, coupled with skills of peculiar sensitivity. It was a task more likely to be performed by a Conservative than a Labour leader, as was shown when Harold Wilson attempted to review and restrict the powers and privileges of trade unions. The unions had become a fairly solid power block whose political impact was negative: they rarely got what they wanted in major industrial disputes or in legislation but, when in substantial agreement among themselves and particularly when Labour was in office, they had collectively enough influence to stop changes which they did not like. A number of them were run undemocratically and the spectacle of a handful of leaders casting block votes (sometimes against the wishes of their own members) was attractive to nobody but themselves. A few unions had substantial power, notably in public utilities where they could monopolize the labour force in an industrial monopoly. Wilson propounded reforms but lacked the determination or courage to persevere with them in the face of opposition in his own party. Thatcher went to the other extreme. One of her virtues when she first became Prime Minister was the bluntness with which she acknowledged the long-term weaknesses of the economy and her evident determination not to be deflected from doing something about them. In relation to organized labour she had no opposition in her own party; she was herself attracted by the combative nature of the exercise and conscious of extensive public support, accentuated by the serious violence engendered during recent industrial disputes. She had, therefore, no difficulty in introducing and carrying legislation to impose drastic changes in the internal affairs of unions and in their conduct of industrial disputes (notably the right to picket) and to strip unions of their assets if they exceeded their newly constricted rights. She used the need to curb violence as a means to curb powers. These measures, together with the advent of massive unemployment, curbed wage claims and strikes, dulled the spirit of the unions and turned some of them against one another.

The power of the unions, whether exaggerated or not, had two aspects. It harassed management and it contributed to cost inflation by pushing up wages. British management was much criticized and Thatcher's assault on unions and their leaders (often designated bosses or, even more pejoratively, barons) was designed to give managers the freedom to manage and to improve their performance. For a time it did so, but since workers may have genuine grievances as well as cussedness, managers cannot be permanently freed from industrial strife without the abolition of the workers' one effective weapon, the right to strike; and although proposals were mooted to this end the government baulked at so radical a transformation which would elevate boards of directors from a managerial to a command role unbecoming a democracy in peacetime. The second issue, control of wages and so of prices, was regarded by nearly all Conservatives (and not a few on the left) as unattainable by direct government intervention. Incomes policies being therefore ridiculed and ruled out, government was left with the instrument of monetary squeeze and its inescapable accompaniment, unemployment.[2]

2.   The aim of an incomes policy is to regulate rises in wages and salaries in such a way as to ensure that the aggregate increase in wage bills does not exceed the aggregate value of increased output. If and so far as industrial costs rise faster than industrial output prices rise too. This is cost inflation. The prerequisites for an incomes policy are, first, techniques for measuring current economic performance and, secondly, mechanisms for adjusting the overall increase in wages accordingly. These mechanisms may be set in a legal framework but need not be: a statutory framework is no more than an additional constraint towards compelling compromise between competing economic forces – employees who want more pay, employers who have to find the money, and government which is responsible for balancing economic pressures at national level. The obligation to discuss, followed if necessary by obligatory and binding arbitration, may be imposed by contract or statute; what matters is that it should come to seem normal. The biggest obstacle to an incomes policy is that it operates over the whole economy by seeking to regulate wage increases in a multitude of separate industries which themselves are composed of a multitude of separate companies. No incomes policy will produce a precise equation between aggregate rises in pay and output, but it may produce a tolerable approximation and has done so in a number of countries: for example, West Germany from the middle of this century, Australia from its beginning. In Great

But disciplining labour was not the sole or even the main way to make the economy healthy. Margaret Thatcher's economic qualifications were no lower than those of most her predecessors but her drive was as narrow as it was sharp. She was obsessed by inflation, which she identified as an economic problem on its own rather than as one problem within a complex of problems. This obsession was an instinctive and not surprising reaction to the rate of inflationary growth in the 1970s. Europeans, other than Germans, had had little experience of galloping inflation which they supposed to be a phenomenon peculiar to incompetent and

Britain incomes policies were effective in the immediate postwar years and in the lifetime of the Prices and Incomes Board (1967–70), but both experiments exposed their limitations. They were introduced in special circumstances: in the first case the aftermath of war and a continuing mood of self-abnegation and discipline; in the second case because enough people were scared about the state of the economy – but they did not stay scared long enough to allow the policy to go on. A few years after Edward Heath abolished the Prices and Incomes Board in 1970 Harold Wilson's Labour government tried to create new mechanisms based on a quasi-contract with the unions, but half the government and more than half the union leaders were mistrustful, Wilson retreated rather than split his party, and the policy was destroyed when the Ford Motor Company gave its workers rises of 17 per cent in the face of the norm of 5 per cent prescribed by the government. These failures reinforced the view that incomes policies cannot work and left the way clear for the next Conservative government to adopt the alternative of doing nothing directly to regulate the pay–output equation. On this view pay rises in particular companies and above commensurate increases in production had to be resisted by the particular company which, if it so raised wages, must also reduce its workforce; only by paying the higher wage to fewer people could it keep costs, and so prices, down. Unemployment replaced incomes policy as the mechanism for evading inflation, and full employment as a national policy had to be abandoned on the grounds that it was incompatible with price stability.

A subsidiary absurdity of the policies tried in Great Britain was the habit of calculating wage rises as percentages of current wages. This procedure necessarily widened the gap between the better paid and the lower-paid and, when applied to cost-of-living increases as distinct from merit increases, carried the implication that the increased cost of necessities was ten times greater for the man with ten times greater pay; that the same loaf cost the rich man more than it cost the poor.

venal Latin Americans; and they were commensurately alarmed. For Thatcher here was another battle. She was not so much a monetarist as a deflater. Inflation was a dragon to be fought and slain. But tackling economic issues as though they were military encounters was, if bracing, not sensible and could turn into a massacre. The theoretical base for what followed was a simplistic caricature of monetarist thinking. It precipitated disasters which the government itself did not foresee and, even when more than half abandoned, continued to thwart recovery.

The monetarist debate is about how a money economy, as distinct from a barter economy, works. That the quantity of money in circulation greatly affects the way the economy works is a proposition denied by no economist; all economists are in some degree monetarists. But some ascribe a bigger role to the money supply than do others. Monetarists may even ascribe to the volume of money so preponderant a role as to exclude other factors in relation to fluctuations in prices. Thus a pure monetarist (if there be such a person) would maintain that an increase in the money supply has a direct and precisely commensurate effect on prices, discounting altogether the effects of other factors such as, for example, fluctuations in exchange rates. He would then conclude that control over the money supply suffices to control price inflation. He might add that the money supply is the only economic factor which government can control.

The modern debate over the role of money stems from the work of Keynes in the 1930s which vigorously attacked prevailing theories about money but did not annihilate them. Keynes was an exceptional man. He was a generalist rather than a specialist but so clever that he might be taken for a specialist as well as a generalist – a combination not unlikely to cause irritation. He was by nature an intellectual explorer, by early accident a political polemicist, and through practice an able administrator who took as much delight in running things as in thinking about them. He was also a compelling writer and articulate speaker at both recondite and popular levels. Culturally and politically a liberal, he was a believer in the effectiveness of free market forces and the capitalist system, but in the 1930s – his two principal books on economic theory appeared in 1930 and 1936 – he contested the view that the market and the system worked automatically and satisfactorily if left to themselves.

As an economist Keynes was formed in the classical school. He never doubted that the money supply had a major impact on the level of prices and employment, but he denied a basic precept of academic economists: their belief that a money economy tends to equilibrium through market forces. He called in question the effect and benignity of these forces and so postulated a need for some intervention by government in the working of the economy.

The starting point of his argument was the special nature of a money economy in which – in contrast to a barter economy – people get money and not goods out of an economic transaction and may decide to keep some of it. If they do, they reduce demand and so prices and, in Keynes' argument, do so cumulatively and without an automatic redressing factor: lower demand leading to lower output and lower employment without automatic redress. So government needs to intervene in order to reverse progressive regression. Manipulation of the money supply was one of the available means but not the only one. Keynes regarded this means as always crude and often unnecessarily destructive.

Keynes' concentration on these problems was caused by his temperament. He was an academic with a strong concern, part civic responsibility and part intellectual keenness, with the practical application of academic expertise; and this proclivity was sharpened by his revulsion against the unemployment of the Depression years. He questioned and revolted against the notion that an ailing economy can be cured only by creating massive unemployment which he regarded as an affront to human intelligence, socially horrible and economically wasteful.[3] He argued that to squeeze and deflate an economy could do more economic harm than good; that unemployment beyond a certain point was economically malign as well as socially evil and that it should not be regarded as a

---

3.   Keynes distinguished two kinds of unemployed: those who did not work because they had too high an opinion of their worth and so chose not to do the work on offer at the going price, and those who could not get work through no fault of their own. He believed that the former amounted to about 5 per cent of the workforce and that it was the business of government to coax or bully them into contributing their labour to the community. He implicitly asserted that unemployment above a certain level might be a more serious economic disaster than inflation above a certain level. He did not accept the more traditional view that any degree of unemployment to eliminate inflation must be endured – that is to say, that in economic straits the poor pay and nothing can be done about it, that in Thatcher's famous phrase 'there is no alternative' to deflation by monetary squeeze.

passing pain to be endured of necessity with gritted teeth and lachrymose rhetoric; that it was avoidable without recourse to uncontrolled inflation. He sought a formula for determining the point at which deflation became counterproductive and a point at which measures to create jobs automatically created unacceptable inflation. Keynes enlarged the sphere of economics by stressing what was often only reluctantly perceived: that economic, social and political questions could not be treated in separate departments either by academics or by politicians. Some of the distrust which he roused, particularly among politicians, arose from the fact that he himself was more attuned to the social than the political end of the socio-economic–political spectrum. He was neither a good politician nor fond of politicians. He also offended economists by seeming to inject irrelevant dimensions into their studies.

Keynes' influence was so magnetic that his theories attained almost the status of axioms, particularly in Great Britain during his later years and after his death in 1946. But in Great Britain and in the United States, particularly in the University of Chicago (Professor Milton Friedman leading), older orthodoxies persisted and they were reinvigorated, within and then beyond academic fields, by economic failures and disappointments in the 1960s and 1970s. These neo-monetarists maintained that Keynes himself and his post-Keynesian followers had gone too far in their depreciation of the role of money. They sought, therefore, to redress this imbalance by re-emphasizing the primacy of monetary factors and by denying the ill effects of an unregulated system (unregulated, that is, by anything other than control over the money supply). Their message to politicians – or the message that politicians thought they were getting – was that interference with the economy otherwise than by the money supply was either otiose or harmful, but in applying this message politicians ran into two difficulties. Curbing the money supply entailed defining money, and monetarists did not agree on how this should be done. Keynes for one had stressed that in a modern economy money means more than the sum of coins and paper in circulation but what should be added was contentious – and was varied more than once by the Thatcher administrations.[4] If, however, money could not be defined, then

4.   The problem was not modern. Sources of money such as cheques, bills of lading, contracts of insurance, etc., came into use in Italy in the Middle Ages. Capitalism attained its enormous force in the modern world by adding credit to cash as a means for money transactions.

neither could its supply be controlled, since it is not possible to control something which cannot be defined or measured. (In practice measures aimed at controlling the money supply proved to restrict it on one definition of money but to do the reverse on another.) A second obstacle to applying monetarist recipes was their cost. Deflating an economy is comparatively simple, but deflating it in such a way as to cure ills without creating worse ills is not easy, for deflation which is too severe or too precipitate beggars businesses, makes the survivors uncompetitive, puts people out of work and by raising interest rates axes investment and savings, crucifies borrowers and wrecks the external balance of payments – and revives inflation. All these things the Thatcher administration did in the cause of reducing inflation which nevertheless in her third term was on the rise once more.

The application of monetarist measures was not new in Great Britain. What was new was Thatcher's increasingly insistent claim that inflation must be controlled only by high interest rates. A foretaste of the problem occurred in 1957 when, in response to a sudden drain on the reserves and rising inflation, the Chancellor Peter Thorneycroft demanded a credit squeeze, an investment freeze, higher Bank Rate and cuts in government spending on forces' pay and health and other social services. Macmillan, and a majority in his cabinet rejected this medicine, all the Treasury ministers resigned, and in the event the situation was retrieved without the extreme measures at which Macmillan had baulked at least as much on grounds of social as economic policy. In the 1960s a Labour Chancellor, Roy Jenkins, used monetary and fiscal instruments. Edward Heath and his chancellor, Anthony Barber, then presided over a boom in credit and speculation, an ominous conjunction since the new money made available by the credit boom went not into making things but into speculation, particularly speculation in property. The bank rate rose to 11.5 per cent. Numerous banks collapsed and their depositors and creditors had to be rescued at a cost of at least £1 billion. The pound had to be floated. Labour returned to power in the resulting turmoil and in the middle of a world recession. In the mid-1970s the price of oil quadrupled in a matter of months and shot up again in the aftermath of the revolution in Iran when it passed $40 a barrel on the spot market where it had been little more than $2 a decade earlier. Governments were perplexed whether to meet the increased cost by inflating expenditure or to cut expenditure by cutting oil imports and domestic economic activity. Since other imported primary commodities also rose steeply in price in these years every importer of raw materials was faced with the menace of inflation at alarming rates – a problem which did not abate until the 1980s when these prices were sharply reversed to the great relief of the industrialized world. In these countries the chief source of inflation was external to them and so was the relief when it came. In Great Britain another Labour Chancellor, Denis Healey, had recourse to monetary restraints and by the late 1970s industrial investment and GDP were rising again, the bank rate was back to 5 per cent, the balance of payments was in surplus and unemployment was falling, but the Labour government's attempts to control wages and prices failed with the result that the economy was threatened with its perennial bugbear, cost inflation.

The failures of the 1960s and 1970s paved the way for the disordered reaction of the 1980s under a prime minster who was determined to be as unlike her predecessors as possible. Harold Wilson and Edward Heath, who between them spanned the years 1964–76, were intelligent and industrious prime ministers who nevertheless failed in two important respects. They did not command the loyalty of their cabinet colleagues and their attempts to find a workable pay policy collapsed. Both took office with every appearance of decisiveness but were branded as ditherers before they left it. Wilson became prime minister with an exceptionally promising record but in the knowledge that most of the men and women whom he picked for his cabinet had voted for somebody else as the leader of the Labour Party on the death of Hugh Gaitskell. His determination to hold his party together – a determination which, given his own ambivalent position, inclined him to weld or patch rather than lead – had much to do with his failure to press trade-union reform or to maintain control over the rate of wage increases. Heath's pay policy was torpedoed by his colleagues when it seemed to be succeeding and was followed by a disastrous consumer boom engendered by his Chancellor of the Exchequer. Wilson's Chancellor, Denis Healey, on resuming office recovered control of prices and inflation, but only temporarily. A policy of restraint by annual agreements with the unions was increasingly difficult to maintain and ended when, at the third time of asking, prosperous companies such as Ford preferred to concede large pay rises rather than risk strikes to please the government. Upon Wilson's sudden resignation Callaghan backed spending cuts and monetary curbs but the government had lost control of industrial policy and lost a general election in 1979 after a winter of alarming industrial strife.

On taking power the Conservatives' economic task was to intensify Healey's recourse to monetary measures but for political and ideological reasons Mrs Thatcher wished to characterize her policies as diametrically different from Labour's and she carried these policies to calamitous extremes. Raising interest rates to 15 per cent the Conservatives condemned Great Britain to a needlessly deep depression, wiped out a fifth of manufacturing capacity and created levels of unemployment from which they would have shrunk if they had realized what they were doing. The main source of these disasters was an opinionated, helter-skelter imposition of half-baked remedies: the bull let loose in the china shop was not even a well-groomed bull. Inflation, inherited from Labour at 10.3 per cent, rose to 22 per cent and was still above the Labour rate three years after the change of government. Direct taxes were cut but the cuts were financed by increases in indirect taxes (VAT was doubled) and it has been plausibly conjectured that only the aberration of the Falklands War saved Thatcher from electoral defeat.

By 1982 the government felt compelled to abandon its monetarist shibboleths and its so-called Medium Term Financial Strategy – devised to cover this retreat by Nigel Lawson when still deputy to Sir Geoffrey Howe at the Exchequer. No monetary targets had been made and some overshot by 100 per cent. Although new targets were set and new ways of measuring money were invoked, policies degenerated into ways of handling figures rather than measures to improve them. Financial institutions, including the Bank of England, openly admitted the mistakes of earlier policies and the government abandoned tight money as an election approached. This manoeuvre was assisted by three pieces of singular good fortune – singular in the sense that no other country enjoyed all three. They were the reduction in world prices of oil and other commodities, the flow into the Treasury of taxes and special levies on North Sea oil, and the proceeds of privatization. The reversal in commodity prices began around 1980; the last two bonuses averaged respectively £12.6 billion and £5 billion a year in the 1980s. The privatization programme, adopted initially for ideological reasons, became a fiscal necessity in order to meet government spending which Thatcher had promised but failed to reduce (as a proposition of GDP). It was justified by the argument that by taking the proceeds of privatization into the budgetary accounts the government reduced the amount it had to borrow to balance these accounts (the Public Sector Borrowing Requirement – PSBR) and so reduced inflation; but this argument was weak, if not entirely fallacious, since the expansion of the money supply came overwhelmingly from the private, not from the public, sector.

Inflation, measured by the retail price index, came down to 2.3 per cent and the stricken economy began to recover, even to boom, but the surge was misdirected and brief. Growth at around 4–5 per cent was mainly – about two thirds – in service sectors and not in manufacturing. The revitalization of industry was once more missed and when recovery wavered the government's single-minded insistence on trying to regulate it by interest rates alone produced a new bout of high interest rates which hobbled indus-trial growth. By treating as income not only the ephemeral oil taxes but also the once-for-all proceeds of privatization the Chancellor of the Exchequer was able to claim that he had balanced the budget while at the same time reducing taxes. In fact, although income taxes – particularly the higher-rate taxes on the rich – had been substantially reduced, Thatcher's promise to reduce the overall burden of taxation was not redeemed and as she entered triumphantly on her third consecutive term as Prime Minister investment in industry was still no higher than it had been in 1979 and in the intervening years there had been no net investment at all; much of British industry was reduced to being uncompetitive abroad; the balance of payments was reversing into unprecedented deficit;[5] public health and education, research and the economic infrastructure were in decay; and the cycle of recession set in motion in 1979–81 was beginning again. Thatcherism offered alter-native ways to death: on the one hand renewed inflation, on the other tackling inflation by raising interest rates and therewith the exchange value of the pound and so inflicting on industry an over-valued currency, a hurdle which no country dependent on exports can live with. Most damaging in the longer term was the failure of the new radical Conservatives to comprehend that in a

5.   So was the American, but the two cases were different. As the most productive economy in the world the United States could attract foreign funds with relative ease, but foreign investors and speculators found sterling much less attractive than the dollar. The vice of American administrations was profligacy in an economy of plenty; the vice of Thatcher's administrations was squeezing productivity and the tax base to create a straitened economy.

complex modern society some things cannot pay for themselves, notably education and the infrastructure of road, rail and other forms of communication, and that attempts to make them do so are crippling.

Abroad this wayward performance caused wonderment and doubts about the value of the British connection. These doubts were intensified by Thatcher's rising hostility to the aims of the European Community and her brusqueness towards European leaders, in evident contrast to her adulation of Ronald Reagan. Thatcher wanted, and was right to want, the best of all worlds but trying to get the best of two incompatible worlds is a folly that must lead to tears. Thatcher wanted the benefits of European association without the clogs, but the association in the making – the only one on offer – was not one in which economic integration could be divorced from sizeable political, organizational and legal implications: the treaty creating the Community said as much and Great Britain had adhered to this treaty. How far and how fast economic integration might require political integration was uncertain, not so much because of varying and fluctuating will in the several national capitals but because what was being constructed was without precise precedent. Thatcher rightly derided concepts of European union akin to the United States of America, but this kind of union was neither practicable nor advocated: it was a red herring. By asserting that such a union was to be ruled out for her lifetime she was expressing a fairly widespread English distrust of any form of internationalism which trenched on British sovereignty, particularly in defence and economic policies and notwithstanding that British independence in both areas was long past. But this opposition necessarily diminished Great Britain's power to influence the shape and pace of developments within the Community to which Great Britain was bound by treaty and by self-interest; revived continental suspicions of British commitment to a truly give-and-take partnership; and raised the question how far British participation was worth the sniping and subversion emanating from London. Thatcher marginalized Great Britain.

Yet the lasting effects of Thatcherism could be exaggerated. A country which had recovered from the Second World War might weather Thatcherism, even though the latter catastrophe lasted twice as long. Much of the economic damage was inflicted over a short period at the beginning of the *Thatcherzeit*. Missed opportunities might never be wholly retrieved and Great Britain's position among industrialized states might have been lastingly impaired, but a considerable part of the total cost of Thatcherism lay in a congenital failure to count, or to care much about, the social cost of economic experiment and mismanagement; and social damage, however deplorable, is not the same as economic damage. Once the economy had been redefined by expelling several million people from it, what was left recovered for a while, so that the straitened British economy began to grow once more and to grow briskly. The dominant question was not whether this was so but whether it was growing in the right way and whether the growth would continue. The Thatcherite version of monetarism had been gradually and stealthily diluted. Overall growth looked promising, even if too little of it was industrial. On the other hand the belief (another article of the Thatcherite faith) that yesterday's industries could be replaced not by tomorrow's industries but by services from banking to tourism was a forlorn hope since, quite apart from the generally lower returns in the service sector, Great Britain's share in the worldwide provision of financial service had fallen in the postwar years by more than a half. By 1990 invisible exports were not only failing to cover the deficit on trade but were in sight of, or actually in, deficit themselves for the first time in two centuries, thus producing a cumulative deficit on payments forcing down the value of sterling which could be maintained only by raising interest rates as a counter-attraction in the short term to the long-term decline in the acceptability of sterling at its current rate. The belief that London might provide financial services on a par with Wall Street and Tokyo was a lingering remnant of the post-imperial delusion which gave the British the Suez and Falkland wars: the replacement of manufacturing by Disneylands was a desperate illusion. The unreality and uncertainties in the British situation were most clearly shown after Thatcher's third electoral victory in 1987. Cuts in personal taxes, both before and after the election, gave half the country a feeling of well-being but also swelled a consumer boom which had already been set in train by the removal of restraints on credit. For the first time in its recorded history the nation was living beyond its income. Nemesis hovered as this boom, which a truncated industry could not satisfy, swelled imports, more than nullified a rising tide of exports, and so threatened to renew inflation, dearer money, the squeeze on industry and high unemployment. Electoral calculations had triggered a second recession just as some recovery from the devastation of 1979–81 was appearing. Penal interest rates made loans lethal. A capitalist system which had flourished mightily on the invention and expansion of credit was being ruined by the cost of credit. The outstanding feature of Thatcher's stewardship was instability: wide fluctuations in the rate of inflation, in interest rates, in the balance of payments and even in the money supply.

The most unsettling thing about the new conservatives' revolution was that it was no revolution, only a conservatism which dodged the underlying problems. After a decade of Thatcherism these problems – the renewal of industry and its competitiveness, employment, the scope and quality of education and research – were the same except for the passage of lost years. Faced with the central question of how to combine price stability with economic growth the government had been able to achieve sometimes the one and sometimes the other but never both. This failure was compounded by disarray in government as disputes between the Chancellor of the Exchequer and the Prime Minister's personal economic adviser became public abroad as well as at home and the Prime Minister herself appeared unable, because ill equipped, to decide between them. The British economy's underlying malady was cost inflation, for which the Thatcherite remedy at the beginning of the decade was an indiscriminate attack on industry and, when the symptoms reappeared at the end of the decade, a campaign *faute de mieux* to stifle retail trade through high interest rates. These remedies aggravated the malady.

Thatcherism, however, was more than radical economics. It was no less essentially an attempt at social transformation. The sources of this venture, whose thrust was more felt than formulated, were both deep and recent. At one level it was a reaction against the trivialities of the Macmillan–Wilson era, but it was also and more profoundly an assertion of the values and claims of the class or sub-class which Thatcher herself personified – that section of the middle classes (the commercial rather than the professional element in the bourgeoisie) which rejected the synthesis of the upper middle and upper classes which had constituted the ruling class of the nineteenth and twentieth centuries. Thatcherites resented the exclusivity and pretensions of this ruling class and were impatient with its values and attitudes. At the core of their challenge was the belief that money is the measure of most things, and this commercial ideology was applied with a drive as determined and narrow as Lenin's doctrine of democratic centralism, with similar destructiveness, with increasingly authoritarian by-products and with increasing resort to secrecy in the exercise of executive power. The Thatcherite state was characterized by an overweening central executive which neutered local government, sought to use the law and the judiciary for its social and political purposes, harried broadcasting and the press, curtailed freedom of expression through old and new secrecy laws, and discarded the traditional British principle of government through checks and balances. Thatcherism therefore was a belated British example of a more general trend in twentieth-century Europe, of which a mild and ephemeral example was Poujadist petty bourgeoisism in France in the 1950s. But the principal prototype was provided by Benito Mussolini, the self-important peasant's son who regarded the Italian establishment as flabby and negative, was much given to swatting his colleagues and replacing them by ill-chosen mediocrities, was ignorant of the world beyond his own country but fascinated by it and eager to remodel it, and entertained grand ideas for restructuring society – particularly by eliminating socialism (by, in his case, the crudest methods). Yet the new conservatives, in Italy and elsewhere, were not admirers of capitalism, whose chiefs they distrusted. Their radicalism was destructive, without an intelligible long-term programme and, as the Italian example well demonstrated, tended to decline into pointless tinkering with state institutions and public services. What the modern industrial state needs is the demolition neither of socialism nor of capitalism. Socialism and capitalism are not alternatives. Capitalism is a way of organizing the production of wealth, the most effective way of doing so in the modern world. But it is not concerned with the distribution of the wealth and the more successful it is in creating wealth the more reprehensible does the inequitable distribution of it appear. Capitalism does not pretend to be about the distribution of wealth but it gets the blame for blatant unfairness. Socialism, which is about the distribution of wealth, is therefore a necessary corrective to capitalism – necessary both in absolute moral terms and to the acceptability of capitalism. Attempts to eliminate the one or the other are equally hare-brained.

Thatcher fell from power in 1990, abruptly, when half her own party in the House of Commons revolted against her in an accumulation of grievances: the onset of a recession, obtuseness over Europe, a too blatant scorn of her colleagues and the principles of cabinet government, and the prospect of electoral defeat. She had made a large mark as a phenomenon in politics, but when she was forced unwillingly to resign none of the contestants for her place was in political terms a true successor and in spite of her evidently positive qualities she was more likely to be remembered for her personality than her achievements. Great Britain's declining strength and peevish temper under her rule had consequences for the world as well as for Great Britain itself. A marginalized Great Britain meant a diminished western Europe and a distorted European Community. A Community without a substantial and reliable British component must carry less weight in the world. It could give Germany a position at once too commanding in western Europe and not solid enough in Europe as a whole or in the world. With such a distorted Community Germany might be pressed to supplement a Franco–German entente in the west with a Russo-German entente in central and eastern Europe. British prevarications over the Community, by delaying its maturity, forced on Germany the need to develop eastern policies while the policies of western Europe were uncomfortably fluid.

CHAPTER ELEVEN

The European Community

The European Community, created in 1957 by a treaty signed by six states, was a logical expansion of the European Coal and Steel Community, created in 1951 by the same six states. A European Atomic Community was created at the same date as the Economic Community. All three were merged in 1967. On the surface they were industrial and economic associations but they had also a portentous political origin. If on the one hand they aimed to profit their members materially through economic cooperation, they enshrined also a novel attempt to deal with Europe's perennial problem of the single overmighty state. They looked forward to a time when Germany would once more be in a position to rule the roost and might wish to do so.

The first move towards this permanent partnership between European states was tentative, limited and largely political in inspiration. In 1943 Belgium mooted a plan for a customs union with the Netherlands and Luxembourg, which among other things was a device to bring pressure to bear on Great Britain to pay attention to the views of these smaller states on how Germany, their large and economically essential neighbour, should be treated after the war. The Dutch in particular did not want Germany to be pauperized and went so far as to renounce any claims to reparations in return for a small cession of territory. The Belgians, if more slowly, came to the same conclusion but Great Britain and France remained for some years insensitive to this reasoning. While the principal combatants were still wondering how to keep Germany weak militarily, Germany's smaller victims realized that they needed an economically strong Germany and that in any case Germany would recover its strength sooner or later. In the 1950s

France abandoned the idea of taming Germany by weakening it and this reversal of French attitudes was the spark which animated the seed of a western European union whose chief purpose was to exorcise the menace of German nationalism. The ghost of the old German problem attended the birth and adolescence of the European Community.

The first aim of the Coal and Steel Community was to join forces in order to expand production and reduce costs, to profit from cooperation and common management instead of competition. This aim was common to the six and primarily economic. The second aim was specifically French and political – to protect not just a section of French industry but France itself against a recrudescence of German national ambitions powered by German heavy industry. The treaty of 1951 instituted a degree of supernationalism by establishing, alongside a governmental Council of Ministers, a High Authority empowered to fix prices and financed by levies on production. A third body, the Community's Assembly, was a pale reflection of a national parliament, which might in time become less pale.

The Coal and Steel Community was a tribute to the functional approach in international affairs, an approach which advocated the internationalization of specific and particular economic sectors one by one. In this case coal and steel provided a useful first step owing to their historic importance in nationalistic competition, particularly between France and Germany, but the step was obviously a first one, if only because coal was becoming less important than oil, gas and nuclear power in the overall production of energy. Behind this pragmatic approach was the broad impetus to integration which came from each state's fear of being left on its own, not least in the ever-accelerating race in technical research and development.

The Treaty of Rome which created the Economic Community had three primary goals: a commercial and customs union, an economic union, and creeping political integration. Its first concerns were the creation of a common market for goods, services, capital and labour and a common agricultural policy. Next came the expansion of the Community by the accession of new members, the establishing of associations short of full membership (mainly in the Third World), and joint activity in world affairs (mainly in the Middle East). Thirdly and at the same time, the Community edged uneasily towards economic and monetary unification via the alignment of currencies to curb fluctuations in exchange rates and towards a single currency and central bank. The Community needed also to attune its own constitution and the distribution of political power within itself to the evolution stage by stage of its economic and political purposes.

Common Market and Common Agricultural Policy

The customs union was to be attained in twelve years by the elimination of all trade barriers and the imposition of external tariffs common to the whole community, these measures to be followed by free movement of capital and labour. The initial steps were taken within the prescribed period. There were gains and alarms. Industries were regrouped and refashioned and industrial exports flourished, particularly between members of the Community, but the pace of this industrial acceleration created nasty towns or accretions to towns and threatened to impoverish remote or less favoured areas (for whose relief a special fund was established). But the statistical outcome justified the aspirations of the Community's founders as annual growth averaged more than $4\frac{1}{2}$ per cent in the 1950s and nearly 6 per cent in the 1960s.

When the Community came into existence, agriculture was a prime candidate for communal integration and regulation, both by reason of its economic and social importance and because aggregate agricultural production was below the Community's needs. Over the next ten years a Common Agricultural Policy (CAP) was elaborated which converted under-production first into sufficiency and then, almost ruinously, into over-production. By the 1980s the Community was spending 70 per cent of its budget on the CAP and much the greater part of this money was being spent not in direct subsidies to farmers but in buying up the surpluses which were then thrown away or re-sold at a heavy loss. (Direct subsidies have accounted for about one quarter of the Community's total expenditure.) The policy had run away with itself. So long as it amounted to a transfer of resources into the agricultural sector it was fulfilling the Community's intentions, but with the production of surpluses the policy developed into a transfer of resources to the purchasers or recipients of these surpluses. However desirable it might be for the Community to sell foodstuffs to the Third World at bargain prices, it had not been the Community's intention to produce surpluses on such a scale that they had to be offered at almost any price to the Third World, the communist block or anybody who would take them. The problem was aggravated by two independent factors. First, fluctuations in exchange rates within the Community led to the invention of a special currency for calculating agricultural payments, a device which proved wasteful and open to corruption. The second factor was the fact that farmers in the United States were also subsidized beyond the need to safeguard domestic self-sufficiency and were competing with the Community in the disposal of their surpluses at bargain prices or even by dumping (i.e. selling at prices below the cost of production). The CAP became, therefore, an item in the commercial competition and illwill between the Community and the United States.

At the centre of the CAP was the setting annually of prices for farm products by the European Commission in Brussels. These prices were set above world prices in order to assure farmers a decent living. The Commission also undertook to buy surpluses at fixed minimum prices and it levied duties on imports from outside the Community whenever prices fell below given levels. This régime achieved the aim of raising production from the low levels of the 1950s but it also inevitably encouraged farmers to produce more than they could sell within the Community and landed it with surpluses which it was obliged to buy and – most foodstuffs not being suitable for stockpiling – re-sell. In 1974 Dr Sicco Mansholt, the Dutch member of the Commission, tried to grasp this nettle by proposing a drastic reduction of the agricultural area over ten years and the coalescing of the residual sector into larger units, but member governments quailed and rejected his plan. They were afraid of losing votes. They were also inhibited by the peculiar intractability of any attempt radically to reform the agricultural industry.

Reform meant reduction and radical reform meant big reduction soon. The governments upon which the cost of the CAP fell most severely (Western Germany, Great Britain) wanted radical reforms; others, more lukewarm, were prepared to back changes or limitations (for example: a quota on the total of milk subsidies) which hardly amounted to reform at all; the countries where agriculture bulked largest in the economy (Denmark, Greece) wanted no reform or indefinitely postponed reform. These difficulties represented human and social problems. Farmers constituted Europe's oldest and most sentimentalized body of workers. Those in remote or comparatively inaccessible areas – who were usually small farmers whose sturdy outdoor toil evoked popular admiration – were apt to constitute a region's sole economic activity, so that any threat to their existence was automatically a threat not only to themselves but to the entire community. They were, however, inescapably the victims of reform as soon as the problem of under-production turned into its obverse and required the cutting of the subsidies upon which these farmers and communities depended.

This dilemma was compounded by an older one: the pressure to modernize an industry which had been particularly slow to acknowledge an industrial revolution. Modernizing agriculture – more machinery in few but larger farms employing fewer workers per acre – was not like transforming a declining manufacturing industry into a new and more active one. In the manufacturing case the need was to change the product, but in agriculture the problem was not (except within narrow choices) what to produce but how, and how much less. Here too the impact of change was bound to be regional unemployment and depopulation by taking whole areas out of the economy.

This was what was demanded by the economy in one sense and rejected by the economy in another. The economy, interpreted as the sum of market activities, demanded more production in pro-ductive areas and less or none in others. The economy, in its basic sense (Greek for *Lebensraum*) of the totality of human and natural existence, required some protection against such destitution. In Norway concern for the small fisherman, the local equivalent of the small farmer, led the Norwegians to reject by plebiscite their government's decision to join the Community. Norway as a whole, it was judged, would benefit by joining the Community, but the Norwegians preferred to forego these benefits if they were going to destroy the fishermen's livelihood. (The fact that, a few years later, when North Sea oil had transformed the Norwegian economy and patterns of employment, the Norwegians veered towards another conclusion, does not alter the fact that such arguments and calcu-lations may need to be faced.)

After the Second World War agriculture in western Europe had been transformed, largely by amply capitalized farmers or new agro-businesses which, obedient to the precepts of market forces and their own profit motives, caused their farms to flourish and increased their productivity (often a polite word for sacking expensive human workers and replacing them by cost-effective machines). But the good fortunes of the luckier and richer areas blighted the poorer and forced governments to weigh the human pain, and the cost of unemployment relief, where it existed, against a superficially logical impulse to press ahead with agricultural reform. Only an obsessive preoccupation with markets and profits, and a correspondingly blind eye to the human and social consequences, could sanction the post-haste radical reform of the CAP which the fulfilling of its original purpose seemed to impose.

The testing point came when the cost of the CAP outran the Commission's capacity to pay it. The Commission's annual income came from import duties and levies on foodstuffs plus a contribution by each member state of a sum equal to 1 per cent of its GDP. When these sources of revenue fell short of expenditure the Commission might (from 1979) require from each member a further contribution not exceeding 1 per cent of its receipts from VAT. In the 1980s the last item proved insufficient to bridge the gap and the Commission asked for the ceiling to be raised from 1 per cent to 1.4 per cent of receipts from VAT. The fiercer critics of the CAP, vociferously led by Thatcher, saw in this situation a means to force radical reform of the CAP by refusing to give the Commission the extra resources needed to balance its budget. She miscalculated, for although she had much sense on her side, her brashly arithmetic approach to a complex human and social problem won little sympathy and less support, and in 1984 Great Britain agreed to the increase in the VAT ceiling in return for limits on its own contribution to this increase. But the CAP and its excesses remained. Measures to protect farmers and agricultural and rural communities were a legitimate transfer of resources from one sector of the economy to another, but the export of surpluses at subsidized prices angered competitors and threatened the attempt under the aegis of the GATT to free trade in foodstuffs as well as manufactured goods. The GATT's Uruguay Round (1986–70), which covered fifteen areas of international bargaining, was brought to a standstill by conflicts between the Community and American and other exporters of foodstuffs over the level of support given by the Community to its producers and exporters.

Expansion

The European Community was born outward-looking. Its six founder members envisaged from the start the growth of the Community by the adherence of more members in western Europe.

The six became nine from the beginning of 1973 and were joined later by Greece (1981) and Spain and Portugal (1986) – but Greenland seceded. The Community's industrial heartland needed a less developed hinterland where goods might be sold and capital invested. In the original Community of the six, southern Italy constituted the requisite under-developed area waiting to be developed. Where the Italian north had failed to create a mutually advantageous partnership between north and south, foreign (mainly German) capital and skills were successfully allied to Italian to meet the needs of the Italian south and open new fields for German enterprise. But more such areas were needed. Central and south east Europe had been familiar areas before the war, but the political risks and uncertainties were daunting, creditworthiness precarious and the export of capital in return for stakes in capital assets contrary to both communist doctrine and capitalist instinct. The Third World was a vast and needy field but at least as risky financially as the communist block. Much more promising were unattached parts of Europe itself: Spain (like Italy) partly industrialised and partly not; Ireland, Greece and Portugal barely developed at all. All these countries were desirable fields of opportunity and all were incorporated in the Community, making it a community of 320 million consumers.

The Community also developed, soon after the start, a comprehensive special relationship with many states in other continents. And the members began to try to concert common foreign policies, notably in relation to the Middle East whose oil was crucially important to all of them. The members of the Community, some of the smaller as well as the larger, had long histories of knocking about in the wider world and little inclination to stop doing so. Provided the Community could establish and expand a healthy common economy and common policy, it might become not only a fruitful self-help cooperative but also some sort of world Power. This was part of the vision.

Ever since ancient Greeks rounded the Cape of Good Hope, if not earlier, Europeans have ventured beyond their continent to satisfy curiosity, extend knowledge, seek wealth or display power. In modern times the scientific revolution which gathered pace in the seventeenth century fostered learned bodies (including the Royal Society in England) whose members debated all kinds of knowledge and financed expeditions to get more knowledge from all over the world. The great voyages of discovery of early modern Europe, culminating in the three voyages of Captain James Cook, were devoted to charting and exploring, to botany, astronomy, elementary anthropology and numerous other activities which could broadly be embraced in the term 'physics'. Besides physics were economics, beginning with trade and leading to empire. The end of empire in the twentieth century meant the end neither of far-flung economic interests nor of the habits of mind which linked Europe with other continents and seas. Post-imperial Europe was bound to seek new ways of being active all over the globe, for post-imperialism altered the context without altering the imperatives. In one area of special importance – the Middle East – which had for centuries combined the fascinations of mystery and wealth the imperatives were sharpened by the crucial importance of oil in the period between the age of coal and the age of nuclear power. In a second area – the Third World – links and new opportunities combined to create a special relationship between the European Community, the former colonies of its members and, by natural extension, the whole undeveloped world of which these colonies constituted a substantial part. Here were still markets.

European interests beyond Europe had been won and secured by power. For many generations the interest and power increased *pari passu*. A new problem arose when the interests went on increasing but the power diminished.

The heyday of power was short but memorably massive. It was for the most part exercised by sea; it was military power brought to bear by sea power. (The exception was Russian expansion which, like that of Rome, proceeded almost entirely by land, south to the Black Sea, east into Asia and west over Finland, the eastern shores of the Baltic and half Poland.) Power was first brought into the equation as an element in contests between European states – the British against the French, for example, in India and North America in the Seven Years War. It was also used to subjugate and then control the non-European people upon whose lands Europeans trespassed. It was always questioned on the grounds that it was exploitative, unjust, and the source of infections from venereal and other diseases, the trade in drugs and arms, and wars. Such criticisms were met by claims that Europeans also carried with them the only true religion, superior principles and moral qualities, superior knowledge and powers of organization, and the notion of progress and the keys to it. But these counter-claims, although originating in a vision of a world made better by Europeans, could not escape the whiff of self-serving exculpation and by the twentieth century the thrust of economic gain was too heavily impeded by a revulsion against colonialism which was all the more pressing for being grounded in the European's own dogmas of liberty, self-determination and self-help.

Consequently, when the first Great War ended, territorial acquisitions – the traditional reward of the winners – were frowned upon and the debris in Europe of the Habsburg and Ottoman empires were distributed among their inhabitants rather than being annexed by the principal victors. Outside Europe, however, a halfway rule was invented which allowed the victors to have effective, if temporary, control over other parts of the Ottoman empire and over the African, Asian and Pacific possessions of the defeated Powers. This was the mandate system. It acknowledged in principle the right to independence of these territories but decreed that the time was not yet: some might expect independence soon, others not so soon, a few not at all. They were administered but not annexed by European states, and these states were obliged to accept international inspection of their administration by a Permanent Mandates Commission, whose members were international functionaries and not representatives of national governments.

This regime was pushed a step further by the Second World War. At Yalta in 1945 it was agreed that mandated territories which had not achieved independence between the wars should be transferred into UN trusteeship. The practical effect was a strengthening of the international element, the trustee being obliged to submit annual reports to the UN Trusteeship Council which could also despatch investigating missions to the territories and receive petitions from them. The change from mandate to trusteeship was significant in that it was no longer easy for the administrator to treat a trust territory as part of its property. Eleven trust territories were constituted after 1945 and all proceeded quite rapidly to independence. The Trust Territory of the Pacific Islands, composed of previously Japanese mandates and placed under American administration, survived the longest (until 1986) and its ports retained a special association with the United States. The United States at first wished all colonies to be given independence but abandoned this stance in favour of a declaration on non-self-governing territories which brought colonies into the international compass without too much inconveniencing the colonial power. The US government became more tolerant of European colonialism as it became more anxious to enlist Europeans in the Cold War against the Soviet Union and to establish American military bases or listening posts in territories outside Europe but under European control. Colonial asperities were reduced when France and the Netherlands abandoned their attempts to repossess their prewar empires, Great Britain gave independence to most of its colonies with unexpected speed, and the Spanish and Portuguese empires too dissolved. (When the war ended the British empire comprised four self-governing dominions, two pieces of empire – India and Burma – and 55 colonies. These, almost in their entirety, were incorporated in the Commonwealth which, after Pakistan rejoined it in 1989, had 49 sovereign members. The Commonwealth was a political reality of a peculiar kind. It had a Secretary-General with a modest staff in London and was held together by the accidents of history which had formed it and a sort of clubbiness which survived even Margaret Thatcher's pert belief that when forty-eight members thought one way and Great Britain another, one counted for more than forty-eight.)

The Community's first major venture in world affairs was a direct sequel to imperialism and was initiated by the Treaty of Rome itself. France, unlike Great Britain, did not see the end of empire as the end of political influence and economic opportunities in Africa and elsewhere outside Europe. For the British the Commonwealth was the empire's residual shadow, an epilogue, not (in spite of some postwar romancing) a power centre. But the French set about retaining in new form the profits, prestige and even some of the military presence which had bedecked their colonial activities, and when the Treaty of Rome was being negotiated they ensured the inclusion of provisions for associate membership of the Community. The first associates in 1964 were nineteen (mostly French) colonies in Africa; ten years later their number had grown to forty-six states in Africa, the Caribbean and the Pacific; and by 1990 the Community had sixty-six ACP associates. It was therefore one of the largest international associations in the world and it functioned upon the basis of a different status between permanent members and other states whose association (and its terms) were regulated by short-term renewable treaties. The principal instruments of this worldwide connection were the Community's Development Fund, from which were dispensed loans and grants to the associated states, used chiefly to build roads, hospitals and schools, and develop water and energy supplies and forestry; non-reciprocal preference agreements; and schemes for stabilizing the prices of more than twenty of the principal exported commodities of the associated states and of their exported minerals. The first Convention, that of Yaoundé in 1969, was followed by four

Lomé Conventions of 1974, 1979, 1984 and 1989. The aid provided through these agreements muted, if it did not entirely extinguish, complaints that these were neo-colonialist devices which kept poor countries dependent on the rich and fixed their economies in old colonial patterns instead of diversifying them. In political terms the relationship cut two ways. On the one hand it helped recipients; on the other the aid and preferences were never enough and the bureaucratic trappings caused no little irritation. The overall result was to continue European links which had been expected to fade away but – after the inflation and recession, collapse in commodity prices and massive indebtedness of the 1970s and 1980s – to do so only in the expectation of a major overhaul which was slow in coming. The Community's aid to the ACP countries was a relatively small and diminishing proportion of the total amount of aid drawn by them directly from European and other states and from the larger international agencies, but it was far from insignificant in their straitened circumstances.

A second and more specific area of European concern was the Middle East, once more a special case. The Middle East was economically more important to Europe than any other part of the world and its importance was indefinitely prolonged by the failure of nuclear power to supplant oil as the main source of domestic and industrial energy. For western Europe the Middle East was more important even than the rest of Europe. The Soviet occupation of central and eastern Europe was extremely unpalatable, but a Soviet occupation of the Middle East would be a disaster and a cause for war.

The French had been removed from the Middle East during the war, mainly by the British, and after the war the British failed to renew the special relationships reserved to them by prewar treaties with Egypt and Iraq and retreated from Palestine in the face of Jewish violence and because they no longer had the stomach to go on trying to accommodate Arabs and Jews. In Palestine the creation in 1948 of the state of Israel crowned the endeavours of modern Zionism but led also to seemingly endless wars in a part of the world where outsiders particularly wanted stability. It led too to divergent European and American perspectives on the Middle East and to a sharp awareness of the hazards of pursuing policies running counter to American policies and preferences.

Modern Zionism, which took shape at a conference in Basel in 1897, stemmed from atrocities in anti-Jewish pogroms in Russia, Romania and Russian-occupied Poland in 1881–84. The founder,

guide and presiding spirit of the movement was Theodore Herzl,
a Viennese Jew (in the racial sense, but an agnostic in religion) who
devoted his life and worldly goods to finding somewhere for the
threatened Jews of these areas to go and have a decent life. Herzl
was tireless and self-sacrificing but also naive and unable to secure
wholehearted backing from the disparate segments of the Jewish
diaspora (including leaders of the Russian segment). His preferred
asylum for persecuted Jews was their ancient biblical homeland,
at this time under Turkish rule, but he was prepared to consider
other parts of the Ottoman empire and also refuges in the British
empire. He hoped to attain his aim by diplomatic negotiation with
the rulers of these empires, whom he visited and misinterpreted.
The Turks, including the Sultan, were politely ready to receive
him and listen to him but they were never willing to permit any
substantial number of Jews to settle in Palestine: this Herzl did not
realize. The nature of the settlement sought was discreetly veiled
by the Zionists who called it a homeland notwithstanding that from
the start of the movement they were resolved to found a state. Few
of them – the immensely learned and respected Ahad Ha'am of
Odessa was the outstanding exception – called attention to or even
appreciated the existence of Arabs in Palestine or their attachment
to Jerusalem as one of their most holy cities after Mecca.

The defeat of the Turks by the British in the first Great War did
little to advance the Zionist cause since the British, although in
1917 they gave a conditional promise to sponsor a Jewish 'home'
in Palestine (the Balfour Declaration), were never prepared to give
the Zionists what they wanted if it were unacceptable to the Arabs,
which it was. Consequently, the removal of the British became a
pre-condition for the success of Zionism.

The Second World War fortified the Zionist case to the point
of swamping the Palestinians' objections to it. Hitler's atrocities
against the Jews far exceeded in horror the earlier pogroms in
eastern Europe and created a wave of pro-Zionist emotion which,
in Europe, owed something to Christian guilt over anti-Semitism
and, in America, was marshalled by the numerically and financially strong Jewish community. The Jews, who had refrained
from taking up arms against the British and Arabs so long as
the former were fighting Hitler, did so as soon as Hitler was
defeated and succeeded in evicting the British and half the Arabs
from lands which Zionists claimed as theirs by divine decree.
Their campaigns, the prototype of what would later be called
terrorism, were in a manner legitimated when the United Nations

purported to create the sovereign state of Israel, a political act of uniquely obscure legal significance since the United Nations had no authority to make states. In truth the new state of Israel was created in a more traditional way, by conquest. The twin state of Arab Palestine, similarly evoked by the United Nations, did not come into existence since the Zionists and the emir of Transjordan (later King Abdullah of Jordan) conspired to apportion it to the latter. Thereafter the state of Israel refused to envisage a Palestinian state or recognize the Palestinians as a people.

Between 1897 and 1948 Zionist ambitions had expanded steadily. Zionist prospects were enhanced by the end of the Ottoman and British empires over Arab lands and also by Hitler's savagery. But, following the rule that savages tend to brutalize their victims, the Nazis brutalized Zionism and helped to endow it with new leaders whose ruthless and ideological obduracy were the reverse of the gentle and diplomatic Herzl. The Jewish state consisted of what they were able to conquer in 1948 together with what they might add to it later in fulfilment of what they saw as their God-given right. They were opposed not only by the Arab inhabitants of the lands they conquered or coveted but also – if neither unitedly nor wholeheartedly nor consistently – by Arabs at large. The ensuing wars destabilized the Middle East, disrupted commerce and eventually affected the price of oil and the pace of world inflation. Israel prevailed over its enemies but could not make peace with them (except in the case of Egypt: Menachem Begin's treaty with Egypt in 1978 was Israel's one diplomatic victory in a history more notable for military victories). This failure to come to terms with its neighbours made Israel dependent financially and militarily on the United States and made American policy in the Middle East dependent on Israel.[1]

For Europe this unresolved conflict entailed loss of influence both with Israel and with Arabs, and mounting economic damage. The Middle East therefore entered into European affairs not merely, as heretofore, because of its proximity but because of its impact on war and wealth. Europe's loss of influence in the Middle East, coupled with its undiminished economic concern in

1.   The migration of the Jews to Israel looks like a further act in a terrible tragedy. It was a natural urge made irresistible by the Nazi holocaust in Europe, but it was too late to prevent that holocaust and sowed the seeds of another disaster far away from a Europe which had become a safer place for Jews than Israel could ever be.

the area, impelled western European leaders into tentatively joint action. Since the springs of such action were essentially economic the European Economic Community was a natural forum for discussing and concerting what best to say and do. But the problem of bringing their influences to bear was compounded by marked differences between Europeans and the United States, which were far greater in Middle Eastern affairs than over anything in Europe itself.

The United States was deeply committed to the existence and defence of Israel, even to the extent of adopting uniquely lenient standards for judging Israel's conduct. Between the wars the United States held wisely aloof from British problems in Palestine but in 1942 the American Palestine Committee, formed the previous year with impressive Congressional support, adopted the Biltmore Program on Palestine for the Jews. A surge of support for Zionism drowned other voices and arguments and many inconvenient facts; was strong enough to derail American attempts to construct a joint American-British declaration and postpone the issue until after the war; and convinced Arabs that the United States government was no mediator but was manipulated by Jews and intent upon establishing a power base in the Middle East through a Jewish satellite state. President Roosevelt met King ibn Saud of Saudi Arabia after the Yalta conference of 1945 but failed to arrange a meeting between the King and the Zionist President Chaim Weizmann. Roosevelt wanted to proceed only in consultation with Arab leaders, but he discovered, as had the British, the impossibility of getting an Arab-Jewish accord. Arab kings and presidents were united in adamant opposition to unlimited Jewish immigration into Palestine. Roosevelt concluded that no Israeli state could be created without war and probably reconciled himself to abandoning the Zionist cause. Truman, however, less cautious and inclined in the first stage of his presidency to discount the advice of the elder statesmen around him, became the first in a line of American presidents to back the Jews unequivocally against, first, the British and then the Arabs. The American attachment to Zionist pleas and Israeli ambitions became a profound emotional and political factor throughout the United States and a major element in world affairs. At the root of this attachment was Hitler's holocaust. As the ghastly facts gradually became known their impact was sharpened by a guilty feeling that the United States might have done more to prevent or mitigate them. Whereas in Europe similar feelings of shock and guilt were dissociated from the conduct of policy, in the United States they were allowed to shape policies for a generation or more. Israel became for the United States a special case – not so much an independent state as a ward – and this special relationship, which was not felt by Europeans, entailed opposition to Arabs and, as the Cold War developed, a Middle East policy based on the non-Arab states of Israel and Iran. To Europeans this was a myopic policy which aggravated instability in an area which economically was an extension of Europe.

Governments apart, Americans and British were suspicious of one another over oil, particularly in Iran where the British near-monopoly was broken to American advantage (Americans retaining, however, a monopoly in the newer oilfields of Saudi Arabia). During the war Iran, whose monarch was evicted by the British, got food and other basic economic help from the United States. American troops built or improved roads, railways and ports. Iran was the main channel for American aid to the Soviet Union. After the war American military and financial missions replaced the Europeans who had overshadowed Teheran before the war, and Anglo-American commercial rivalry was welcomed by Iranians as a means of getting rid of the Anglo-Iranian Oil Company. None of this pleased the British, although they got used to thinking of Iran as no longer a British sphere of interest.

In the 1950s and 1960s the western allies, European and American alike, feared that the Soviet Union would take advantage of conflicts in the Middle East to extend the Cold War and Soviet influence to the area. Soviet interventions, however, were partial and short-lived (Iran as the war ended); or ill-fated (Egypt from 1956 to 1972); or less useful to the Soviet Union than to the other party (Iraq, Syria); or catastrophic (Afghanistan in the 1980s). The Soviet Union hovered about the area with increasingly little to show for its policies. This reduction in Soviet effectiveness left the field clear for western disagreements, while in the same period the Arab–Israeli conflict developed an interminability which seriously alarmed Europeans and, so far as American policies were concerned, irritated them. Europeans trod warily. On the one hand they avoided explicit condemnation of such American actions as the United States' complaisance towards Israeli excesses (even the invasion of Lebanon and the atrocities in the refugee settlements round Beirut in which Israel appeared at least to acquiesce) and the bombing of Libya in 1986; on the other hand they formally acknowledged in 1975 that the PLO represented the people of

Palestine and in 1980 the chairman of the Commission, Gaston Thorn, made a tour of the Middle East after a meeting of the Council of Ministers in Venice where European opposition to American policies and attitudes was expressed with unaccustomed openness.

The Arab–Israeli conflict was not the only area where European and American interests and perceptions clashed. Pressed by the United States to impose sanctions on Iran after fifty-two American diplomats were taken hostage in Teheran the members of the Community did as little as they decently could; they judged the proposed measures pointless. They applauded the initiative of the so-called Contadora states to negotiate an end to hostilities in Central America (1984) notwithstanding that the United States was doing its best to scupper that initiative. And they challenged and defeated Reagan's attempt to penalize European companies participating in the construction of a Soviet-European gas pipeline. Taking joint positive stands around the world was not without its embarrassments.

Economic union and political integration

The members of the Community were states. As such they regarded internationalism as a useful accretion but not an over-riding principle. Their governments had no inherent impulse to transfer their authority to a Community, nor were they pressed by public opinion to do so. When Americans talked of a United States of Europe as though such a phenomenon had only to be conceived in the image of their own prosperous society they passed over the fact that the perennial characteristic of Europe's states had been that they were not united and did not much want to be. They were not the same kind of 'state' as the American states at the date of their union, when they were not sovereign states but colonies. By a happy piece of legerdemain the Americans dubbed their colonies states and then united them and called a union of colonies the United States. Nothing so simple was possible in Europe where a state, almost by definition, was a unit which had a different language from the next state and a history of fighting it. Even if they had reached the stage when they were no longer minded to make war on one another, that did not mean that they had no feuds or that they were ready to abdicate to a supranational authority the right to adjudicate their conflicts, order their internal affairs, change their laws. Political leaders in particular, who had reached the top of their national trees, were outraged by the idea that anything might be allowed to grow higher.

Yet against these factors were others: the small size of Europe and its excellent communications; a high and well-spread level of administrative competence; wealth; a common culture making communication easy and predisposing influential, if minority, sectors of society to greater unity; and a potent fear – the fear of economic decline, of being left behind. It was far from clear how great this propellant fear might be, but the combination of fears, vision and resources enabled the Community to survive a wounding political crisis in the 1960s, the recession of the 1970s and 1980s and an acute financial crisis in 1983, by which date it had been in existence for a quarter of a century.

Yet distrust remained and was easily evoked by opponents who made play with two emotional deterrents: the threat to national sovereignty and the threat to national identity. Sovereignty is a legal status. It is far from co-extensive with the capacity to exercise sovereignty, which nearly all states in the world have lost to greater or lesser extent, or never had. In so far as the Community eroded sovereignty it did so in areas where the capacity to exercise sovereignty had vanished or was fast vanishing. More real and no less emotional was the concept of national identity. People are what they feel and like to feel that they will go on being what they are. But national identities are persistent hardy annuals, powerful enough to resist homogenizing pressures for centuries. Thus the Scots have remained recognizably different from the English in spite of nearly four centuries under the same monarch and nearly three centuries under a union government. No Scot likes being told that he has lost his identity.

A number of western European governments wanted the kind of cooperation which fell well short of anything that could be called a union. They wanted a common market but no economic union and certainly no financial or monetary union.[2] Under British leadership

2.   A commercial union need have no more than minimal political and bureaucratic implications, but an economic union requires continuous decision-taking and policy-making of a governmental nature. A common market means the elimination of barriers to trade – customs duties, quotas – within the market area and identical regulations at all points round the periphery of the area. An economic union is both wider and vaguer. Problems arise when measures which

they created a European Free Trade Area (EFTA) which, however, was a failure. Some EFTA members thereupon applied to join the European Community. They did so not because they had been converted to the case for an economic union but because their alternative had failed and they judged that they could not afford to stay outside the Community which, contrary to their expectations, was not a failure. Consequently the Community's membership was increased in 1973 by 50 per cent and one of the new members was Great Britain.

This major change coincided with another. The economic weather turned rough, and it remained rough throughout the 1970s and 1980s. Economic growth faded away, currencies became unstable and unemployment rose alarmingly (it exceeded 10 per cent of the workforce by the early 1980s). Internal disputes, such as a Franco-Italian wine war (1975) and attempts to restrict the over-production of milk, became more difficult to handle and gave the Community a bad name. France refused to accept an agreement concluded in 1974 between its European partners and the United States for sharing oil in a crisis such as the crisis of 1973 when war in the Middle East quadrupled the price of oil and made it hard to get. The Community failed to concert an energy policy. Relations with Japan were soured by the latter's continuing economic triumphs (when the trade imbalance between the Community and Japan reached $14 billion in a year (1982) the Community complained formally to the GATT about Japanese trading practices). The big world of economic blocks was getting abrasive before the Community was fully organized to engage in it.

One consequence was to retard integration. Monetary union was a victim of this turbulence. In 1969–70 a series of reports (two over the name of Raymond Barre and a third over that of Gustav Werner) proposed a programme for assimilating currencies and credit policies. The Werner Report recommended full monetary and economic union at the end of a period of ten years, during

flow from a commercial union or common market require broad harmonization (such as safety regulations or hygienic standards); free movement of capital; restraints on exchange rate fluctuations pointing to a common currency; common guidelines and eventual central authority over some areas of taxation (rates of VAT, for example, or the size of budget deficits); and the creation of a central bank – all of which measures decrease the ostensible freedom of action of national governments.

which currency fluctuations would be narrowly confined, national budgetary and economic policies would be increasingly subject to communal consultation, and capital movements would become unrestricted. The Council of Ministers was prepared to endorse parts of the report but it was wholly submerged when the West German government allowed the mark to float (following the suspension of the convertibility of the dollar into gold), and although the plan was revived a year later, it flagged until revived once more by a new chairman of the Commission, Roy Jenkins, in league with Valéry Giscard d'Estaing and Helmut Schmidt. In 1978 Schmidt proposed a European Monetary System (EMS) in which currencies would be allowed to fluctuate only narrowly, a new reserve currency – the European Currencies Unit or ECU – was invented, and the member states would pool reserves of gold and foreign exchange to form a central reserve of $50 billion.

The EMS was designed to achieve in the narrower sphere of the Community what the Bretton Woods system had failed to achieve in a wider world. The Bretton Woods system combined internationally fixed exchange rates with national control over national economic policies. This balancing act broke down. It was maintained by allowing national governments to operate controls over the flow of capital between national economies: national governments, unable to fix exchange rates, imposed exchange controls in order to reconcile their policies with the facts of economic life. One consequence was increased speculation in money markets – anathema to financiers. Then, in the 1970s, national governments lost control over capital movements, largely as a result of the oil price rises from 1973 onwards which created waves of footloose capital washing across national boundaries and washing away existing exchange rates. This time the consequence was unpredictably floating exchange rates – anathema to commerce and industry. As the management of currencies returned to favour the principal concerns of the wider world were first to regulate the soaring dollar and then to check its decline and stabilize it through ad hoc agreements (the Plaza and Louvre agreements). In the narrower world of the Community the EMS was an attempt to manage and at the same time to provide a new institutionalized framework for monetary management. It was created by all twelve members of the Community but four of them – Great Britain, Greece, Spain and Portugal – stayed outside the mechanism (the Exchange Rate Mechanism – ERM) devised to operate the system. The function of the system was to keep currencies fixed in terms of one another, subject to permissible variation and to annual review and, if necessary, readjustment.[3] The system's prime purpose was to effect a compromise between floating and fixed rates, between flexibility and predictability. It was a way of controlling fluctuations in order to prevent uncontrolled fluctuations whose volatility impeded commerce by making prices uncertain and by encouraging trade rivals to engage in competitive inflation. It was also a step towards a monetary union with a single currency, since the more currencies became fixed in terms of one another the more they constituted a single currency which was merely called by different names in different places. Within a year of the EMS agreement loans were being negotiated and bonds issued in ECUs; and within ten years ECU loans exceeded in value loans in all other currencies other than the dollar, yen, Deutschmark and Swiss franc, and the Council of Ministers had instructed the Commission to prepare the next step towards monetary union. This last decision followed the signing in 1986 – again by all twelve members – of the Single European Act designed to ensure the completion of commercial union by the end of 1992.

But the creation of the EMS took place within a year of the return to power of the British Conservative Party under Margaret Thatcher, firmly opposed to the essential features of a monetary union and committed to the preservation of British sovereignty in monetary matters, even though monetary independence was largely a myth. British interest rates, for example – a key indicator of independent decision-making – were not under the control of a British government. Given the state of the British and West German economies investors and punters might prefer 7 per cent on their money in Frankfurt to 13 per cent in London, and if they did, a rise of the German rate from 6 per cent to 7 per cent would oblige a British government to raise the British rate to 14 per cent. The Chancellor of the Exchequer might announce that he had decided to do this and he might even believe that he had exercised a choice, but in reality his action would be determined by outside forces since if he did not raise the British rate investors

3. The permissible variations were at two levels. Italy joined the mechanism at the wider level before moving to the narrower. Spain joined in 1989 at the wider. In 1990 these tolerances were 2.25 per cent and 6 per cent. Britain, joining in 1990 in spite of Thatcher's opposition, chose the wider.

and punters would sell sterling and there would be a run on the pound. Even if the Chancellor were to try to hold the rate down he could do so only by persuading foreigners to buy sterling at a price which in the circumstances must be above the market price, so that once more the decision-making rested less in London than with foreigners whose willingness or unwillingness to buy sterling (in the cause of financial stability) would determine what happened to it. Yet myths can be as powerful as facts, particularly when the myths are allied with strong emotions and weak reasoning. Thatcher believed in Great Britain's economic sovereignty and was resolute in her determination to thwart the Community's advance to financial and monetary integration.

The 1980s recognized therefore that the projected pace of this advance could not be sustained without serious quarrels with Great Britain which, although increasingly isolated within the Community, held a trump card: monetary union required a supplemental treaty. The majority faced a choice between slower advance on the monetary front and forcing the pace at the risk of splitting the membership and even creating a community within the community – a cumbrous and divisive outcome desired by few. The British, therefore, held a strong delaying hand. In the face of this dilemma the Commission's chairman, Jacques Delors, elaborated in 1989 new proposals which envisaged a lengthy process in three stages and without time limits: first, the application of the ERM to all members' currencies and the convergence of these currencies to a point where they would coalesce to form a single currency; secondly, the creation of a hybrid banking system in which a new central bank would co-exist with national banks and would, by joint deliberations, exercise some control over national economic policies, including limits to national budget deficits; and ultimately, a single currency and a central bank controlling monetary policy throughout the Community. To the first stage there was little opposition in principle but disagreements over timing – particularly in the case of Great Britain whose recalcitrance was generally regarded as not merely technical (the British rate of inflation, having risen once more, had to be reduced before an acceptable rate for sterling's entry into the ERM could be fixed) but also as a mask for indefinitely postponing the following stages. The powers of the proposed central bank on the other hand and the degree of its accountability to governments were subjects for profound disagreement in principle, again particularly in Great Britain where the gradual conversion of ministers to economic and monetary integration did not include the Prime Minister.[4] Since no time limits were to be imposed at any stage, even to achieving the initial goal of an all-embracing EMS, these proposals gave each member a veto over any move towards complete integration. The power of veto became, therefore, of overriding importance and therewith the constitution itself of the Community, as laid down in the Treaty of Rome.

Under this constitution the Community has four main organs: a Council of Ministers, a Commission, a Parliament and a Court. The veto operated in the Council of Ministers which is the greatest power in this constellation, exceeding in practical authority the other three combined.

The Court is the guardian and interpreter of Community law, including the right to determine whether a member state is in breach of Community law. (This court is not to be confused with the European Court of Human Rights which, sitting in Strasbourg, is not an organ of the Community but of the older and wider Council of Europe established in 1948.)

The Parliament began as a body of appointees but since 1979 its members have been elected (in Great Britain the first elections came later). It has a single chamber and the groups within it, although they form alliances on familiar right-to-left lines, are primarily national groups – a situation unlikely to be altered until a bicameral system is devised in which national and supranational interests may be separately but collaboratively represented: a desirable reform. The origins of the European Parliament were completely different from those of national parliaments; the former was created at a stroke from above, whereas the latter have grown by gradual process and particularly through their power to accord or refuse to a sovereign the money which he needed to pay his servants or wage his wars. The European Parliament possessed initially the right to debate, the right to dismiss the entire Commission (a right too drastic to be useful – the Parliament may not dismiss a particular Commissioner), no power to tax, the right to reject but

4. European policy was the chief cause of the removal of the Foreign Secretary Geoffrey Howe and the resignation of the Chancellor of the Exchequer Nigel Lawson. A new Chancellor, John Major, produced in 1990 a variant plan designed to achieve integration in a way acceptable to Thatcher. It was inevitably even more complex than the Delors plan – it envisaged a European currency as an extra currency, not a substitute – and found few friends.

not amend the budget (again a right so extreme as to be severely limited in practice), only a limited share in framing legislation, and no power to restrain the executive branch. It was reasonable to suppose that parliamentary powers would be enlarged only slowly, since national parliaments are no less jealous of their status and prestige than national governments, but in democratic terms the European Parliament was woefully weak. The position reached by the 1980s was acceptable *pro tem* but uncomfortably deficient as an example of the European parliamentary tradition, notably in relation to legislation, which was firmly under the control of the Council of Ministers.[5] Laws were drafted by the Commission, transmitted by the Commission to the Council and by the Council to the Parliament. The Parliament might express an opinion which might or might not cause the Commission to alter the measure. The Council then, by a majority, might adopt a text and send it to the Parliament which, by an absolute majority of all its members, might accept or reject it. Next the Commission might within one month express its opinion on any amendment. The Council, again by a majority, might adopt the text approved by the Commission and the Parliament or, alternatively and in this case unanimously, reject the entire text. Under these procedures both the Commission and a majority in the Parliament were given the power to influence new legislation, but the last word lay in the Council which, if in agreement with the other organs, might enact by a majority; if not in agreement, might reject but only unanimously.

The Commissioners, at first one per member state and later two from each larger member, constitute a supranational nucleus, in permanent session in Brussels, fully occupied with the development of the Community and with nothing else, the embodiment of the Community's spirit and drive. The Commissioners have usually held ministerial posts in their own countries but within the Community they are nearer akin to heads of departments of state – senior civil servants or, to those wishing to denigrate them, bureaucrats. Their powers of initiative are considerable, of decision negligible.

5.   Opponents of the Community instance its undemocratic structure but fail to remark that the remedy is to increase the powers and authority of its Parliament and the calibre of its parliamentarians. But increased authority and increased democratic credentials would mean increased independence from national governments. A possible compromise is the creation of a second chamber elected by national parliaments.

The Council of Ministers dominates the Community. It owes this position to the circumstance that the Community was created by states and not by political evolution. The Council's members are the heads of government of the member states and the Council is the stronghold of national particularism and sovereignty. It has the last word in Community affairs. The original French outline for the Coal and Steel Community contained no such ministerial Council, but the Schuman Plan's supranational High Authority was regarded with suspicion by the Benelux states which were unconvinced of the need for so radical a departure. They were attracted to the Plan primarily because a resuscitated Germany was essential to their own economies; they welcomed France's conversion to the goal of a healthy Germany within international constraints; they accepted supranationalism in so far as it might be necessary for these economic-political purposes. But supranationalism was not for them an aim in itself and an essentially national Council of Ministers was added to the Plan in deference to their view that, without it, the Plan was going too far in the direction of supranationalism.

When the Coal and Steel Community was followed by the European Economic Community a similar duality was adopted. The signatories of the Treaty of Rome agreed to create an economic union which should go beyond tariff reductions and other forms of commercial liberalization and they accepted supranational institutions to this end, but they made the new Council more clearly superior to the supranational Commission than the older Council had been to the High Authority. Supranationalism was again an acceptable ingredient but not an end in itself or at any rate not an end to be pressed at this stage.

The Council of Ministers acquired in this way the power to be the ultimate arbiter of how much supranationalism was to be permitted and, given the Council's nature, it was bound to contain some members intent upon keeping the supranationalism to the minimum. Any tendency towards supranationalism would proceed at the pace of the least enthusiastic. Political leaders, particularly those from the larger states, were quick to make a fetish of sovereignty, insisting on the formal rights of national governments even when these rights had been eroded in practice. They cherished the right to decide even where their decisions were conditioned by circumstances outside their control, and they believed that they had a duty to maintain these formal rights even when the assertion of a right meant little more than the postponement of a moment of truth. This attitude was most evident in monetary matters, for whereas the thrust of commercial policies was cooperative and anti-protectionist, the national manipulation of exchange rates and interest rates was difficult to abandon so long as ministers and public opinion continued to believe that such rates could be fixed and maintained independently of external economic forces. The preservation of national independence within the Community had, besides its considerable emotional appeal, the determined support of those political leaders with the more short-sighted economic vision and the inability to see how uncontrolled monetary fluctuations might destroy the Community as, in a wider sphere, they had destroyed the Bretton Woods system. The Council of Ministers was the forum for the resulting conflicts.

These were conflicts over the degree of the transfer of authority from national capitals to a supranational centre, and over the pace of such transfer. While the Commission was the beneficiary and symbol of any such transfer, the conflict itself was not so much between the two institutions – Council and Commission – as within the Council; and the determining factor was the Council's own rules of procedure – in short, whether the Council might take decisions by a majority or only upon unanimity. In the original Community of six the most nationalist of the members had been France which precipitated the first crisis in the Community's life. Although provoked by the Commission, this crisis occurred – and could only have occurred – in the Council. In 1965 the Commission made two bold proposals for strengthening the Community's supranationality and incidentally the Commission's own independence: first, that the Council should reach decisions by a majority and, secondly, that the proceeds of agricultural levies should be paid directly to the Commission instead of to national governments for transmission to the Commission. France, much displeased by this initiative, withdrew its ambassador from the Community's headquarters in Brussels and refused for over six months to attend the Council. This action, dubbed the Empty Chair, was tantamount to halting the Community in its tracks and imperilled its very existence.[6] It was brought to an end in

6.   De Gaulle's motives were widely misunderstood. The main source of his intransigence was his conviction that French industry was not yet ready for unprotected competition. His aim was to buy time rather than to arrest the Community or to insist on the permanent

the following year by the so-called Luxembourg Compromise. This was an arrangement, without formal sanction, which enabled any member to insist that a measure deemed by itself to have special importance should remain under discussion until unanimity were attained. It was, therefore, a kind of veto and was the price paid by the non-French members to secure the renewal of French cooperation. Judging French participation to be a *sine qua non* of the Community's existence the non-French members were forced to give way when France insisted. (When, in the 1980s, Great Britain found itself in a similarly nationalist and obstructive position it nevertheless lacked the power to insist because its membership was evidently not a *sine qua non* for a Community which had existed for fifteen years without it. Thatcher did not invoke the Luxembourg Compromise in the disputes over the CAP, the Community's 'own resources' or the British contribution to the budget.)

France, the prime author of the Coal and Steel Community, had not been enthusiastic about a wider economic association until the Suez débâcle and Great Britain's abandonment of the Anglo-French attack on Egypt in mid-stream, at American behest and without notice to its ally. The Treaty of Rome was signed in the same year as the retreat from Suez and although there would have been a treaty without the retreat, the Suez folly and muddle played a part in turning France more purposefully to a continental partnership with wider aims than the Schuman Plan. Wider, but still not precipitate. At first France was satisfied with the limited aims of commercial liberalization and with reviving German (but not independent German) economic strength and almost a generation passed before France showed anything like enthusiasm for a more dynamic integration.

The Luxembourg Compromise had sanctioned an impasse. It bowed to French intransigence by accepting a recipe for stagnation but produced in consequence an embarrassing accumulation of unresolved issues. Even the admission of the latest members,

predominance of the national over the supranational. In his *Europe des Patries* the *patries* were not the only repositories of political authority but de Gaulle was reminding people of the strength of the national idea and asserting the need to pay due regard to it in the course of developing the Community. It also suited him at this time to go slow. But *patrie* is not the French for state.

Spain and Portugal, caused protracted wrangling and the Council seemed to be following the UN Security Council into becoming a forum for profitless squabbling and getting on with nothing. But in the same period French attitudes altered. France decided that it was now strong enough to assume a positive part in Community development and abandoned (to Great Britain) the role of peevishly jamming on the brakes. Mitterrand believed in the Community and intended to rely on it more than any of his predecessors, and in 1984 at Fontainebleau the Council resolved with French encouragement to appoint a special committee (the Dooge Committee) to consider and make proposals for changes in its procedure. At the beginning of the next year Jacques Delors, a former French cabinet minister with a zest for action, assumed the presidency of the Commission with a plan for committing the Community to the completion of a single integrated market by the beginning of 1993. The Parliament had already produced its own draft Treaty of European Union, so that the two major issues of economic advance and constitutional change became linked and early in 1985 the Council recognized the combination by endorsing the Delors proposals for 1993 in addition to its appointment of the Dooge Committee. The decisive role was played by France and West Germany: France gave the lead but West German cooperation was essential. Bonn, initially undecided, sided with France and the smaller members who wanted above all to see an end to stagnation, and against Great Britain which (with some Dutch and Greek support) wanted the completion of the internal market but no constitutional or institutional reform. The Council agreed to convene an inter-governmental conference which would consider even amendments to the Treaty of Rome. These moves were the prelude to the adoption in 1985 of the Single European Act – in effect a supplemental treaty – which affirmed the completion of a single unified market by the end of 1992 and opened the way for more integration of financial and monetary policies – in taxation, land and air transport, manufacturing and environmental standards, a single currency, integrated company law. The Act also abolished the veto in the Council in matters concerning the completion of the single market.

The mid-1980s therefore were hardly less decisive than 1957 in the Community's life. The two most powerful members joined forces to push the Community forward, even at the cost of offending Great Britain and relegating it for the time being to the role irritant. West Germany's decision to accelerate integration was potentially as important as any step taken in Bonn since the creation of an independent West German state in 1952. It affirmed, even if it could not guarantee in perpetuity, West Germany's choice of an integrated western Europe as its primary field of international operation; and it did so at a time when revolutionary changes in the Soviet Union and its satellites were reshaping European affairs by exposing the frailty of Soviet power, signalling the re-emergence of Europe's soft centre into a halting independence, and reversing the partition of Germany after the Second World War.

Those Dutch and Belgians who, over forty years earlier, had imagined a new pattern in Europe in which the strong would not be destroyers might find here cause for tremulous optimism. Nevertheless the reunification of Germany roused alarm in varying degrees in neighbouring countries and among Jews. In so far as it meant the reunification of the separate states which emerged from Germany's defeat in the Second World War and the Cold War it betokened something which was neither unexpected nor very substantial. It amounted to an extension of the Federal Republic which was already the strongest state in Europe, adding to it seventeen million people, commensurate territory and long-term economic opportunities (but short-term economic embarrassments). It restored in large measure pre-1938 Germany, but without restoring the lands lost to the USSR and Poland in 1945. In the absence of a treaty Poles had grounds for uneasiness but in 1990 Germany formally renounced all claim to these lost territories, thus supplementing promises already made not to use force to change Polish-German frontiers.

In a wider sense the unification of Germany implied the creation of a nation state embracing all Germans, but in this sense Germany had never been unified. There was no German equivalent to the unified French or Spanish or Italian state. Bismarck stopped short at the *Kleindeutsch* solution – a pragmatic choice which was unpopular with many Germans within and outside the Reich but only briefly reversed by Hitler. A unified German state would embrace, besides Austrian Germans, the millions of Germans who lived in other foreign lands and whose existence played no small part in Hitler's political and strategic thinking: irridentism is about people rather than land. These Germans, however, were either killed in the war or driven westward into Germany (six million of them out of Poland, three million out of Czechoslovakia) and the threat to stability which they represented had by 1989 long since disappeared. If in nationalist terms Austria remained an anomaly it was one incapable of causing war. The vaguer, if more pertinent, question of the German mood or temper was (as indicated in an earlier chapter) conditioned less by unification than by the success, prosperity and confidence of the great majority of Germans who displayed no ambition to use their growing weight in the Community to drag it into adventures in *Mitteleuropa* nor any ambition to use their growing weight in Europe to do without the Community. In all the Community's main tasks for the 1990s – the completion of the single market, economic and monetary integration, political integration, concerted aid for central and eastern Europe – Germany put its weight in favour of common and accelerated action.[7]

7.   The Community created in 1989 a European Reconstruction and Development Bank. In 1990 the original six members other than Italy made permanent the abolition of frontier controls introduced five years earlier by the Schengen agreement.

CHAPTER TWELVE
Europe and the World

Unlike this book Europe does not begin with Bismarck. The best starting point is Rome. The Greek world was a Mediterranean world, but the Roman world was European. It did not cover all Europe or even half of it, but the sum of its parts was a European domain as large as any that the continent has known, and the marks of that empire still exist. Minor fluctuations apart, it was delineated physically by the two great rivers of the Rhine and the Danube which, rising quite near to one another (the source of the Rhine is south east of the Danube's) flow in very different directions. Europe east of the Rhine and north of the Danube was not Romanized, excluded by the disaster to Augustus' legions under Varus at the battle of the Teutoburger Wald across the Rhine in AD9 and by the empire's inability later to sustain Trajan's conquests north of the Danube. In the far north, in the Roman province of Britain, the limit wavered between the more ambitious designs of Agricola and the more prudent policies of Hadrian but embraced the greater part of the British Isles for several hundred years. Within these bounds the Roman empire was for many purposes the world, although the Greek-speaking east retained a distinct and self-conscious identity.

The Romans established the un-Greek idea that big is good. Although southern Italy was arid, Italy north of Rome and the lands conquered beyond the Alps were fertile and the Romans disseminated, among other things, up-to-date agricultural practices and techniques.[1] They found in Gaul areas to which they

---

1. The Romans, great soldiers though they became, began as farmers. The oldest Roman noble families were Junkers.

could move the surplus poor of southern Italy. (Julius Caesar was a forerunner of the organizers of Italian emigration to the United States and *Gastarbeiter* to postwar Germany.) By greatly improving communications and agricultural yields the Romans turned local restricted rural economies into an ampler agricultural-commercial economy. The wheel turned when they overburdened this economy with heavy military budgets to defend lengthening frontiers and by allocating more and more good land to time-expired servicemen who were not necessarily good farmers and were not required to pay taxes. The western half of the empire became a military organization, and the barbarians – whom Gibbon correctly blamed for half the empire's woes – were able the more easily to knock it about because what they attacked was already weakening. As the Romans withdrew from the fifth century onwards the economy was once more fragmented into separate rural units with diminishing commercial connections and horizons. The Roman military-agricultural complex dissolved into a multiplicity of local holdings which eventually crystallized and reappeared under the lords and abbots who later characterized the agricultural system of landowning feudalism. The Roman empire provided a foretaste of the swing between a united and extroverted economy and, on the other hand, poorer tighter local economies. The forces making for unity were military power, political organization and geography – easy movement of men, arms and commerce. The forces making for fragmentation were the ambition to maintain a military power beyond the limits of economic resources and the consequent breakdown of centralised political and economic organization. Because the economy was inadequate and misman-aged, the political organization faltered and failed, and when the political organization failed there was no longer an empire.

There were, however, memories of the empire and they were memories of its better days, of its prosperity and order rather than the decline which fascinated Gibbon. The impact of Rome was so formidable that the Roman empire has remained for nearly two thousand years the largest single event, cultural as well as physical, in the history of Europe; and foremost among its char-acteristics has been the notion that it put parts together and that the parts prospered in consequence. The Roman empire has been remembered as, in its heyday, a zone of peace and prosperity. Some of this nostalgia has been specious. It is one thing to acclaim Latin literature and Roman law, but it is foolish to suppose that these high achievements are inseparable from Rome's conquests, or that the heirs of Virgil, Cicero and the rest possessed a secret key or a divine right to impose themselves imperially, or that the empire was as golden for all its denizens as it was for Rome's senators, bourgeoisie and generals. Rome knew no kind of unification otherwise than by conquest and Romans were as deluded as later peoples in supposing that their successes in arms derived from their superior virtue.

The empire collapsed because it failed to develop the economic sophistication needed to maintain it and because the central government ceased to be a government in the essential sense of a centre making decisions which it had the means to execute. But the causes of the collapse were only superficially understood by its immediate heirs who hoped to resuscitate it. The first attempt was made in concert by its two principal heirs in the west, the Carolingian Franks and the Papacy, who aspired to recombine the old Roman empire beyond the Alps with the even older Roman lands in Italy. Charlemagne, like the Romans, grasped the political importance of efficient administration and communications (roads and posts), but good public services do not by themselves create wealth or power: they help to turn opportunities into achievement, to make the most of existing resources. The Carolingian peace nourished trade in agricultural products but the Carolingian infrastructure, civil and military, was less effective or durable than the Roman, the Carolingian empire proved no more than an episode, and its division between Charlemagne's grandsons attested its inherent weakness. The fragmentation of this empire reaffirmed the Rhine barrier and left the Papacy looking for another partner.

Two hundred years after Charlemagne another ex-barbarian dynasty, the Saxon, tried again. Three Saxon emperors, all called Otto, having checked and confined the Magyars and carried German power eastward across the Elbe, came up against Slavs who were forming a Slavonic empire round the dukes of Poland. Otto III, the most imaginative of these emperors, conceived with his mentor and former tutor, Pope Sylvester II, the idea of a multinational Christian empire: a dream of religious and cultural unity enveloping ethnic diversity. The western Franks had by this time floated away towards a separate identity in what would be France, but in the opposite direction the Slav duke of Poland and the Magyar king of Hungary were captivated by Otto's vision (Slav Bohemia was already part of the Saxon empire). But once again the Roman dream was too flimsy. Otto III died young and the dream evaporated. It rested on the hopes and fantasies of a few individuals, inadequately supported by the organization, resources or communications necessary to substantiate it. The Poles and Hungarians followed the western Franks away from empire and towards nationhood. Between west and east the Germans coined for their zone the title of Holy Roman Empire, but neither Christianity nor Romanism could create a body politic and the pretence of a German empire served merely to delay the consolidation of a German state. Never again was there to appear the possibility of achieving unity in central Europe otherwise than by conquest.

The second Christian millennium was occupied, in one half of Europe, with the consolidation of separate states based on secular kingly power, on language and ultimately on the notion of nationalism. They included some of the most successful polities that the world has ever seen, successful both materially and culturally – and by the nineteenth century western Europe dominated much of the rest of the world directly or indirectly. This success went hand in hand with political diversity within a common cultural inheritance, with the diversity outranking the commonality and with the abnegation therefore of the closer unity characterized by Rome. For all its worship of Rome western Europe foreswore Rome's political example – at first perhaps for mainly technical reasons such as poor communications, but in time because sentiment sanctified the separate secular state. But not without an intellectual struggle. As late as the eighteenth century some massive minds – Voltaire and Gibbon, for example – were describing Europe as a single 'great republic'. By doing so they were emphasizing a cultural rather than a political unity and were putting forward the view that a political system ought to comprehend the whole of a cultural zone.[2] But diversity predominated, and so long as diversity and success were compatible there was no need to look specially hard at alternative patterns. When in the twentieth century the conflicts between states became ruinous and world dominance slipped away, the balance of the argument shifted. By the middle of the century even the strongest of these states was uncomfortably

2.   Voltaire excluded the Turks from his European *respublica* and had doubts about the Russians. The ideal of a cultural unit has classical roots. The greatest of Athenian educators, Isocrates, defined Greeks not by their language or their race but as all those who shared a culture.

less independent in practice than it was in theory and in outward form. The discomfort promoted readjustment. Set minds began to move.

The sovereign nation state is proving to be an interlude between the sovereign monarchy and the community of no longer sovereign states. The achievement of kings was to make kingdoms where would-be emperors failed to make empires. But kings were tempted by empire. The Spanish Habsburgs and the French Bourbons tried to convert dynastic kingdoms into continental empires. They failed in what were essentially ill-judged essays in vanity and greed over the rational assessment of resources. (Lesser sovereigns such as the Venetian republic, when it expanded from its islands to the mainland, made the same mistake.) These miscarriages put paid to any notion of creating by military conquest a western empire and constituted a warning to the nation states which succeeded dynastic states not to go that way.

The king was a state-maker, his kingdom an organizing principle, embodying power, setting goals and incarnating emotions. The king's chief functions, once he had made his state, were to make and enforce laws and to make and win wars; but he could not make money and the more successful his state the more money he needed and the more dependent he became on those who supplied it – tax payers. The body of tax payers eventually supplanted the king as the sovereign power in the state.

Yet the typical European sovereign state was only by courtesy a nation state. It is hard to find a nation state anywhere between Norway and Portugal if the term means a state without an obtrusive ethnic minority. Nationality means citizenship, not ethnic kinship: minorities are ubiquitous and majorities are for the most part content if they can keep the minorities as small as possible. A stronger bond is language, which has changed from being a mark of superior (or inferior) education to being a mark of nationhood. So long as the people who mattered were few, Latin was a unifying force in western Europe, but it represented a universalism at odds with the state and retreated to churches and monasteries as the secular state made ground in the Middle Ages. Vernacular tongues became the allies of state-making monarchs. Northern French conquered the *langue d'oc* of the south as the French king, who was a northerner, extended his power southward. In Italy Provençal and Tuscan vied for primacy; the former seemed set to win but Dante ensured the triumph of the latter which became in time the symbol and instrument of an Italian state. German was eroded at the fringes but not enough to prevent the formation of a widely spoken German language which played a big part in shaping ideas about the proper limits of a German state. National tongues became so much the right thing that a general tongue or *lingua franca* was made to seem debased (dog Latin or pidgin English). Some tongues were promoted, almost invented, with the express intention of binding together a nation in order to lay claim to statehood: thus Vuk Stepanovic Karadzic for the Serbs and Adamantios Koraes for the Greeks (although the one spent much of his life in Vienna, the other almost all of it in Paris.)

Language has been a unifying force in the service of statehood but by the same token language has been a divisive force, marking one state off against its neighbours. This divisiveness of language is in retreat. A stubborn refusal to master a foreign language is no longer a cause for boasting. That languages are different does not make them mutually unintelligible and the twentieth century has seen an enormous increase, beyond narrowly cultivated and scholarly circles, in linguistic skills. It is astonishing how easily television reporters find individuals on the streets of continental countries who can give fluent answers to questions put to them in languages not their own. Language is ceasing quite quickly to be a rampart.

The Community of western European states is an attempt to create a political entity with the strengths, material and emotional, which have in the past distinguished the several states. The need arises from causes internal and external to Europe: internal, in order to prevent resources and lives being wasted by wars and other debilitating conflicts; external, in order to enable Europeans to prosper in a world which is not made by or for Europeans.

The wider world in which Europeans have to operate is not the world which existed before the two great wars of the twentieth century. This fact has been assimilated. Nor is it the bipolar world of two Superpowers which emerged from those wars. That world, although disquieting or worse, had one virtue. It was stable. Its stability was due to circumstances rather than statesmanship, and as the world moves from a two-Power to a multi-Power context the stability will be endangered and the calls on statesmanship increased.

The two Superpowers, however much they may have depreciated, remain unquestionably in a superior league. Their relations with one another, whether gauged by their armaments or their rhetoric, have become less acrid. Both of them now attach more importance to finding ways of cohabiting on the planet than ways of annihilating or terrifying one another. But although their mutual hostility is being conducted in different modes, it will not suddenly disappear. Europeans (and others) have been nervous about the consequences of detente, fearing a Superpower condominium over world affairs in which the interests of others would command scant attention. This fear, which appeared at intervals long before Gorbachev and became a common talking point in the late 1980s (particularly in the light of Reagan's ineptitude during his meeting with Gorbachev at Reykjavik), is absurd. Two major Powers may contrive to live together sensibly without becoming allies or co-dominators. The two protagonists of the Cold War are not only deeply opposed to one another by their systems, values and experiences but have little to offer one another. The Soviet Union's most urgent needs from beyond its own borders are credit and technology, but it is not obviously incapable of developing the latter for itself and is more likely to penetrate the western capitalist world through international institutions (the World Bank and the IMF) than via Wall Street. For the United States the Soviet Union is an almost worthless ally, in every way inferior to Japan whose economic strength and geographical location make it the ideal, perhaps a necessary, partner for the United States in what is left of the present century and into the next. Above all, the United States and Japan are by a long way the world's leaders in the galloping advances of modern technology in many profitable (as well as astonishing) directions, and although these advances breed competition, scientific communities do not have the in-bred adversarial psychologies of military and political castes, while the enormous cost of technological research and experiment are a powerful argument for cooperation. Between the United States and the Soviet Union on the other hand common interests are more limited: disarmament, for which both Superpowers have a similar economic compulsion; and cooperation in trouble-spots where both have reasons for wanting to dowse local eruptions.

Japan has turned the biggest somersault of all, converted from a terrible militarism to unparalleled economic success with no nuclear weapons and relatively modest military expenditure. It is a Great Power but an unconventional one. It presents a menace but not a military one. It has the resources for maintaining a big military establishment but, after being forced by defeat to foreswear the latter, it has discovered the sweetness of using the former to build the most modern industrial base, expand trade all over the world, and create corporations which – unlike their American counterparts – escape the economic shocks of the end of the Cold War. Japan is the biggest supplier of investment funds for the rest of the world. Like Great Britain in the nineteenth century it is not self-sufficient in food or industrial commodities and has to import a high proportion of its energy, but it is confident of supplying these deficiencies by financial and not military strength. With the United States in the Pacific, and with China and Russia in east Asia, it has had conflicts which have led to war but have now little current significance. The outstanding dispute is with the Soviet Union over southern Sakhalin and the Kuriles but this is a dispute which will either be settled diplomatically or go on inconspicuously. Both Soviet Asia and China offer in the long term opportunities, mutually beneficial, for Japanese investment in Soviet and Chinese natural resources and consumer needs, but more immediately Japan's commercial and entrepreneurial activities are directed towards the richer industrialized countries (the United States and parts of Europe) and towards the East Asian and Pacific zone where it is creating a new Co-prosperity Sphere under its tutelage (in competition with North American and West European zones).

China's vastness, together with recollections of past achievements unsurpassed in the history of the world, make it a candidate for Great Power status, but it is at present no more than a candidate. If with the aid of modern communications and techniques it emerges from a long period of being more ramshackle than coherent it will be a Great Power once more, but forecasts of the date and prophecies about the mood likely to accompany this resurgence are too difficult. China's main impact at present is the impression which it contrives to give that it is on the verge of justifying the special position it enjoys as a permanent member of the UN Security Council. Since nobody wants to miss the Chinese boat everybody is crowding the boarding stage well ahead of its arrival. But as the twentieth century draws to its close China is hardly less chaotic than it was when the century began and its government no less dependent on the heavy hand than was that of the appalling empress dowager who died in 1908.

The creation of the European Community is an attempt by half Europe to claim a place with these Powers. It is a compound of vision, intelligence and audacity. It requires exceptional leadership since for most Europeans Europe remains what it has been for centuries – a patchwork of sovereign states, of unequal size and wealth and power, different languages and disparate culture, and discordant interests and ambitions. The Cold War mangled this pattern to the extent of imposing on the patchwork a dyarchy, the two fiefdoms of the post-1945 Superpowers. This is what Europe has looked like from the outside – if not to itself – since the end of the Second World War. The odd spots of neutrality were not significant enough to negate this dual pattern but it exhibited two contradictory aspects which made it psychologically unsatisfying and inherently impermanent. It was, in the first place, uncommonly and unnaturally static. There was a line down the middle and the line was rigid. No state on either side of the line was induced or allowed to cross it. Even the neutrality of the neutrals was uncontested (neutrality having changed from a status chosen to a status imposed). This kind of immobility provided stability at the price of rigidity; but the price seemed high, the stance artificial. Secondly, and in spite of the rigidity, the pattern had an appearance of impermanence. Not only was Europe arbitrarily split into two whereas it used to be multi-faceted; its power centre, Germany, was itself split and this fault created a political freak. In theory this overall pattern, which reflected the Superpower dominance of the continent, might solidify and Europeans might come to see Europe in these terms, but they did not. Superpower dominance never became more than an overlay.

When the pattern weakened there was, in central and eastern Europe, no alternative to a return to a familiar past. The removal of Soviet dominance removed clogs on sovereignty. The recovery of this sovereignty, however limited in its exercise it might be, was one of the two main aims of the revolutions of the late 1980s (the other was the removal of one-party-cum-police rule by communist cliques).[3] Soviet and local communist rule degraded and homogenized the states of this part of Europe, but it neither federated nor obliterated them. On the contrary, Stalin had kept them distinct, adopting the old imperialist principle of divide and rule. Stalinism reinforced the several identities of the satellites,

3. The *nomenklatura* or privileged few cannot be precisely quantified. If the lower levels of safe government appointments are included the total may be 100,000 or even 250,000, but the upper reaches where power is added to security are very narrow, perhaps no more than 1 per cent of the population. In the extreme case of Romania this reach comprised one man and his wife.

whether strongly ethnic as in Poland and Bulgaria or kaleidoscopic as in Czechoslovakia which, as its name (and Yugoslavia's) implies, is an ethnic composite.[4] In economic matters it left them looking outward for sustenance and not at one another. Cooperation with one another cannot much help their material needs. They have sympathetic transnational bonds in their demands – largely satisfied by the revolutions of 1989 – for civil and political freedoms, but to the less easily attainable but no less urgent demands for a better material life – food, clothes, housing at affordable prices – federal schemes are at best marginally relevant. The lack of enthusiasm which torpedoed such ideas (Danubian leagues, for example) in the past persists, and there is little reason to suppose that the misfortunes and miseries of the postwar years have irrevocably submerged national feuds, of which those of Hungarians against Romanians, Serbs against Croats, and Poles against Czechs are only the most notorious. The countries of central and eastern Europe are a long way from any useful union, economic or political. Their ills cannot be cured by incorporating them in western Europe's Community. The Community will provide and coordinate financial, technical and educational aid but issuing tickets of admission to the Community will solve no problems in the east and will weaken the Community. They face too physical commotion on a scale unknown in Europe in peacetime for centuries as central Europeans try to get into Germany and Russians perhaps try to escape chaos and famine by fleeing into central Europe.

In western Europe the trend from sovereignty to partnership derives from the members' own assessment of their own best interests, an assessment made initially against the grain of sentiment. The construction of the European Community entailed an abnegation of sovereignty, but this was a voluntary renunciation. Neither peoples nor governments were moved by an unadulterated desire to give up sovereignty but they were persuaded that it would pay to do so, that the strength of the whole would be greater than the sum of the parts in economic affairs and in influence beyond the bounds of the Community. This was a proposition intellectually plausible but impossible to prove without being put into operation. The nearest approach to hard supporting evidence was provided by the united front presented by members of the Community

4.   The creation of Czechoslovakia after the First World War substituted a Czech-Slovak for a Czech-German partnership.

in negotiations within GATT. In political and diplomatic affairs there was evidence pointing the same way, if only negatively; it was hardly conceivable that, in the Middle East for example, any member of the Community on its own could have had even the limited effect attained through concerted action. The doubters did not deny the benefits of operating as a Community on the lines laid down by its basic treaty, but they jibbed at the price. The more authority seeped away from national centres to the Community the less did they like it. Thatcher even went so far as to lodge objections in terms which were barely compatible with continued membership. Since, however, it was highly unlikely that Great Britain could secede without doing itself enormous damage, these objections served only to clog the Community's development.[5]

The Community's population exceeds that of the United States by half. Its GNP equals that of the United States and is much larger than the Japanese or the Soviet. It is the largest trading entity in the world, it leads worldwide in a number of manufacturing areas, and it has a larger share of world production than the United States, Japan or the Soviet Union. Although it contains grievous regional disparities, these are no greater than the disparities within the United States. But it lacks two things: authoritative central government and firmly fixed frontiers.

The constitutional position has been described in an earlier chapter. The Community's central organ is a committee of representatives of national governments. The essence of government is the power, the will and the ability to take decisions. An international committee will take few decisions and those only after lengthy preparation and discussion behind the scenes: it is a ratificatory body, not an executive. In Brussels the European Commission may initiate and implement but it may not assume the intermediate function of deciding. That right is reserved to the Council of Ministers who are collectively better at blocking than proceeding and have in recent years allowed their meetings to degenerate into occasions for demagogic pronouncements and photo oppor-

5. How many of the Japanese plants established in Great Britain in the 1970s and 1980s would stay there if they found themselves outside the Community or even in the outer rim of a two-tier Community? Their departure would be a lethal blow to British industry, employment, exports and prospects. Hardly less damaging to banking and other financial services would be the creation of a European Central Bank in Frankfurt, not London.

tunities – a caricature of government which recalls once more the cautionary tale of the Roman empire whose decay in the west was evidenced by having a government incapable of taking decisions which meant anything at a distance from Rome itself.[6]

At some stage those members of the Community who wish to see it thrive may have to take the painful path of creating a new body with substantial, although rigorously defined, powers. Such action will be discriminatory because its aim will be to form a small directorate from which some members will necessarily be excluded. The model is the UN Security Council in which some member states have a permanent seat while the rest compete at fixed intervals for a limited stint on the Council. In the Community the three biggest and strongest members should have permanent seats in its directorate together with, perhaps, two other members representing the Community's northern and southern zones. Five is enough. An association of states which observes the principle of equal representation for all members is doomed to stultification. Initially the terms of reference and powers of such a directorate would be strictly defined since otherwise governments will not create it. The allocation of permanent seats to major states will go some way to securing their necessary consent.

Fixing the geographical size of the Community entails keeping new members out. The original Community of six was compact and homogeneous, and this homogeneity was essential since the Community was bound together by a range of common interests and not by a single sharp overriding purpose (such as Nato had). The addition of Great Britain, Ireland and Denmark did not erode this homogeneity. Thereafter, however, new members were admitted for secondary political reasons and on the bizarre calculation that membership would inoculate them against anti-democratic coups from the left or right. For their part these later recruits joined either because they did not want to be left out or in order to get what they could out of it. These were not disreputable motives but their accession vastly complicated the business of growing together and has not been a source of strength to the Community as a whole. As even more candidates for membership queue up, the strains and contradictions must increase at the expense of good administration, good temper and communal strength.

Expansion has logic as well as pitfalls. The problem is to decide when the pitfalls cancel the gains, at which point expansion should

6.   See R. MacMullen, *Corruption and the Decline of Rome* (1988).

be halted. A vigorous economic association requires a core and a hinterland. At the core of the European Community are its industries which thrive by making and exporting manufactured goods over and above the needs of its own consumers and by exporting capital to places where it can generate more profit and acquire valuable assets. In the Community of six southern Italy provided an impoverished zone which was rescued by German capital to the benefit of German investors and Italian consumers alike. The greater the Community's economic success the more outlets of this nature and new fields to conquer must it seek. The newer Mediterranean members and Portugal have attracted funds and the fact that they are within the Community has been one reason (among others) why the richer members prefer to put capital and businesses in them rather than in central or eastern Europe or the Third World. Surplus capital seeking assets to buy and profits to reap finds an easily acceptable and easily understood development zone in the Community's outer ring.

There is, therefore, a contest, only half acknowledged, between adventurous financiers and industrialists on the one hand who regard the Community as an expanding enterprise zone with no predetermined limits, and on the other hand administrators and politicians whose primary concern is for a manageable community which will work only if it is finite and known to be. If Norway reverses its decision in 1972 not to join, the Community must welcome it and will have no difficulty in doing so, but practical good sense dictates that thereafter the ranks of the Community be closed. The larger the Community the looser, to the point where communality disappears and Europe turns back into a collection of states such as it was in the nineteenth century, but with this difference: that instead of being states in the first, second and third class they will be in the second, third and fourth class, increasingly subordinate and vulnerable in a world not shaped by them.

A hundred years ago there was a European states system constituted by the European Powers. That system has vanished. After an interval which has included two Great Wars a wider system has emerged. Only one of the European Powers – Russia – graduated into the top class in the new system and it is sinking to the bottom of the class and could slip lower still. The other European Powers cannot reach that class but a European Community may.

If it does it will be a Power with a difference. The other World Powers are nationalist. Ronald Reagan was at his most appealing to Americans when telling them that they were the greatest: the

Soviet Union is founded on Russian nationalism and the one part of Stalinism which it will not denounce is the nation's triumph under Stalin over Germany: Japan is seen by itself and by all its Asian and Pacific neighbours as a thrusting nation: the Chinese have been more nationalist for more centuries than any other people on earth. But a nationalist European Community is a contradiction in terms.

If Europeans are to continue to play a noticeable part in world affairs they will do so through some such association as the European Community. They have no other way. Even reunited Germany would on its own be no more than a regional Power. The strongest reason for supposing that Europeans will make a serious bid for a place at the top table is that they have evinced a steady desire to do so. The will exists and so do the resources, skills and education. There is also a contrary will, nourished by emotions with deep roots and by the vested interests of politicians, but this contrary will emanates from pride and prejudices which are in conflict with material interests and it is not implausible to suppose that the latter will prevail. The Community's greatest obstacle is its very strangeness. Nothing like it exists or has existed. It is either a great invention or a sorry freak.

What is in question for the people of western Europe is not simply power or prestige, the elemental but superficial attributes of national success. These may be dispensed with. A nation may live happily and safely at a lower level of power and many nations do. But nations which have developed a certain kind of economy and have achieved a certain standard of living cannot choose to relapse into pastoral bliss, because for them it is not available. Nations whose living comes from industry and commerce must manufacture and trade to the hilt if they are to continue, at the least, to provide for themselves at the levels that they have reached and, further, to improve the standards of the less fortunate among them. The European Community is a necessity on these grounds and its opportunities may not be scouted in the false belief that its members can keep what they have by standing still and standing separate. The Community is what it was first designated: an Economic Community. Its success may place it in the front rank of Powers but its justification is not the attainment of that rank but the persistence of the European drive over the past two to three centuries to make life better for more people, beginning at home but not forgetting abroad.

This book makes two assumptions about the future of Europe

which have not been argued at length because they appear almost incontrovertible. They need to be restated bluntly and with the caveat that, for all their plausibility, they are nevertheless assumptions. The first is that Germany will not again disrupt Europe: and the second is that central and eastern Europe are, as they have been from time immemorial, profoundly different from western Europe, economically much inferior and politically attuned to a national sovereignty which is fast losing ground in the west.

If the first proposition is correct and if, as seems certain, there is no other potential disturber of the peace of western Europe, then this part of the world is now what it has never been before. There is no other part of the world of which it can so confidently be predicted that war within it is a thing of the past. Consequently, very considerable energies, hitherto much employed in the preparation and perpetration of destruction, are available for other activities, physical and intellectual.

The second proposition leads to the conclusion that the European Community will not become pan-European, since it is inconceivable that its stronger western members will allow it to be overrun by weaker newcomers. But demands for a more cooperative and more generous association of some kind will increase and the Community faces therefore a multiplicity of problems whose concurrence is unfortunate: its own development and its relations with the other half of Europe. The next twenty years will demand extraordinary political and intellectual ability.

About the Soviet Union no assumptions are made except that it is so severely overstretched that the consequences of this (and other) mismanagement cannot be expunged in less than a generation, and that many non-Slav parts of the Union in Europe and Asia will drop off. Yet even if shorn of all twelve of its non-Slav republics the Soviet Union will remain a massive presence in both continents (Siberia is part of the Russian Republic) and Europeans will continue to be afraid of it, less afraid than they were, but with the proviso that fear has not gone away for good. The Soviet Union may retain the status and some of the military capacities of a major power but only in the same sense as Italy was reckoned one of the European Great Powers – that is to say, as a player in the big league but without the power of independent initiative in that league. If, in the alternative, the disintegration of the Soviet Union were to sunder its three Slav republics from one another the consequence for Europe could be severely disruptive since war on the Soviet borders could not be ruled out.

The lead in Europe, if it lies anywhere, lies with the principal states of western Europe in association with one another. The government of the European Community will continue to be by committee (as in any properly functioning democracy) but it has an urgent need to make its executive organs more effective in fact and in appearance and to create a recognizably democratic parliament with legislative and budgetary authority. It must also ensure that its material appetites do not eclipse its social needs and duties: its success in the world depends on its industrial, commercial and financial vigour but for success at home it is not enough to make profits. Uncertainty about Great Britain's will to remain in the Community or to act the part of responsible partner is one of the Community's bigger problems but not big enough to threaten its existence. Neither Germany nor France has anything to gain by abandoning it and that circumstance alone should ensure its continued existence. The growing weight of Germany predisposes Germany to strengthen the Community of which it is the leading light and virtually obliges France to do so too for want of anywhere else to go.

Too much can be made of the Community's destiny as a World Power, if that term connotes an exclusive or preponderant world role such as Great Britain's in the nineteenth century or the United States' in the twentieth. There is a difference between playing in the top league and running it. The necessary aim is the ability to be in – not to be – the top league. Most of the Community's members have never been or tried to be World Powers in the larger sense and the Community's prime aims were other: to collaborate for prosperity and to exorcise the German problem. Prosperity makes power and western Europe needs power in and beyond its borders in order to secure prosperity; but power worldwide, if it is achieved, will be a consequence of the Community's prime aim and is not the aim itself. World power is gratifying and remunerative but not a necessary condition for the degree of prosperity which most western Europeans seek.

The Community's other prime aim, at least as important as status, is stability. A peaceful Europe is more valuable than a dominant Europe. Great Powers have in the past done more to upset the peace than keep it and none more so in living memory than Germany. The German problem is not what it was, but for just that reason it is difficult to say what it now is. A new German bid for hegemony is no longer a serious fear. On the other hand Germany is still in a sense different since it is the one major

European state which may, in the not too distant future, find itself in a position to choose between alternative policies and if Germany were to choose a neutral posture between west and east that choice would be profoundly disturbing to other Europeans who would regard it as endangering the stability, perhaps even the peace, of Europe.

The prevailing view in western Europe, including Germany, is that European stability is best served by a strong European Community whose strength is guaranteed not only by economic power but also by exceptional and overriding political bonds. But for Germans, unlike the rest of western Europe, there is an alternative view, whose greatest exponent was Bismarck, and which asserts that European stability is best served by German-Russian accord. Bismarck worked to rescue Russia from the isolation into which it had lapsed after the Crimean War and to handle the antagonism between the Russian and Austrian empires by diplomacy rather than by confrontation. He allied Germany with Russia and the reversal of this policy by his successors has been held by many in Germany to have been their greatest mistake. German-Russian collaboration was submerged by the two great wars of the twentieth century and seemed an irrelevance in 1945 owing to (among other things) the enormous disparity between the two states. But since then Germany has grown steadily and vigorously while the weak places in Soviet power have been increasingly exposed. There is therefore still foreboding about the balance of power in Europe and its exercise, and the answer to these forebodings is to encapsulate Germany in a European Community. The development and coherence of the Community are the antidotes to fears of a detached and detachable Germany and the revival of uncertainties in what has been a singularly stable part of the world for half a century.

The resurgence of Germany has roughly coincided with the decline of the Soviet Union, an equally portentous event. This decline, issuing in the Gorbachev revolution, has transformed the politics of central Europe not merely by easing the Soviet yoke but, amazingly, by making a Soviet leader a popular figure among reformers in those countries – the one outstanding triumph of Soviet over American diplomacy. In turning his remarkable abilities to western Europe Gorbachev has canvassed a view of the Soviet Union as one among the family of Europe's states. But that is hardly how Europeans see it. While accepting Russians as Europeans the rest of Europe sees the Soviet Union as more than European, the Soviet record as repulsive and Soviet military might as still frightening. Against this inherited background Gorbachev has stood Soviet policy on its head. He attaches more importance to economic relations with western Europe than to military dominance of central and eastern Europe. His bugbear is not an anti-Soviet alliance so much as a western closed shop rebuffing Soviet needs for capital and technology. His method has been to build on useful elements out of the past. He has resurrected Brezhnev's slogan of a Common European Home and turned a phrase into a policy.[7] He has harked back to the Helsinki Final Act of 1975 and its appeal for economic, social and technical cooperation throughout Europe, and he has gone so far as to propose a European conference on civil rights to he held in (of all places) Moscow. He has explicitly accepted the United States as a necessary participant in European affairs. On a visit to the Council of Europe in Strasbourg he proposed Soviet adherence to some of the Council's international conventions and collaboration in its specialized agencies. He has addressed himself particularly to Germany as the most likely source of investment and managerial and technical aid. A Soviet-German *rapprochement* of this nature is not inherently harmful to French or British interests (or to those of the lesser members of the Community) but the progress of Soviet-German cooperation independently of the Community alarms western Europe by shifting the focus of European affairs from western Europe, where the more prosperous Europeans suppose it to be, to *Mitteleuropa* where Russians and Germans alone count.

These shifts present Germans with a challenging and special responsibility: how to respond to events in the east while maintaining solidarity with the west. West Germany's attachment to the west, inaugurated by Adenauer, has always been tempered by an open eye to the east, first formalized by Brandt's *Ostpolitik*. The challenge is to combine the two aspects of Germany's essential centrality without giving non-Germans the impression that German policy is about choosing rather than about combining. That a German *Ostpolitik* need not be inimical to the west is sufficiently shown by the fact that de Gaulle had an *Ostpolitik* before Brandt did.

Europe lived in fear of the Germans for the first half of the

7.   Dar ul-Islam is the Common Muslim Home. But the prospect of a European counterpart vanished around the year 1000 and the Common Muslim Home is not an alluring example.

present century. This fear was removed by the outcome of the Second World War, whereafter Europe lived in fear of the Soviet Union. The Soviet Union owed this position to its victories in that war but another half century later Germany, the loser in both the century's great wars, is arguably Europe's greatest Power. It is not feared as it once was, but it could be. The fear departed with the verdict of 1945; it has remained submerged because of the Soviet Union's rise to Superpower status and because of West Germany's relatively small size, non-nuclear armaments and evidently pacific temper. But, unlike the Soviet Union, West Germany has tailored its commitments to its resources, has magnified those resources and in this essential equation has become a major Power, raising the question whether it may not one day be a frightening Power. The recovery of Germany from the Second World War has been even more spectacular than its recovery from the First and looks like being more enduring. Since the Soviet Union on the other hand looks like suffering the fate of the Ottoman empire after 1918 the future of Europe may again be posed in terms of the German Question. The Community is the answer to that question – not an utterly conclusive answer (none could be) but a powerfully promising answer and the only one in sight.

Bismarck created a German Power in the middle of Europe. It is still there. What has changed is the context. Psychologically: Germans have been afflicted by two great wars which delayed the growth of German power and which they lost. Environmentally: Germans find themselves with no enemies to the west, no superiors to the west, no need to bother about war on two fronts. Politically: Germans have embraced a new order in which they have bound themselves in permanent partnership with erstwhile enemies. To the east they have, as they had a hundred years ago, conundrums and the biggest single question in Europe at the turn of the twentieth century is how they will deal with these conundrums, whether as members of that new partnership or once more on their own. And the biggest single element in resolving that crucial question is their assessment of the reality and effectiveness of the partnership in the west which at present they prefer to untrammelled national sovereignty.

The future of Europe will be settled by Europeans. Even the relatively powerless Africans and disorganized Asians have more say in the regulation of their own affairs than do outsiders who, most of the time, stay outside. Western Europe is pacific and relatively prosperous and stable. Eastern Europe is less prosperous, less stable, far less united and possibly less pacific. It is in the process of throwing off the rule of entrenched and conservative communist cliques, a process entailing some violence which varies from country to country and in its timing and its consequences. Gains in civic liberties and political pluralism will not automatically produce the economic relief which many of their citizens long for as much as they value freedom. Whether governed by communists or not these states are all economically fragile and some of them are ethnically distracted – in the case of Yugoslavia to the verge of civil war. They have little desire or incentive for the cooperative unification in vogue in western Europe. On the more optimistic side they may experience a wave of energy and goodwill such as is often engendered by an escape from tyranny – the rise of the Netherlands after the collapse of Spanish imperial rule is Europe's most conspicuous example but the Netherlands in the sixteenth century had resources and opportunities far exceeding anything to be found in central or eastern Europe in the twentieth. Flaring resentment against the Stalinist order and economic needs which the Soviet Union cannot satisfy have combined to make central and eastern Europe look west, for sympathy easily given and for money not so easily available in the amounts needed to reverse nearly fifty years' mismanagement and misdirection.

Western Europe, backed by generations of success sufficient to confront the comparative decline in its fortunes, possesses the material and imaginative resources needed to think confidently and constructively about the future – a rare gift. It has accepted the limiting condition, which is the abandonment of formal sovereignty and the politics of the international jungle, in favour of permanent collaboration and common regulation. It is recovering corporatively that power to influence world affairs which some of its states once exercised individually and then lost. It is safer than any other part of the world from internal wars and external aggression. And for all its domestic disfigurements and defects it is socially better balanced than any other part of the world and alive to the need to provide equitably for yet more of those good things which money buys – education, health and the freedom to pursue happiness.

Other Books

This list is not a bibliography. It is a short list of books of special quality which will point to yet other books.

Andrieu, C. *Le Programme Commun de la Résistance: Des Idées dans la Guerre* (1984).
Aron, R. *Les Dernières Années du Siècle* (1984).
Balfour, M.L.G. *West Germany: A Contemporary History* (expanded version 1982).
Barker, E. *Churchill and Eden at War* (1978).
Barker, E. *Macedonia: Its Place in Balkan Power Politics* (1950).
Barnett, C. *The Audit of War: The Illusion and Reality of Britain as a Great Nation* (1986).
Bartlett, C.J. *The Global Conflict: The International Rivalry of the Great Powers 1880–1970* (1984).
Bartlett, C.J. *The Long Retreat: A Short History of British Defence Policy 1945–70* (1972).
Berezhkov, V. *History in the Making* (revised English trans.) (1983).
Biddiss, M.D. *The Age of the Masses: Ideas and Society in Europe since 1870* (1977).
Bond, B. *War and Society in Europe 1870–1970* (1984).
Bryson, T.A. *Seeds of Mideast Crisis: The United States Diplomatic Role in the Middle East during World War II* (1981).
Buchan. A. (ed.) *Europe's Futures, Europe's Options: Models of Western Europe in the 1970s* (1969).
Bull, H. and Watson, A. (eds) *The Expansion of International Society* (1984).
Butterfield, H. and Wight, M. (eds) *Diplomatic Investigation* (1966).

Calleo, D. *The Atlantic Fantasy: The United States, Nato and Europe* (1970).

Calleo, D. *The German Problem Reconsidered: Germany and the World Order 1870 to the Present* (1978).

Dawisha, K. *Eastern Europe, Gorbachev and Reform* (1989).

Dibb. P. *The Soviet Union: The Incomplete Superpower* (1986).

Evans, R.J. *In Hitler's Shadow* (1989).

Freedman, L. *The Evolution of Nuclear Strategy* (2nd edn) (1989).

Hathaway, R.M. *Ambiguous Partnership: Britain and America 1944–1947* (1981).

Hillgruber, A. *Deutschlands Rolle in der Vorgeschichte der beiden Weltkriege* (1967). English translation: *Germany and the Two World Wars* (1981).

Hughes, H.S. *Consciousness and Society: The Reorientation of European Social Thought 1890–1930* (1959).

Joffe, J. *The Limited Partnership: Europe, the United States and the Burdens of Alliance* (1987).

Johnson, R.W. *The Long March of the French Left* (1981).

Joll, J. *Europe since 1870: An International History* (1973).

Kaiser, D.E. *Economic Diplomacy and the Origins of the Second World War* (1980).

Kaser, M.C. (ed.) *The Economic History of Eastern Europe 1919–1975.* Vol III *Institutional Change within a Planned Economy* (1986).

Kitchen, M. *British Policy towards the Soviet Union during the Second World War* (1986).

Landes, D.S. *The Unbound Prometheus: Technical Changes and Industrial Development in Western Europe from 1750 to the Present* (1969).

La Serre, F. de *La Grande Bretagne et la Communauté Européene* (1987).

Lichtheim, G. *Europe in the Twentieth Century* (1972).

Lottman, H.R. *The People's Anger: Justice and Revenge in Post-Liberation France* (1986 – US edn *The Purge*).

Louis, W.R. *Imperialism at Bay 1941–1945: The United States and the Decolonization of the British Empire* (1977).

Lowenthal, R. *Social Change and Culture Crisis* (1984).

Mastny, V. *Russia's Road to the Cold War: Diplomacy, Warfare and the Politics of Communism 1941–1945* (1979).

Milward, A.S. *The Reconstruction of Western Europe 1945–51* (1984).

Mommsen, W.J. and Kittenbacker, L. (eds) *The Fascist Challenge and the Policy of Appeasement* (1983).

Neidhart, G. (ed.) *Kreigsbeginn 1939: Entfesselung oder Ausbruch des zweiten Weltkrieges* (1976).

Palmer, A.W. *The Lands Between: A History of East-Central Europe since the Congress of Vienna* (1970).

Parker, G. *The Geopolitics of Domination* (1988).

Paz, V. *One Earth, Four or Five Worlds: Reflections on Contemporary History* (1985 – expanded version of *Tiempo Nublado*, 1983).

Pearton, M. *The Knowledgeable State: Diplomacy, War and Technology since 1890* (1982).

Roberts, J.M. *Europe 1880–1945* (1967).

Ross, G. *The Great Powers and the Decline of the European States System* (1983).

Rostow, W.W. *The Division of Europe after World War II* (1982).

Rusinow, D. *The Yugoslav Experiment 1948–74* (1977).

Sainsbury, K. *The Turning Point: Roosevelt, Stalin and Churchill in 1943* (1985).

Seton-Watson, H. *Eastern Europe between the Wars 1918–41* (1945).

Stone, N. *Europe Transformed 1878–1919* (1984).

Tucker, R.C. *Political Culture and Citizenship in Soviet Russia from Lenin to Gorbachev* (1987).

Wight, M. *Power Politics* (1986).

Yergin, D. *Shattered Peace: The Origins of the Cold War and the National Security State* (1977).

Zeman, Z.A.B. *Pursued by a Bear* (1989).

Index